South Africa's Dreams

South Africa's Dreams
Ethnologists and Apartheid in Namibia

Robert J. Gordon

berghahn
NEW YORK · OXFORD
www.berghahnbooks.com

First published in 2021 by
Berghahn Books
www.berghahnbooks.com

© 2021, 2024 Robert J. Gordon
First paperback edition published in 2024

Library of Congress Cataloging-in-Publication Data

Names: Gordon, Robert J. (Robert James), 1947– author.
Title: South Africa's Dreams: Ethnologists and Apartheid in Namibia /
Robert J. Gordon.
Description: New York: Berghahn Books, 2021. | Includes bibliographical
references and index.
Identifiers: LCCN 2020053932 (print) | LCCN 2020053933 (ebook) |
ISBN 9781789209747 (hardback) | ISBN 9781789209754 (ebook)
Subjects: LCSH: Apartheid—Namibia. | Ethnology—Political
aspects—Namibia. | Namibia—History—1915–1946. | Namibia—
History—1946–1990. | Namibia—Colonization.
Classification: LCC DT1556 .G67 2021 (print) | LCC DT1556 (ebook) |
DDC 968.8103—dc23
LC record available at https://lccn.loc.gov/2020053932
LC ebook record available at https://lccn.loc.gov/2020053933

British Library Cataloguing in Publication Data
A catalogue record for this book is available from the British Library

ISBN 978-1-78920-974-7 hardback
ISBN 978-1-80539-149-4 paperback
ISBN 978-1-78920-976-1 epub
ISBN 978-1-78920-975-4 web pdf

https://doi.org/10.3167/9781789209747

For Etai, Asher, Graham, and Elliot

The political aim of Imperialism was "ruling space" not "living space."
—Moritz Bonn, 1945

Contents

Acknowledgments

This volume is the product of a long-term research interest in what became known as Namibia. Apart from interviews with former military personnel, ethnologists, ordinary Namibians, and on-site visits to the former Operational Area and the former "homelands," I was privileged to enjoy the hospitality of a number of archives and collections, especially the National Archives of Namibia and those of the Namibian Scientific Society in Windhoek, the Sam Cohen Library in Swakopmund, the South African National Archives, and the SANDF Documentation Center in Pretoria, the Special Collections at the universities of Cape Town, Witwatersrand, Stellenbosch, and Johannesburg, and at the University of South Africa. Bloemfontein offered perhaps the most surprisingly rich lode of material in the University of the Free State's Institute for Contemporary History, now known as the Archive for Contemporary Affairs, and the downtown National Literature Museum.

In particular I am deeply indebted to a large number of friends, colleagues, students, informants, some-time collaborators, and strangers who contributed in various, often unanticipated ways to bringing this volume to fruition. This includes but is not limited to the following: Parfait Akana, Martha Akawa, Michael Akupa, Zeka Alberto, Heike Becker, Heike Behrend, William Beinart, Marion Berghahn, Gertrud Boden, Michael Bollig, Max Bolt, Pia Bombarella, Shirley Brooks, Kuno Budack, Marieta Buys, Jane Carruthers, the late Peter Carstens, Ben Carton, Allan Cooper, Andrew Corbett, Richard Dale, Tilman Dedering, Lieneke de Visser, Chris de Wet, Thea de Wet, Ute Dieckmann, Gregor Dobler, Saul Dubow, Andre du Pisani, Ben Eastman, Bob Edgar, the late Johann Els, Piet Erasmus, Casper Erichsen, Petro Estherhyse, Anthony Feinstein, Kileni Fernando, Deon Fourie, Matthia Fumanti, the late Alex Gaomab, Jan-Bart Gewald, Claudia Gastrow, Andre Goodrich, Hugh Gordon, Keith Gottschalk, Biddy Greene, Geoff Grey, Albert Grundlingh, Patricia Hayes, Jennifer Hays, Dag Henrichsen, Werner Hillebrecht, Bob Hitchcock, the late Josiah Hoebeb, Dianne Hubbard, Pierre Hugo, Crispin Inambao, Margie

Jacobsohn, Deborah James, Jonathan Jansen, Fanie Jansen van Rensburg, Chris Jasparro, Hergen Junge, Preben Kaarsholm, Bennet Kangamu, Sarel Karsten, Peter Katjavivi, Nehoa Kautondokwa, Evert Kleynhans, Reinhart Kössler, Carol Kotze, Fabian Krautwald, Adam Kuper, Hubre Lambrecht, the late Brigitte Lau, Richard Lee, Ian Liebenberg, Gwen Lister, Louise Lombard, Jannie Loubser, the late Anton Lubowski, Stuart Marks, the late John Marshall, Mike McGovern, Henning Melber, Werner Menges, Giorgio Miescher, Udo Mishek, Dunbar Moodie, David Moore, Martin Murray, the late Melwa Musambachine, the late Mbulelo Mzimane, Ellen Namhila, Ghirmai Negesh, Coen Nel, Zed Ngavirue, Isak Niehaus, Francis Nyamnjoh, Willem Odendaal, Bryan O'Linn, the late Nic Olivier, Dan O'Meara, Robin Palmer, Wade Pendleton, the late Kobus Pienaar, Roberto Polli, Louwrens Pretorius, David Price, Ciraj Rassool, Steven Robins, Peter Rowny, Martin Ruehl, Hartmut Ruppel, Beatrice Sandelowsky, Chris Saunders, Carlien Scholtz, Carmel Schrire, Wolfgang Seibel, Joe Serekoane, John Sharp, Napandulwe Shiweda, Jeremy Silvester, Sian Sullivan, Julie Taylor, Kent Thorburn, Norman Tjombe, Johan van den Berg, Cees van der Waal, Piet van Rooyen, Chris van Vuuren, Steven van Wolputte, Ilana van Wyk, Dick Werbner, Wolfgang Werner, Andre Wessels, Louise White, Thomas Widlok, Polly Wiessner, Christian Williams, Christine Winter, and several who chose to remain anonymous. I sincerely apologize to those whom I have overlooked.

Special acknowledgment is due to those unsung heroes of research facilitation, the librarians, especially Lisa Brooks at the University of Vermont, who would willingly walk the extra mile. The manuscript has been much enriched by the deep reading and superb editing of Caroline Jeannerat, whose skills in these matters exceed any that I know of. To Marion Berghahn my heartfelt thanks, not only for publishing this book, but also for the way she has steadfastly expanded her list of anthropology and history books, and to my Berghahn editor, Tom Bonnington, the proverbial good shepherd, my gratitude.

The University of Vermont's (minor but critical) and the National Research Foundation's munificence significantly shaped this research, while a semester-long fellowship at the Stellenbosch Institute for Advanced Study provided the ideal space to complete this manuscript, although the intellectual stimulation was such that I frequently had to rethink several of the ideas central to my argument.

Finally, Rinda, my long-suffering spouse, who deserves recognition for having to bear with my obsessions and having to read my drafts with a good red pen in hand, my thanks, gratitude, and love!

Some material has been published before, and I am grateful for permission to use some of it. This includes "Collecting the Gatherers," in *Worldly Provincialism: German Anthropology in the Age of Empire*, edited by H.

Glenn Penny and Matti Bunzl (Ann Arbor: University of Michigan Press, 2003); "'Tracks Which Cannot Be Covered': P. J. Schoeman and Public Intellectuals in Southern Africa," *Historia* 52, no. 1 (2007): 98–126; "How Good People Become Absurd: J. P. van S. Bruwer, the Making of Namibian Grand Apartheid and the Decline of *Volkekunde*," *Journal of Southern African Studies* 44, no. 1 (2018): 97–113; and "Protecting the Borders: Etiquette Manuals and Ethnology in the Erstwhile South African Defence Force," *Anthropology Southern Africa* 40, no. 3 (2017): 157–71.

Notes on Text

All translations from German and Afrikaans are my own. An important note on nomenclature: I have retained the terminology used in the original sources, the compilers of the documents, who generally referred to themselves as Southwesters and to the territory as South-West Africa, finding it difficult to utter the word "Namibia" right up to the time the country became independent. This is not to be reactionary, but to emphasize the dissonance between the documentalists and the people they were objectifying. I have also quoted extensively rather than paraphrased much of the documentation, not only to highlight how absurd some of it was, but also in the belief that if one gives these experts enough rope, they will hang themselves.

Abbreviations

AB	Afrikaner Broederbond
ANC	African National Congress
BAD	Department of Bantu Administration and Development
BOSS	South African Bureau of State Security
CAP	Civic Action Program
CCB	Civilian Co-operation Bureau
COMOPS	Directorate of Communications Operations, Department/ Division of Military Intelligence
CSI	Chief of Staff, Intelligence
DST	Directorate of Special Tasks
DTA	Democratic Turnhalle Alliance
FAK	Federasie vir Afrikaanse Kultuur
ICJ	International Court of Justice
INCH	Institute for Contemporary History (Now Archives for Contemporary Affairs)
LPs	Local populations
NAN	National Archives of Namibia

NIS	National Intelligence Service
NP	National Party
PMC	Permanent Mandates Commission
SABRA	South African Bureau of Racial Affairs
SAIRR	South African Institute of Race Relations
SADF	South African Defence Force
SANA	South African National Archives
SANDF	South African National Defence Force
SSC	State Security Council
SWA	South-West Africa
SWANLA	South-West Africa Native Labor Association
SWAPO	South-West Africa People's Organization
SWATF	South-West African Territorial Forces
UCT	University of Cape Town
UN	United Nations
UNTAG	United Nations Transition Assistance Group
US	United States
USSALEP	United States–South Africa Leadership Exchange Program
WHAM	Winning Hearts and Minds
Wits	University of the Witwatersrand

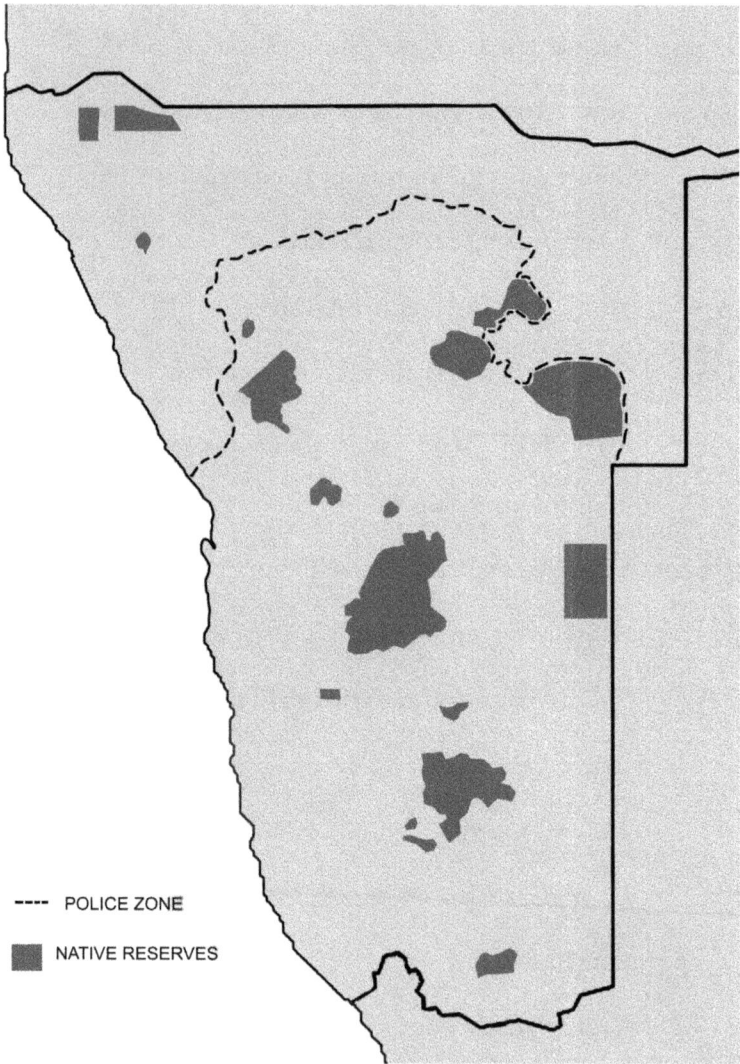

Map 0.1. *Native reserves 1939. Map by Hugh Gordon.*

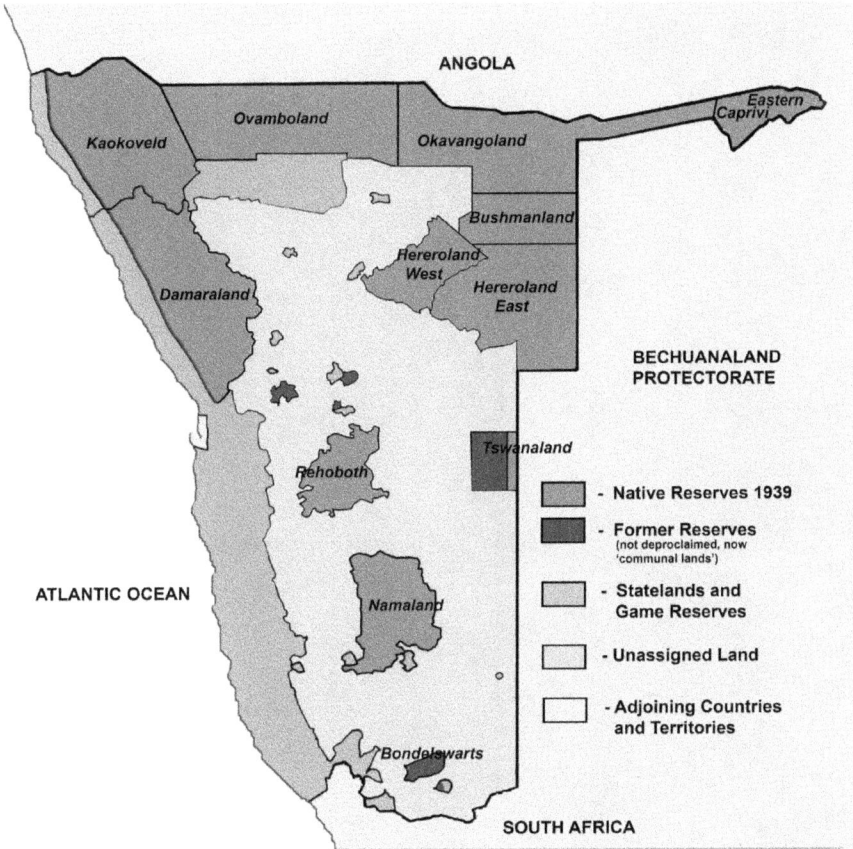

Map 0.2. *Land allocation following the Odendaal Commission. Map by Hugh Gordon.*

Introduction

Why focus on anthropological scribbles about a piece of marginal land like Namibia? Precisely because peripheral vision can allow one to see critical issues more clearly. Recent histories of the rise and demise of apartheid have either ignored or dismissed the significance of South Africa's colony, the mandated territory of South-West Africa.[1] *South Africa's Dreams* redresses this fault by pointing to the significance of South-West Africa (SWA) for understanding the development of apartheid and the role of experts in its elaboration.[2] John Ellis, in his classic *The Social History of the Machine Gun* (1975), showed how military technology was first tried out in frontier or colonial areas before being brought back to the metropole, with deadly results. I suggest that a similar pattern can be detected with regard to the technology of internal pacification. The social technology for internal pacification was field-tested in Namibia and then transferred back to South Africa as part of its strategy for suppressing internal dissent.

How anthropology is imbricated in the practice of apartheid, and more broadly colonialism, is a vexing and contentious issue. It has been discussed in numerous articles, reviews, and essays but generally in a rather piecemeal fashion. *South Africa's Dreams* proposes a different tack. It focuses on a single space on the globe and examines how, in the course of time, the space became a colonial place, eventually named Namibia, and how people commonly known as "native experts" helped imagine, shape, and consolidate this colonial enterprise. I place this historical inquiry into the development of vernacular anthropological knowledge within a larger project of understanding the ways knowledge practices shape and, in turn, are conditioned by interaction between heterogeneous worlds in a colonial setting. I am interested in how geopolitical formations shaped the work of these experts and led to occlusion: how their work led to concealing, blocking, and closing off understandings of SWA society through the deployment of conceptual grammars that rendered certain situations visible while making others invisible. What were the political logics and epistemic assumptions that rendered some events or actions visible? Occluded histories can take varied forms, as Ann Stoler (2016) points out, but especially in Namibia through benign mislabeling. Occluded knowledge, she suggests, leads to aphasia, a political condition that simultaneously allows one to know and not to know, a space between ignoring and ignorance. It is something more than self-delusion. Such a perspective ties in with an emergent discipline called agnotology, the study of the social production of ignorance (Proctor and Schiebinger 2008). These questions then shape the second focus of this book: Why and how did these experts, often highly intelligent, good Christian men, not see, or at least articulate, that their work and recommendations flew in the face of reality, even with the wisdom of hindsight?

An Afrikaner variant of anthropology called *volkekunde*, an effort at a decolonized and indigenized anthropology, came to dominate this exercise. My concern is not with volkekunde per se, or with ethnology, as *volkekundiges*, its practitioners, glossed it in English, but rather with the relationship between self-proclaimed "native experts" and their (potential) patrons and how this relationship shaped their creation of knowledge. Except for a smattering of articles and a rather dated book (Schmidt 1996), volkekundiges have largely been ignored or dismissed by English-speaking anthropologists and historians as pursuing a fringe activity, especially with regard to how they went about the business of creating material. One can go further and argue, like Peacock (2002), that one can see the center more sharply by engaging in peripheral vision, so this is also a critical appreciation of volkekunde. After tracing the historical roots emphasizing the contested role of "native experts," especially in the international sphere as constituted by the League of Nations' Permanent Mandates Commission (PMC), this volume examines how the only large-scale effort at grand apartheid—the large-scale consolidation of native reserves to create homelands—was attempted in SWA. The intellectual midwife and initial administrative wet nurse in this exercise was the volkekundige Johannes P. van S. "Hannes" Bruwer, who also doubled as the main expert witness called by South Africa to justify apartheid at the 1962–66 International Court of Justice (ICJ), or World Court, case concerning South Africa's jurisdiction over the territory.[3] When this homeland policy failed, the ensuing long-drawn-out low-intensity guerrilla war resulted in the South African Defence Force (SADF) becoming one of the largest employers globally of ethnologists, who were engaged in assorted civic action programs and covert operations. The lessons learned and experiences gained here were then taken back to South Africa and applied to countering anti-apartheid protest in the seventies and eighties. A number of the rising stars in the South African security/internal pacification establishment also cut their teeth on Namibia before being promoted to key positions in South Africa. This book serves as a corrective to previous analyses of apartheid (itself a cottage industry) that have ignored the colonial connection. I examine how, through time, native experts, especially volkekundiges, imagined, described, advised, and helped create the edifice now known as Namibia. I scrutinize how they created information that was used, often uncritically, by others, ranging from colonial speculators, to government policy advisers, to expert witnesses at the World Court, to writers of tourist guides. Such a discussion forces one to consider ethics and the role of anthropological knowledge in the contemporary world.

I show how attempts to use ethnology and cognate disciplines in social engineering took place, not always or everywhere, but in specific places and times where they can be investigated in detail. *South Africa's Dreams* examines activities not only on the public front but also backstage. Looking at how these experts operated allows one to infer how policy makers thought, how the state assessed the threats to its monopoly of power, and how it tried to cope with these threats.

History is a narrative construction that calls for a reflection on the convolutions of the sources used. What was the context in which the source was created, by whom, and for what purpose are some of the many questions that need consideration. Despite the scarcity of documentation, not only were many of the official police files, reports, and photographs concerning the "bush war" destroyed in 1993, but the archives of the South African National Defence Force (SANDF) were also infamously purged of much material considered sensitive, and even the material still on file had to be cleared, mostly by Warrant Officer Blaauw, to whom I owe my thanks. However, to paraphrase the historian Robert Darnton (2014, 13–19), given the rich run of evidence, one can tease out the underlying assumptions and undercover activities of those charged with undertaking these activities. I seek to show the unspoken attitudes and implicit values as they were inflected in their actions. This is done by interrogating certain experts by recovering their voices from the archives and questioning them while reading documents, asking how they worked, how they understood their work, and what effect their words had. Apart from interviews and on-site visits, I was privileged to work in other archives and collections, especially those in Windhoek, Swakopmund, Pretoria, and Cape Town over the last fifteen years.

Personal experiences were critical in shaping this book. I have long been intrigued by how "difference" and "identity" were culturally constructed and reinforced, since my earliest days growing up in southern Namibia where, especially on the school playground, we, the English and Jewish kids, got beaten up by bullies from among the Afrikaner majority. Only later did I realize this was a matter of exclusion, the flip side, if you will, of their self-identification. Eventually I was packed off to boarding school in Cape Town. It was there, in grade nine, that I decided that anthropology might be a good career choice. It suited my emerging political and anarchist sensitivities, as it emphasized the opposite to what apartheid stood for: here was a career that required one to meet and talk across the racial and cultural boundaries. Needless to say, my father was none too excited by my wish to become an anthropologist and dispatched me to Stellenbosch to read law and become "bilingual," although his fear that I might become a "Communist" if I went to an English-language university factored into the equation. Stellenbosch, which styled itself as the Harvard of Afrikanerdom, was where I developed an appreciation—more, a love— for the Afrikaans language. It provided an unexpected education, not so much from the professoriate, who, except for one or two, were a rather dull and pretentious bunch, but on how politics worked. In my third year my father relented and I was allowed to major in anthropology along with Bantu law and administration. Eventually I was allowed into that sacred sanctum of the Department of Bantoekunde (Bantu studies), the tearoom, as junior lecturer (temporary), and thus exposed to the oral history of the rather contentious and contested role of this particular department in the elaboration and activation of the ideology of apartheid. It was here that I first heard of P. J. "Piet" Schoeman and Bruwer, two anthropologists whose careers were closely intertwined with developments in Namibia. My junior lectureship did not last long, and I was downgraded to a technical assistant (half-time), ostensibly because someone better qualified had been found, but no doubt the fact that one of my colleagues referred to me as "that Semite" probably also played into the equation, abetted possibly by, shall we say, some political (mis)adventures. However, by this stage I had already decided to leave the country, with the notion of studying the Afrikaners in Patagonia, a group of people who after the Anglo-Boer war decided that they could not live under the yoke of British imperialism and sought their Calvinist utopia in Patagonia, only to find that they had landed in a Catholic hell. Regrettably, funding and opportunity did not align, and I wound up doing my dissertation on a Namibian copper mine (Gordon 1977).

A second formative episode was when, after being awarded my doctorate, I wound up in Papua New Guinea, where, as stated in my application, I intended to do an anthropological comparison of Australian and South African colonial policies, since both New Guinea and South-West Africa, as former German colonies, had been administered as Class C mandates under the League of Nations. Apart from the fact that both mandatories had to answer to and provide annual reports to the PMC and thus provided similar comparable data, both South Africa and Australia had themselves recently been colonies, and I wondered how this experience had factored into their administrative techniques and strategies. In proposing this research, I was undoubtedly influenced by the radical anthropology of the seventies, in particular Laura Nader's (1969) seminal essay on the importance of "studying up" and Asad's (1973) classic edited volume *Anthropology and the Colonial Encounter*. Over time my position has matured: rather than study down or up, one should study around. While I never managed to do this project, it did lead to my examination of the PMC activities and was to lead to chapter 1 of this book.

A third event occurred in early 1981 when Cultural Survival, an anthropologically based human rights organization, asked me to write a short essay concerning a *Science* article reporting on the controversy that had erupted at the first International Conference on Hunters and Gatherers when Richard Lee presented a petition protesting the militarization of the Bushmen. Not knowing much about the situation, I wrote to the heads of all the anthropology departments in South Africa, enclosing the *Science* article and asking for their comments. The response was an eye-opener. While the English-language anthropologists pleaded lack of knowledge, the Afrikaner anthropologists were effusive in their criticism of Lee, one going so far as to write a ten-page critique, which even referred to statements made by Lee in the Canadian press (in a pre-Internet age, suggesting possible connections to the South African intelligence services?). Another sent South African newspaper clippings about how the SADF was protecting the Bushmen and improving their living standards. Most significantly, my query was forwarded to the chief ethnologist of the SADF, who responded with a five-page letter about how the SADF was "uplifting" the Bushmen. Needless to say, I opened a file on this matter and in 2015–18 was able to visit the SANDF archives to collect further information to complement the recent flurry of books on Bushman soldiery.

The fourth experience that molded this book was an invitation to spend two years at the University of the Free State in Bloemfontein in 2012. Many colleagues dismiss Bloemfontein as a scholarly desert, but it does have its pleasures, including the National Literature Museum, which houses the P. J. Schoeman papers and, more importantly, the holdings of the Institute for Contemporary History (now known as the Archive for Contemporary Affairs), which contain the personal papers of many prominent Afrikaner leaders, including those of Bruwer and Hendrik Verwoerd, the assassinated hard-line apartheid prime minister. Consequently, I spent many engrossing hours going through these reams of files. Bruwer turned out to be critically important for understanding events that shaped modern-day Namibia. In 1961, as a rising star in the Broederbond, a secret society promoting Afrikaner nationalism, he wrote a study piece for the organization arguing that SWA was a good testing ground for grand apartheid, as the different ethnic groups had not yet undergone "large-scale mixing." He anticipated that a public referendum would eventually resolve the territory's legal status, and thus it was crucial to convince Indigenes of South Africa's good intentions through a massive propaganda and development effort in order to persuade them to reject the United Nations (UN). Sued by Ethiopia and Liberia in the ICJ for failing to implement the League of Nations mandate to administer the territory in the best interest of the Indigenes, South Africa decided to use this as a forum to convince an increasingly skeptical global audience that apartheid was indeed the only viable solution. In this selling of apartheid, Bruwer was the star witness. Bruwer was also instrumental in developing the only serious, coordinated large-scale effort to impose grand apartheid, with the purchase of some five hundred white-owned farms.

When this strategy failed in the face of mounting resistance to South African overrule, the situation became militarized, and the SADF developed the Civic Action Program (CAP) as part of its Winning Hearts and Minds (WHAM) counterinsurgency campaign, drawing on the advice of many ethnologists and other social scientists. While these ethnologists failed to gain much credibility, they served an important supporting role in special operations, which were largely devised by an educational psychologist, one Dr. Louis Pasques. After successfully field-testing this counter-mobilization campaign in Namibia, according to the South African Truth and Reconciliation Commission, it was later implemented in South Africa to counter anti-apartheid resistance. But Namibia was a testing ground in another way as well. Many of the irritations and obscenities entailed in what was known as petty apartheid were first abolished in Namibia and then, having been judged successful, ended in South Africa. Thus, in 1967 the ban on the sale of alcohol to non-Europeans was lifted, but the big social innovations came ten years later, when one of the first acts of the newly appointed administrator-general nullified the notorious Masters and Servants Proclamation and repealed the immorality and mixed marriages laws, as well as the pass laws and influx control. In addition, the Bantu Education Act and urban segregation were scrapped, while equal wages for equal work was introduced. When these changes did not signal the collapse of heaven for whites, they set the precedent for similar actions in South Africa.

I mention these details, biographical and chronological, to show how they have molded my interests and approaches in shaping *South Africa's Dreams*. This work can best be characterized not as ethnography or historiography, but as pornography. The *Oxford English Dictionary*, that great arbiter of matters of this nature, defines "pornography" as the "description of the life, manners etc. of prostitutes and their patrons," while "prostitute" is defined as "one who debases her/himself for the sake of gain" and, more intriguingly, as "a base hireling, a corrupt and venal politician." At the same time, the case could be argued that these "native expert" prostitutes in turn (re)present their subjects as prostitutes, since in their accounts they present Indigenes as "debased by being made common or cheap," despite their professed intentions to do the opposite.

If there is one common denominator running through this account, it is that I see the role of the anthropologist to be that of challenging the comfortable assumptions of those in power about difference. I make no great claims for social scientific knowledge, and less for anthropology as an interpretive science. On the contrary! In this era of late capitalism, the best the anthropologist can hope for is to be a trickster: not only speaking truth or alternatives to those in power, but challenging the certainties that everything is a question of black and white, literally and figuratively.

Framing Notions

Three notions frame this project. First is an insight by an obscure political economist, Moritz Bonn. Largely forgotten nowadays, in the interwar years Bonn was considered to be one of the foremost experts on colonialism.[4] Unlike most armchair theorists of colonialism, Bonn had done extended research in the colonies. In 1907, while clicking his heels in the dusty streets of Windhuk, capital of German Südwest-Afrika, and frustrated by an obdurate bureaucracy, Bonn had an epiphany: colonialism was not only racist and exploitative but also ridiculous. It was uneconomical on both the macro- and the interpersonal level. Indeed, he found the colonial situation so ludicrous that he became the first scholar to seriously discuss the necessity of decolonization (Gordon 2018a). It was the ridiculous rules governing etiquette between colonizer and colonized that inspired many of the pioneers in the anti-colonial movement (Shutt 2015). There is also a growing body of literature showing how important joking and satire were for survival in the colonial situation. I take this perspective as a starting point to read against the grain the major forms of knowledge settlers had of "the native."[5] Foolishness is far more common than we realize. In 1984 the historian Barbara Tuchman published her classic *The March of Folly: From Troy to Vietnam*. Misgovernment, she claimed, came in the form of tyranny, excessive ambition, incompetence and folly, or perversity, which was the pursuit of a policy contrary to the self-interest of the group or constituency. In the Namibian case, all four characteristics were present, guided as they were by folly, which is distinguished by "wooden-headedness, the source of self-deception, . . . a factor that plays a remarkably large role in government. It consists in assessing a situation in terms of preconceived fixed notions while ignoring or rejecting any contrary signs" (Tuchman 1984, 7). I confess sly pleasure in this concept of "wood head" because its Afrikaans version *houtkop* was an offensive mode

of address or reference to black Africans. One measure developed as a prophylactic to folly was the professionalization of the civil service, but this
can easily boomerang, as bureaucracies can also become a field enclosed
by protective stupidity, repeating simply what it did yesterday, so that, like
a vast computer, it rolls on ineluctably, having once been penetrated by
an error, duplicates it forever. She concludes, "The problem may not be
so much a matter of educating officials for government as educating the
electorate to recognize and reward integrity of character and to reject the
ersatz" (Tuchman 1984, 386–87). The point about treating colonialism as
ridiculous or foolish is not to belittle the suffering, indignities, or exploitation of the colonized but rather to accentuate the trauma in the tragedy.
The challenge is to understand why colonials did not see their actions as
ridiculous. This calls for a careful analysis of the social situation in which
they found themselves.

Second, as a number of scholars, most notably Steinmetz (2007,
2008) and Mamdani (2012), have argued, the defining feature of modern colonialism was not economic exploitation but native policy that was
based on two fundamental conditions, namely that sovereignty was an
alien imposition and that the Indigenes are treated as different and inferior. Viewing these actions and utterances as ridiculous or, to be more
euphemistic, as examples of temporal dissonance provides a fresh perspective on important issues. It provides a scalpel with which to dissect
the colonial fantasy world that was so crucial for colonialism to work
(Naranch and Eley 2014). The anthropologists and native experts discussed in *South Africa's Dreams* were obsessed with cultural difference
and, at the same time, tried to make a difference in consolidating settler
rule; they saw themselves as scholar-activists. Colonialism thrives, and
indeed is only possible, by dividing people into different categories, and
anthropologists of the "translation of culture" mode have indeed made
a profession out of being experts on the boundaries of these culturally
constructed categories.

Bonn's frustration with the colonial bureaucracy was prescient. One of
Bismarck's greatest legacies was the creation of a new form of bureaucratic
organization. Taking his cue from the Prussian military, he militarized the
civil service, insulating it from the swing of politics and giving its officials
a clear incremental career path in which one was not rewarded for doing more than expected but punished for stepping out of line. Bureaucrats lived in a Weberian iron cage (Sennett 2006). A related Bismarckian
legacy that had important consequences, not only in colonial affairs but
also in bureaucracies globally, was the invention of the professional native
affairs expert. In 1908 the first professional school for training colonial
officials was opened in Germany. Inspired by the new scientific manageri-
alism, the Colonial Institute created the new discipline of *Kolonialkunde*

(colonial studies), which merged theory with practice (Pugach 2012). A variant clone was established in South Africa with the establishment of schools of African life and languages, or *Bantoekunde*, at English and Afrikaans universities in the twenties, which had as one of their principal aims the professionalization of "native administration," signaled by the appointment of a government ethnologist in 1925.

Modern colonialism was legitimized both locally and internationally by invoking expertise in "knowing the native." Colonial policy was premised on what Mamdani (2012) termed "define and rule." Native policy became the centerpiece of modern colonial rule and gave rise to the native expert. Steinmetz (2007) has explained variations in German colonial policy by showing how different European social groups competed for a specific form of social or ethnographic capital, the rather vague claim to "knowing the natives." Credentialed "native" expertise gained further traction in the early twentieth century, with the establishment of the League of Nations and later the UN (Mazower 2012).

Third, taking the lead from recent studies both in the history/sociology of science and latterly in anthropology (Carr 2010), expertise is conceived not so much as intellectual knowledge but as performance. These experts demonstrated their knowledge to a multitude of audiences, local and international, real or imagined. As Robert Frost put it in *A Masque of Reason*:

> Society can never think things out:
> It has to see them acted out by actors,
> Devoted actors at a sacrifice—

While experts certainly are crucial in policy making, they also perform two types of symbolic role (Boswell 2009, 7–8). First, the perception that the administration possesses reliable and detailed information creates confidence that their policies are well-founded, thus leading to legitimizing and bolstering the administration's claims to jurisdiction, or what is known as "epistemic authority." Second, proclamations of expert knowledge could lend authority to particular policy positions by substantiating South Africa's policy preference and undermining alternative policy options. Of course, while experts might have enhanced the administration's credibility, this does not mean that they necessarily improve the quality of the administration's performance, as Boswell points out.

Apart from audiences, real or imagined, context and conditions, especially the sociopolitical and scholarly situations, shaped their expert products. Simultaneously, however, these overlapping and sometimes distinctive situations enabled experts to claim some autonomy, frequently expressed as self-doubt, hence making some of their decisions, and actions, moral. Was the response I got from volkekundiges concerning the militarization of Bushmen largely a consequence of their search for recognition?

The international arena provides a stage for performances ranging from the PMC, the UN, and especially the ICJ to local village-level performances. These presentations are especially fertile for understanding how colonialism works. For one thing, they illustrate how colonialism, which depended on "the white man's burden" for its moral justification, did not simply occur but was dependent upon and influenced by audiences, local and international (Rutherford 2012). These international audiences had the capacity to profoundly affect the practice of colonial policy. Reading documents in the Namibian archives, one cannot but be impressed at how seriously the South Africans took any (potential) international criticism, especially after the so-called Bondelzwarts Rebellion (1922). Even a report alleging Bushman slavery by the Anti-Slavery Society would provoke a full and detailed report. For many years after World War II, foreigners were barred from doing social research in the territory for fear of what impact their findings might have on international audiences. Colonialism had to play to different audiences, including Indigenes and local settlers, as South African prime minister Verwoerd showed with the festive launch of the Odendaal Commission recommendations that, I would suggest, had less to do with promoting the welfare of the Indigenous inhabitants than impressing an international audience, especially those located in the halls of the UN.

Experts, specifically ethnologists, were to profoundly shape how Namibia was imagined. However, their claims to expertise were to be constantly challenged, exposing their fragility, which leads to the main concerns of this monograph: How did these authorities get their expert evidence so wrong that it made them ridiculous? Moreover, why were these absurd ideas believed to be credible? Using a situational analysis perspective, I trace the networks of a number of interlinked personnel and ritual situations in which volkekunde came to imagine a utopian *apartheid* state. In sum, if colonialism is the history of the gradual emergence of state structures and societal forms and geographic expansion, what role did ethnology play in this exercise at least in one particular country, Namibia?

Overall the case can be made that a historically informed anthropology and an anthropologically informed history enrich, enliven, and provide fresh insights into old shibboleths and taken-for-granted flat historical descriptions. But, then again, while I do not think the chapters in this book are particularly innovative, they do show how a certain perspective can bring new insights to bear on old problems and problematize simplistic answers that can easily take on the character of myth or urban legend. Treating colonizer and colonized, military occupiers and *plaaslike bevolking* (local populations, or LPs) as being part of the same historically grounded social system allows one to appreciate more fully acts of resistance, by knowing at least partially what they were up against and how the structures they resisted were created, organized, and maintained.

This volume contributes to a new subfield in anthropology, the anthropology of colonialism. While the anthropology of colonialism is of recent vintage, going back perhaps a decade or so, its roots go back much further. Its emergence was perhaps inevitable given the alignment of a number of contingent disciplinary interests in literary studies and history and, of course, most importantly, the critical or self-reflective nature of anthropology. Given the self-reflective nature of anthropology, a turn to the historical was inevitable. Indeed, if there is one overarching concern in this collection it is that anthropologists and policy makers ignore histories at the peril of getting things gloriously wrong.

The Order of Chapters

Chapter 1. "Beleaguered Knowledge: The Interwar Irrelevance of Anthropological Expertise"

The League of Nations ushered in the era of scientific colonialism in which international expertise was valued. Awarded the territory as a C Class mandate by the league, South Africa had to submit annual reports to the PMC and justify its native expertise. There is nothing like a scandal to bring the experts to the limelight. The Bondelzwarts Rebellion, in 1922, when an impoverished Indigenous group was brutally suppressed, was one such example. This chapter examines how South African claims to expertise on the basis of 250 years of "contact" were justified. Ridiculousness in its full theatricality was manifest not only in the field but also in the hallowed halls of the League of Nations in Geneva. The PMC hearings of mandatory reports were highly scripted, but also absurd, events dealing with important matters. The South Africans cynically played to the formulistic scripted rules of legalism, but the suspicion emerges: Were they so taken in by their own performances that they eventually believed it themselves? As the Canadian novelist Robertson Davies (1974, 251) observed:

> We all create an outward self with which to face the world, and some people come to believe that is what they truly are. So they people the world with doctors who are nothing outside of the consulting-room, and judges who are nothing when they are not in court, and businessmen who wither with boredom when they have to retire from business, and teachers who are forever teaching. That is why they are such poor specimens when they are caught without their masks on.

While the administration belittled professional "native expertise," for the remaining German settlers, especially those belonging or aspiring to the *Bürgertum* (middle class), such expertise became a significant mark of distinction and an important rationalization for why they felt the mandate should be returned to Germany. Key to this exercise was the missionary ethnologist Heinrich Vedder, who after World War II was appointed to the South African senate as an expert on the natives of the territory. Much of this activity was concentrated in the South-West African Scientific Society. Significantly, the ethnic group highlighted was that labeled Bushmen, the forgotten victims of a series of genocidal actions ranging from 1911 to 1915. They were the quintessential "Other." The case is made in this chapter and the next for the importance of that cultural construction known as the Bushmen as crucial for settler identity. The importance of Bushmen is underlined by the contradictory and troublesome relationship settlers had with them and how this was enveloped in a distinctive mythology often supported by a scholarly imprimatur. The assumed uniqueness and scarcity of Bushmen allowed settlers to develop what I term the Leporello syndrome. In the opera *Don Juan*, Leporello was Don Juan's procurer in chief, and what these largely amateur scientists in SWA did was to procure raw material for the metropole. While Bushman imagery extends back to precolonial times, this era marked the increased velocity of recycling of images and written representations of Bushmen for various purposes, creating more robust tropes of their alleged characteristics.

Chapter 2. *"Post–World War II Ethnological Dispositions in a Disputed Territory"*

Refusing to relinquish the mandate to the UN after World War II and fearful of international embarrassment, South Africa started to bring professional experts onto the stage of world opinion. The initial stimulus was the well-funded International Africa Institute's Africa Survey, which led to the appointment of a German ethnologist, F. Rudolph Lehmann, who was later succeeded by the German expatriates Günter Wagner, Oswin Köhler, and Kuno Budack, who, as foreigners, made ideal servants of power. They conducted a number of district surveys in areas that had a sizable Herero population, notable for being "troublesome" by petitioning the UN. At the same time, Dr. Nikolaas J. van Warmelo, the chief ethnologist in the South African Department of Native Affairs, made the regions beyond the Police Zone—the densely populated Ovamboland and Kavango—the major sources for contract labor and the isolated Kaokoveld into his personal realm of expertise, making frequent visits, to advise on chieftaincy problems especially. Of more immediate concern, though, was the perceived imminent demise of the Bushmen, now recast as an increasingly important scientific commodity, which needed to be saved. A Commission for the Preservation of the Bushmen was created and chaired by Pieter J. "Piet" Schoeman, an Afrikaner anthropologist heavily influenced by Bronislaw Malinowski. This single-minded emphasis on Bushmen served to divert international attention from problems in other parts of the country.

Chapter 3. *"Performing for All the World to See: Bruwer and the Fashioning of Modern Namibia"*

In the late fifties and early sixties, pressure mounted on South Africa, both internally, through the formation of Indigenous nationalist political parties, and internationally, at the UN and in various court cases heard at the ICJ. The most famous case was when Ethiopia and Liberia sued South Africa for breach of Article 2 of the mandate, which stipulated that the mandatory had to administer the territory in the best interest of its Indigenous people. At the World Court hearings, South Africa mounted a major campaign to justify apartheid to an increasingly skeptical international audience. Three of the thirteen expert witnesses they called were anthropologists, of whom one, J. P. van S. "Hannes" Bruwer, was the key figure, spending more time giving evidence and being cross-examined than anyone else. Bruwer is crucial for understanding the shaping of modern Namibia. He was the driving force behind the Odendaal Commission, which represents the only serious attempt to implement grand apartheid, the South African nationalist utopia. Archival research shows that one of the commission's main purposes was to mollify international audiences, and Bruwer was appointed commissioner-general to guide this effort. This chapter examines how Bruwer's network and key role in organizations like the Afrikaner Broederbond (AB), a secretive organization promoting Afrikaner nationalism, framed his anthropological praxis, which led him to make statements that were patently absurd.

Chapter 4. *"From WHAM to Countermobilization"*

Failure to find a diplomatic solution for the territory's legal status led to the so-called Border War, an eighteen-year low-intensity war on Namibia's northern boundary. This represents what Agamben (2005) would term "bare colonialism": while oppressing the population, the authorities were also trying to enlist their support for the regime. The favored strategy in this regard was the SADF's Civic Action Program, a notion that was borrowed largely from the US military in which social scientists played a crucial role. The SADF became the largest employer in Africa of ethnologists, who were drawn almost exclusively from volkekunde departments. From the archival record, their major activity appears to have been developing etiquette guides for how to interact with the local population and organizing youth camps. They also tested and developed covert counter-insurgency projects, which, according to the South African Truth and Reconciliation Commission Report (1998), were later applied in South Africa to counter anti-apartheid resistance. While there is a substantial literature on violent covert action by the regime (see, e.g., Schutte, Liebenberg, and Minnaar 1998), especially the activities of the infamous 32 Battalion, the notorious Civilian Co-operation Bureau (CCB), the brutal Koevoet police unit (modeled on the Rhodesian Selous Scouts), and police hit squads, my focus here is on the oft-neglected soft psychological operations in which front organizations and the above-mentioned youth camps featured. This chapter, based on interviews and material from the SANDF archives, critically evaluates the role of anthropologists and psychologists in what was ultimately a futile and ridiculous exercise.

Chapter 5. "Bringing Bonn Back In"

Building on the insights of Moritz Bonn, who produced the first scholarly counter-narrative of colonialism, the praxis of these volkekundiges is critically evaluated. Settler *Umwelt*, the social space around people from within which signs for alarm can come, created the dominant ethos in settler colonies, which Agamben (2005) calls *état de siège*, or besiegement. Volkekundige concern was not with appreciating cultural diversity or Indigenous ingenuity, but rather with "undercurrents" and uncovering the "secrets" of the Other. These attempts, however, amounted largely to the production of "potted knowledge" produced by acts that resembled that of divination. Like the officers in Jaroslav Hašek's classic anti-war novel *The Good Soldier Švejk*, settlers and their volkekundiges could not decide whether Indigenes were stupid or having them on.

Conclusion. "'Have We Met the Enemy and (S)He Is Us?' (Pogo)"

A significant factor leading to an inability to see and to aphasia is the result of "group think," a concept developed by Yale psychologist Irving Janis and what Max Gluckman termed a closed system of thinking in which contrary information is either discarded or incorporated to strengthen the closed system of thought. Perhaps the most effective way of dealing with such purveyors of what is now known as fake news is to raise doubt and thus to stimulate their curiosity about how others might see or act on similar problems. One way to do this is to act as privileged jester in the late capitalist world, but with appropriate intellectual and moral humility, as the slippage between jester in the court of neo-feudalism and buffoons in the circus of neo-fascism is very easy. Indeed, while I ridicule volkekunde, I also seek to show how it became ridiculous and suggest that its value lies in revealing deep uncertainties and anxieties in settler society; the lesson is clear: there by the grace of God go we. Should anthropologists simply write an exposé describing the pornography of power within the discipline in an effort to simply engage in the politics of embarrassment, a strategy that seems to work in reasonably democratic societies? Should they become jesters in the court of neo-liberalism?

Notes

1. The authoritative two-volumed *Cambridge History of South Africa*, edited by Carolyn Hamilton, Bernard Mbenga, and Robert Ross (2011), does not even list Namibia or South-West Africa in its index.
2. Here tribute is due to the pioneering historiography examining South Africa's imperial role as epitomized by the special issue of the *Journal of Southern African Studies* entitled "Rethinking Empire in Southern Africa" (Henrichsen et al. 2015).
3. This book serves to recap and develop some ideas first published in Gordon 2018b.
4. Colonialism was a part of the imperial project, which Bonn defined as the employment of the engines of government and diplomacy to acquire territories, protectorates, and/or spheres: "The economic essence of imperialism is predatory; plunder, not profit, is its aim, while the political aim was 'ruling space' not 'living space'" (Bonn, "The Economic Basis of Imperialism," n.d., Nachlass Moritz Bonn N. 1082, Bundesarchiv Koblenz, Germany [hereafter cited as NMB]). For imperialism to succeed, wrote Bonn, the collaboration of the Indigenes was necessary, obtained either coercively or voluntarily, and typically occurred on two fronts: political colonization (*Herrschaftspolitik*), entailing conquest and administration and focused on territorial expansion; and capitalistic colonization (*Handelspolitik*), manifested in financial reorganization and capitalistic development and largely concerned with trade. Both modes of control rely on superior strength, technology, and knowledge. The purpose was "to squeeze out an income for the mother country," and this exploitation was in open contradiction to Christian principles and emerging beliefs about democracy. European industrialization shifted the equation somewhat by emphasizing the search for markets. Growing surplus generated by industrialism needed investment to grow. As capital moved to backward countries, it needed security achieved through open or disguised political control. With remarkable prescience in the interwar years, Bonn was claiming, "The business of Empire was converted into the Empire of business" (Bonn, "The Twilight of Economics," n.d., NMB).

   It was the agrarian variety of colonialism that was to be Bonn's métier. Colonialism transpired, whether by the conquistadors or Canadian pioneers, when people sought items of value beyond their native territory. Initially the colonial project was not to deal with excess or overpopulation, rather the *auswanderungslustige Elemente* (those willing to emigrate) were drawn from the (aspiring) middle classes and the nobility, especially younger sons who were cut out by the inheritance system but who had some capital and dreamed of setting up a latifundia system to lord over large estates. At root it was not genuine capitalism but rather a mock capitalism, a concept that Bonn unfortunately did not elaborate upon but that displays kinship with Marxian primitive accumulation and Weberian adventure or booty capitalism. The moral justification for colonialism was invariably "'the white man's burden,' a profitable though onerous task laid upon the back of a masterful race of white men . . . whose strong altruistic feelings tempted them to take it upon themselves in the interest of mankind, as long as it was a paying proposition," noted Bonn (1925, 19). Where Indigenes such as North American Indians or South African Bushmen did not fit into the activities the colonials wanted them to undertake, they are declared unworthy and incapable of adapting to higher forms of production. Dilettantes proclaimed that it was the "law of nature" that the less capable "races" had to die out before the more capable ones (Bonn 1909). These "votaries of cheap Darwinism" forgot to mention the spread of contagious diseases, the sale of alcohol and firearms, and the decimation of game (Bonn 1938, 280). After years of colonial pressure, Indigenes started accepting the inevitability of their fate: it entered their consciousness (Bonn 1909, 675).

5. My approach shares kinship with J. M. Coetzee's reading of Geoff Cronje, a major sociological theorist of apartheid, as mad (Coetzee 1996, 163–84). Initially those about to be colonized also saw colonizers as ridiculous (Rutherford 2012). It was this burden of absurdity that made colonialism intolerable. See also Alison Shutt's excellent *Manners Make a Nation* (2015).

CHAPTER 1

Beleaguered Knowledge

The Interwar Irrelevance of Anthropological Expertise

Setting the Stage

With rapidly expanding globalization after World War I, the necessity of legitimating colonialism to Europeans, locally and internationally, took on a dimension that opens the space for considering the absurdity of the colonial project as it was performed in the sittings of the League of Nations where Woodrow Wilson (1919, 73) proudly proclaimed that "for the first time in history the counsels of mankind are to be drawn together for the purpose of improving the conditions of working people." The rise of formally recognized expertise concerning "natives" emerged in the early twentieth century and, with the establishment of the erstwhile League of Nations, provided "native experts" with a solid grounding and assumed expediency (Mazower 2012; Pedersen 2015). In her 1936 paean to progressive native administration, anthropologist Lucy Mair ([1936] 1980) argued that there was a need in Africa for a system of control over colonial administration, not only because of the German colonial atrocities but because of deficiencies in all existing systems. The body best equipped to do this, she argued, was the League of Nations' Permanent Mandates Commission (PMC), which demanded more than lip service and readily criticized colonial administrations. In the "deliberate manipulation of society" (later known as "social engineering") that was called upon by the "Sacred Trust," as the mandates were glossed, science was to play a key role. Mair ([1936] 1980, 286) concluded:

> The ideal union between science and policy would be one in which action was taken only in the light of all knowledge available as to its possible consequences, where such knowledge carried greater weight than the clamour of conflicting desires, and was accepted as a reason for abandoning desires that in achievement must be disastrous.

Awarded a Class C mandate over South-West Africa, the South African mandatory managed to camouflage its brutal and exploitative policies toward Indigenes through the skillful use of bluff disguised as "expertise" in its reports to the PMC, the body charged by the League of Nations to oversee the mandates. Through the prism of ridiculousness, this chapter questions the authority of colonial power and its representatives. Contemplating the mandatory's policies as ridiculous and absurd provides a perspective to describe and analyze the authority and power of the mandate as a complex play with its legal and administrative rule. What is striking is how the practice of colonial policy, especially when marketed as ethical imperialism, was influenced by audiences, real and perceived, local and especially international.

Members of the PMC were mostly experienced colonial officials, supposedly independent, and elected on the basis of personal qualifications by the league's council. Their task was to examine annual reports submitted by the mandatories and make suggestions and recommendations to the council. They suffered under a variety of constraints, notably a lack of familiarity with the territories and, given the time lag in the submission of reports, tended to focus on judging past events rather than prescribing future actions. All in all, the situation encouraged legalistic, stereotypical discourses with a concern about the enforcement of particular articles of the mandate (Cockram 1976, 113). While the hearings and discussions were private, since their work was only advisory, the minutes of the proceedings were public and made good copy for the international press aided by the large and effective press section of the league's secretariat.

The Bondelzwarts Scandal

Barely eighteen months after being awarded the mandate, an event leading to considerable embarrassment to the South African mandatory occurred. In May 1922 the !Gami-nun, at the time called Bondelzwarts in the colonial sphere, rebelled. They were an impoverished group who resided in the arid southern part of South-West Africa and had suffered heavily under German colonial rule. Two issues rankled deeply. First, they wanted Jacobus Christian, who had, along with several other Bondelzwarts refugees, returned without permission from exile in South Africa, recognized as chief. Second, they objected vociferously to a dog tax that Gijsbert Hofmeyr, the first civilian administrator appointed by South Africa under the mandate, in October 1920, had imposed on the territory in an effort to encourage Indigenes to seek work with impoverished settler farmers. In itself this tax would not have been important except that an overzealous official started fining and imprisoning recalcitrant Bondelzwarts. In what became a tragicomedy, Hofmeyr, fearing a general uprising, over-reacted and personally led troops, including a South African machine gun contingent and two airplanes, to bomb the Bondelzwarts. It caused some hundred deaths of men, women, and children out of a total population of between five and six hundred (Goldblatt 1971, 216). Despite efforts at censorship, the episode made international headlines and drew adverse criticism, not only abroad but also in South Africa, where Hofmeyr was ridiculed in Parliament as a "prancing proconsul."

At the League of Nations a motion concerning the Bondelzwarts affair was unanimously carried, and the PMC excoriated South Africa. It unanimously regretted the absence of a mandatory representative, which was contrary to the PMC's constitution and rules of procedure and especially frustrating given the brevity of the South African replies to the commission's questionnaire, which specifically asked for information on the cause, extent, and nature of the disorder and its repression.

Given the international outcry, Jan Smuts, the South African prime minister and a key figure in the founding of the league, appointed a commission of enquiry consisting of all three members of the recently created parliamentary Native Affairs Commission, selected for their expertise in "native affairs," namely Senator Alexander Roberts (as chair), Dr. Charles T. Loram, and General Lodewyk A. S. Lemmer. Roberts had long been involved in matters of African education and served as principal of the South African Native College. Loram had a doctorate from Columbia, published in 1917 as the influential tome *The Education of the South African Native*, and was a leading figure in liberal circles. Lemmer, on the other hand, was simply a loyal and trusted supporter of General Smuts.

Appointed on 20 July 1922, the commission of enquiry commenced its investigation in August, traveling to the territory and conducting 124 interviews, ranging from the administrator and the secretary for the mandate, who were especially thanked for their cooperation, to officials, police, and volunteers, and to the Bondelzwarts chief and headmen. The commission visited Windhoek, the capital, and the battlefields and, to avoid intimidation, heard all evidence in private. It found that many people were living at the "extreme edge of destitution" and that the farmer's labor needs could be alleviated by importing laborers from outside the territory and improving conditions of employment. It was generally highly critical of the mandatory administration. One of the commission's chief concerns was that the interface between native-settler and native-official was characterized by gross mistrust; many officials did not possess the qualities necessary for successful administration. The commission thus suggested the necessity of developing a strong native affairs department consisting of three or four men of "good type who would take up the work as a life profession, and remain in their posts long enough to allow the Natives to get to know them" (South Africa 1923, 27).

In every phase of its inquiry and in its main conclusions, the commission split two to one, with Lemmer disagreeing with Roberts and Loram's conclusions, especially their statement that

> the resistance seems to the Commission to be the action of a people driven to extremity by poverty and by an acute sense of injury and injustice, real or imaginary. . . . The whole native problem, not only as it affects the Bondelzwarts, but as it exists throughout the Territory, requires the most careful and exhaustive examination, in order to bring it into harmony with the idea that the native is a sacred trust to the Mandatory State. (South Africa 1923, 33)

Lemmer claimed that such a wide recommendation was not within the commission's reference and "resisted the inference that may perhaps be drawn that the natives are not being treated as they should in a mandated Territory." To him, the mistrust between Bondels and police was not due to the police but due to the character of the Bondels. They were "temperamentally lazy and lacking the stimuli to improve their situation" (South Africa 1923, 30). Overall, Lemmer felt that Hofmeyr had acted correctly and with due diligence. Accompanying the commission's report was a memorandum by Hofmeyr in which he defended his actions. He felt condemned without trial:

> But for the forbearance and tact of the authorities, who were well aware of the peculiar traits of the Hottentots—though the Commission did not think so—a clash of arms would long ago have resulted. (Cited in Cockram 1976, 155)

The Bondelzwarts Report was presented to the South African Parliament in April 1923 and subjected to an extensive and acrimonious debate, with the opposition Labor Party calling the Bondelzwarts affair a "blot on the escutcheon of South Africa." Smuts, in turn, denied that the Bondelzwarts had any "substantial grievances": "[They] are a native people with simple minds—they misunderstand things and exaggerate others, and in one way or another a whole psychology grows up in their minds which in the end brings forth rebellion." With a whiff of patriotism, he remarked that he was

> pained by the discussion which had put the facts out of focus. [It] . . . would go to the outside world and would be read by people who did not know the circumstances and the local situation. The discussion . . . and the charges raised would be used against them in other parts of the world by people who had not given one-tenth of the time or consideration to native affairs that we had (Hear Hear). If those people seriously believed in South Africa, they would get an entirely erroneous conception of the situation. (*Cape Times*, 23 May 1923)

The commission's report, along with Hofmeyr's critical rejoinder, Smuts said, would be handed over to the League of Nations by Major J. F. Herbst, "who knows all the facts," so that the PMC would have all the evidence and thus "full facts." Herbst was clearly considered an expert on "native affairs," having served as secretary for SWA and doubling as chief native commissioner from December 1916 until 1923, when he was rewarded with a promotion to secretary for native affairs in South Africa. He was singularly underprepared for his examination at the PMC, being forced to apologize for not bringing several relevant documents, including obvious material like the report of the recently completed Native Reserve Commission and the evidence heard by the Bondelzwarts Commission.

The PMC was carefully prepared for the hearing on the precedent-setting scandal. It was concerned that the Bondelzwarts Report and the documents received did not answer any of the questions raised by the League of Nations' council and assembly. It held four preparatory meetings to discuss how to audition both Herbst and Edgar Walton, the South African representative at the league. It developed a series of questions that focused on three particular concerns. First, the PMC did not believe that the Bondelzwarts Commission of Enquiry was an impartial investigation as promised, especially since the evidence gathered by the commission was not available for perusal despite repeated requests. It reluctantly accepted the Bondelzwarts Report as authoritative on the grounds that the commissioners had split on all major recommendations. A second concern was that Smuts had simply forwarded the report without endorsing any of the recommendations, although he had vigorously defended Hofmeyr in the South African Parliament. If Smuts did not accept the report as impartial, was he going to order another commission of enquiry? A third issue concerned who should be heard by the PMC. One of the most active parties in seeking a hearing was the Anti-Slavery Society. It was eventually decided not to hear such interest groups, since it was not the duty of the PMC to hold such an inquiry, moreover "it could not hear everybody. It could not appear to throw doubt in advance of the South African report" (PMC 1923a, 62). Apart from the practical issue of bringing in witnesses from Africa, the PMC doubted the impartiality of the Anti-Slavery Society, simultaneously ignoring that South Africa was sending one of the executive officials engaged in suppressing the affair. Lord Frederick Lugard, one of the most influential PMC members, brokered a compromise by which the league's commission agreed not to hear any new witnesses, on the basis that the conclusions of the report were sufficiently severe for the mandatory administration, but accepted a written submission by the Anti-Slavery Society.

In a remarkable display at the PMC hearing, Herbst dismissed the Bondelzwarts Report out of hand as being biased, inadequate, and unreliable: "Nobody in the Union knew anything about the Administration in South-West Africa. Anybody appointed on a Commission would have to go up and enquire locally for information" (*Cape Times*, 22 May 1923). Thus South Africa rejected the commission of enquiry's recommendation concerning revamping the system of native administration with "three or four good men," since the SWA administration had not been consulted; moreover such a consultation was not within the commission's terms of reference. Regarding the recommendation that the Bondelzwarts be given some form of autonomy, Herbst asserted that this was impractical, as the Germans had "broken up" the tribes in the south. "There had been no complaint" concerning the size of their reserve, which he deemed sufficient, as "they had the best land in that part of the country, but they certainly had asked for all the land recently occupied[, indeed] the whole ambition of a native was to own stock. He wished for little more." He dismissed even minor recommendations, like that officials involved in the affair be transferred, since it was best to "let sleeping dogs lie" (PMC 1923b, 129). Addressing one of the central concerns raised in the motion by the League of Nations Assembly about what was being done to restore the economic situation of the Bondelzwarts, Herbst blithely commented that humanitarian assistance was minimal and the Bondelzwarts men were encouraged to go out and seek work (PMC 1923b, 132).

Regardless of Herbst's presentation, the PMC found that the primary cause of the Bondelzwarts affair was distrust between black and white and that Hofmeyr had exaggerated the gravity of the situation. It asserted that timely intervention by the administrator would have prevented the rebellion, the repression of which had been carried out with "excessive severity" (PMC 1923b, 135–36). It was harshly critical of the lack of information and a complete and authoritative inquiry. The administrator was condemned for personally conducting military operations as a civil servant and representative of the mandatory power, since it "excludes in the eyes of the natives the possibility of a supreme appeal to the highest authority, but also, as a consequence the Administrator is deprived of his capacity as an impartial critic and judge of the conduct of operations" (PMC 1923b, 5). As South African representative at the League of Nations, Walton roundly attacked the findings, using what were to become standard rhetorical devices in the South African armory: the PMC had "failed altogether to realize the situation in South West Africa." He argued that PMC statements like "[in] South West Africa even the educated classes regarded the natives as existing chiefly for the purpose of labor for whites" revealed the prejudices of this international body and ignored "the obvious fact that in that development the native is being gradually civilized, and, indeed, that he can be civilized in no other way . . . the maintenance of law and order is an essential preliminary to the inculcation of the principles of civilization." He posited that the criticism in the PMC report, "emanating evidently from inexperienced persons[,] is prejudicial to . . . successful government. . . . It will be resented by the whole of the white population of the territory, and its only effect on the native people will be to make them more difficult to manage and less amenable to civilizing forces." He concluded with what was to become the standard expertise justification:

> For upwards of two centuries the South African people have been brought into close contact with the native races, and it is only just to claim that they have not shirked the white man's burden. It has been said that the white man will never understand the black, but the white man in South Africa may at least claim to have studied the problem for many generations and may also claim a great measure of success. (Walton 1923, 2)

Expertise, as Hofmeyr was to argue the following year, was based on first-hand experience: "This view is confirmed by experienced officers—that the raw and semi-civilised native in South West Africa is treated better than in any other part of South Africa, if not in the world" (PMC 1924, 55).

Clearly the PMC's opinion stung South Africa. Two weeks after the League of Nations issued its rebuke, the *Cape Argus* criticized "another long-winded vindication" of Hofmeyr, this time by his attorney-general, Lennox Ward, who had prosecuted the Bondelzwarts leaders. It concluded:

> These attacks on the competency of the Native Affairs Commission have laid the Union government open to the charge that it failed to carry out its promise to hold a proper, impartial inquiry into the late rebellion. . . . It is very remarkable that while official memoranda are showered upon the Press with the object of casting doubt upon the main conclusions of the report of the Native Affairs Commission, the evidence upon which that report was based is still withheld from the public. (*Cape Argus*, 4 October 1923)

But the lesson was learned. The next year Hofmeyr personally appeared at the PMC, accompanied by his native commissioner, Major Manning, and South Africa was praised for being the first mandatory to send its administrator to be examined. Hofmeyr sought to "disabuse the PMC of hasty action" and charmed them with his exaggerated courtesy. When the PMC complained about the brevity of the mandatory's annual report, he disarmingly replied that his government had instructed him to keep these reports short so as not to waste the PMC's time. He impressed by being well prepared, bringing several maps and a couple of photograph albums. A ritual reconciliation was effected, and precedent was created. Every administrator after Hofmeyr made at least one appearance before the PMC, usually accompanied by a senior official.

Two themes are constantly reiterated in the mandatory administration's attempts to justify its policies in the face of criticism for exploiting African labor to benefit white settlers: first, the belief that work was essential for "progress," and second, the need to get "natives" to respect the "law."

> Civilization will never be developed on idleness and education of the native does not consist of teaching him the alphabet or the bible only. . . . Left to himself he will simply sit in the sun and dream about women and cattle. A good harvest results in liberal brewing of beer, heavy drinking and tribal disorders. Work brings him in contact with civilization and, therefore, necessarily assists the process of civilizing him. (South Africa 1928, 98)

Such discourses have to be contextualized. In particular the notion that "idleness is sin" was well-grounded, of course, in the dominant Christian and evolutionary notions that progress is achieved through "hard work." The mandatory administration emphasized the importance of "work" as development strategy. Labor and poverty were held to be simple polar opposites, and increasing the one would reduce the other.

Administration rhetoric constantly used the phrase "idle and disorderly." Work and order, in short, were cognitively connected. Indeed, one could make a reasonable case that the rhetoric of "idleness and the nobility of work" was shaped for the international audience, who might have looked askance at any rhetoric featuring settler fears or insecurities. Instead, the rhetoric of civilization and its inherent need for controlling labor enabled the colonials to manipulate the situation, not in the name of fear or even exploitation but in the name of the desire to civilize.

Performing Colonial Expertise

The South African claim to expertise was based almost exclusively on the assertion of "long-term experience" that had shown that making Indigenes work was the surest way to civilize them. But how did this work out at the grass roots? With the establishment of the mandate, the administrative world was considerably downsized, from approximately 1,200 civil servants employed in the German colony to 311 in 1923, of whom 212 were hired on a temporary basis, with large anomalies in pay, allowances, and local privileges eventually leading to demoralization (PMC 1923a, 48). Native administration in South-West Africa under the South African mandate was always a shoestring operation. In 1939 it consisted of one part-time (ex officio) chief native commissioner (the secretary for South-West Africa, who until 1928 was also police commissioner), supported by two native commissioners, twelve clerks, and ten reserve superintendents. In addition, the eighteen magisterial districts were administered by magistrates who doubled as native commissioners. From the beginning, quality of personnel was problematic. Sir Edmond H. L. Gorges, the first administrator, complained that "staff matters have been a terrible worry and I have been saddled with a lot of misfits.[1] . . . The tendency on the part of some Departments has been to try to pass off their bad bargains to me. . . . Of the 18 magistrates only 3 were full magistrates in the Union the rest were nearly all clerks" (Smuts 1966, 455). In 1937 South Africa again conceded that most of the magistrates were of the "weakest type," pointing out that it was difficult to attract "good people" to the territory. Efforts to professionalize "native administration" with one- or two-year university diplomas were singularly unsuccessful, despite offering a small bonus, and the diploma was eventually discarded. Indeed, the PMC noted in one of its meetings that professionalism was deemed irrelevant in South Africa, since "some knowledge of native affairs, languages and customs was common among South Africans, and this would perhaps explain why the Government had not considered it necessary to make such studies compulsory" (PMC 1938, 77).

Given the low organizational density in which these officials operated, it was obviously difficult to audit their performances. This meant that they had considerable informal power or, to be fashionable, devolved sovereignty. A visiting South African journalist compared officials in South-West Africa with feudal lords in Plantagenet England: "They were little kings without any check whatsoever on their actions, and they impose their will, right or wrong, on native and white alike" (*Sunday Times*, 23 May 1922).

Feudal lords require ceremonialism and exaggerated etiquette to display their status, and the Bondelzwarts scandal strikingly demonstrated this. This was why Hofmeyr, whose previous position had been chief clerk of the House of Assembly, proclaimed himself colonel despite having no military experience, only commenced hostilities against the Bondelzwarts after his tailor-made uniform arrived, and used the late Transvaal president Paul Kruger's railcar as headquarters. When Lord Lugard asked if Hofmeyr might have "sunk a little dignity and gone to see" the Bondelzwarts leader, Jacobus Christian, Herbst replied:

> It meant more than sinking a little dignity . . . it would have been an intolerable position. . . . The Administrator did not think it was dangerous. He did think, however, that it would have been undignified and that his position with the Europeans would have been absolutely intolerable. . . . He could not have gone back to the Windhoek if that had taken place. (Cited in Cockram 1976, 141)

The Bondelzwarts Commission of Enquiry, despite visiting the terrain of conflict, took evidence of Europeans in Windhoek, "as it was feared that their presence with the commission would give a wrong impression to the natives" (PMC 1923a, 127). Maintaining settler prestige was cardinal. Christian was not recognized as chief because the mandatory administration felt that it would reduce its own prestige (at least in the eyes of the settlers). Herbst declared that

> if the European population now hear that the Administrator has to go to the natives whenever they oppose the law, or the police in carrying out the law, I do not know what is going to be the result. In South Africa one of the first rudiments of policy is to secure respect for the law from the native population. (PMC 1923a, 186–87)

Ceremonialism and everyday rituals of degradation permeated the territory. The two most famous native commissioners of the interwar years, Carl H. L. "Cocky" Hahn and Harold Eedes, were sticklers for etiquette. Reverend G. W. R. Tobias, MC, MA, founder of the Ovamboland Mission of the Anglican Church and later bishop of Damaraland, reported:

> Hahn and Eades [*sic*] are very much on a pedestal and keep aloof and speak through an interpreter—they are very anxious for me to speak just as they do. . . . The Bishop came to me before he left and said that Hahn wanted to speak to me [about] my attitude to the natives. "Speak to them," he said, "like a Sergeant Major, give orders and never hold a conversation and do not be friendly." Hahn also said[:] "Always speak with authority as to a child who is rather in disgrace." Hahn is on excellent footing with the people . . . but his attitude is "I have spoken—there the matter ends." (Mallory 1971, 29–30)

With an Expert Curtsy to Anthropology

As anyone who has extensively used the National Archives of Namibia will attest, one of the most obvious changes accompanying the arrival of the South African administration is the massive decline in administrative documentation. Compared to their German predecessors, South African bureaucrats made poor documentalists, reflected in the civic sector where the South-West African Scientific Society drew its support largely from the German minority. Unlike their British counterparts who proudly emphasized their Oxbridge tradition, the South African administrators made do with minimal educational requirements. Indeed, their most renowned native commissioners, Hahn and Eedes, barely managed to complete their high school education. Moreover, the organizational culture of the state bureaucracy worked against officials from taking an interest in local customs. As Gerard P. Lestrade (1932, 14), the first South African government ethnologist, shrewdly observed, "We live in South Africa with a peculiar complex with regard to our knowledge of the native.

We think we know the native through and through, while in truth we shy away from the magnitude of our ignorance." Efforts in the interwar years by the universities of the Witwatersrand (Wits) and Cape Town (UCT) to offer vacation schools that would professionalize native administration in southern Africa were doomed to wither away. No official from the territory ever attended such a school. Indeed, a Southern Rhodesian official noted with surprise that while the school was sponsored by the South African government, no South African officials enrolled for the one he had attended (Morris 1930). A bonus for officials learning a native language was withdrawn because of the disappointing response (South Africa 1936, 144). They were very much part of the South African mold where Isaac Schapera, professor of social anthropology at the University of Cape Town, complained that for promotion

> officers of the Native Affairs Department must speak the two official languages of the country, and pass the Civil Service Law Examinations; but they are apparently not required either to speak the languages of the peoples with which they are most directly concerned, nor is any special knowledge demanded from them of the Native laws and customs which they have to administer. (Schapera 1939, 102)

Nor was there much interest in amateur ethnography by officials or settlers generally. Natives were apparently too westernized except for those north of South-West Africa's so-called Police Zone, where Hahn served as gatekeeper extraordinaire. When compared to its other African colonial counterparts, the *Journal of the South West Africa Scientific Society*, published since 1926, is remarkable for its lack of ethnographical observations, and if it did include them, these tended to focus on the people considered most exotic, the marginal Bushmen. This was hardly the stuff of practical knowledge. The major work of ethnography and history was done by German-speakers, in particular the Rhenish missionary Heinrich Vedder, who received financial support from the administration to compile a history of the territory, entitled significantly *Das Alte Südwestafrika* (The old South-West Africa) (Vedder 1934), a 685-page tome translated and abbreviated to 540 pages in both the 1938 English version, entitled *The Early History of South West Africa*, and the 1937 Afrikaans one, named *Die voorgeskiedenis van Suidwes-Afrika* (The prehistory of South-West Africa). This book is a fine example of what Brigitte Lau (1995) called colonial apologetic writing, supporting white settler myths and centering on the role and responsibility of the white (largely German) "race as the carrier of Christian civilization." It emphasized precolonial conflict and was clearly the major source for arguments made in favor of apartheid. While the book creates the gloss of comprehensiveness—an effectiveness that is attested to by the fact that it is still printed and sold in Windhoek—Vedder's lack of training as a historian is attested to by his uncritical acceptance of missionary and traveler accounts and its lack of references.[2]

The South African government confidently believed that its own experience in dealing with the "native problem" was the ultimate guarantee of its bona fides and with ceremonial regularity stressed this, but occasional doubt was present. Clearly the mandatory administration had begun to realize that its claims to expertise based on two hundred years of experience and on-the-spot assessments were not going to convince the PMC, and a more sophisticated gesture was called for—a focus on Lugard's active promotion of anthropology. In 1928 administrator Albert J. Werth began by describing the ethnic diversity in the territory and their inherent tribal antagonisms to each other and "frankly admitted" that ethnological knowledge was in its "infancy." He then introduced chief medical officer Dr. Louis Fourie, who was

> probably one of the greatest living authorities on the Bushmen. To indicate the spirit of service which animates the officials of the Administration, I would say that he spends his holidays in the deserts of South-West Africa studying the family and social life of the Bushmen, you will realize what sacrifice that means; and even Dr Fourie will admit to you today that he knows very little about the soul of the Bushmen people. The same applies to probably the largest native race we have in South-West Africa, namely the Ovambo. (PMC 1928, 58)

Werth then proceeded to present the book *The Native Tribes of South West Africa* (Hahn, Vedder, and Fourie 1928), which had been specially prepared for the League of Nations, as well as a collection of photographs showing the "natives in their primitive state" and the conditions they worked under on the mines (PMC 1928, 90). *The Native Tribes of South West Africa* was undoubtedly the major, if only, ethnographic achievement of the mandatory administration. Its purpose, as stated in its foreword, was "to lay before the League of Nations a short sketch of each of the principal tribes, in order that without a great amount of study it can be seen by members of that body the state of development of the natives, their mode of living and the ways in which they resemble or differ from one another." The book consisted of five chapters, proudly listing the credentials of each author. The first chapter, "The Ovambo," was written by Hahn, introduced as "MBE, Officer in Charge of Native Affairs, Ovamboland." Fourie, presented as "MBE, M.B., FZS, Medical Officer to the Administration," provided a chapter entitled "The Bushmen." And Vedder, portrayed as "Dr h.c. and Präses of the Rhenish Mission in Damaraland," contributed three chapters, "The Berg Damara," "The Nama," and "The Herero." The credibility of the volume was enhanced by the citation of all of the authors' titles and awards. In retrospect, it is clear that this ethnographic volume was used more to bolster South Africa's credentials for administering the territory than in the actual practice thereof.

The book, incidentally also still in print, served to smokescreen answers to nagging questions. Sometimes, though, this strategy did not work, as when the indomitable Valentine Dannevig, Norwegian and the sole female member of the PMC, posed a question concerning the situation of native women. When the South African representative to the league, Eric Louw, referred her to *The Native Tribes* and quipped that if, after reading it, she "wished for further information in the next report, perhaps she could request it from the permanent SA representative," Dannevig bluntly replied that she had indeed read the whole book but that it said nothing about the status of native women (PMC 1931, 54).

So how must the book be contextualized, and what does it not say? Even a cursory reading reveals that it is written in the "antiquarian tradition," with its emphasis on speculative historical reconstruction (Ranger 1979), and that its chief purpose was to justify administration policy. Clearly the entities covered were the ethnic groups local Europeans thought significant: Ovambo, because they were the most numerous and an important source of labor; Herero and Nama, because of their reputation for confronting the German colonial regime; and the few thousand Bushmen who were believed to be on the verge of extinction and defined by science as valuable. The book ignores a number of people who would later be accorded distinct ethnic group labels, like those living on the Kavango River and in the Kaokoveld, as well as sizable minorities, such as the Tswana and the Colored and Rehoboth Basters ("troublesome" petitioners to the league). Consider Hahn's conclusion regarding the Ovambo:

> Most of the customs . . . in this brief report are no longer observed to their full extent among any of the tribes. The more revolting among them, such as those which led to an unnecessary and cruel sacrifice of human life . . . , have fortunately disappeared entirely owing to the gradual enlightenment of the native mind under European influence. . . . Contentment and happiness are steadily taking the place of the constant fear for life and property under which the people lived until recently under tribal regime. (Hahn, Vedder, and Fourie 1928, 36)

Not lacking in self-confidence, although he had problems putting pen to paper, Hahn considered his essay in the volume to be the best and most interesting in the volume (Wanless 2007, 80). His public representation of Ovambo was to impose itself on countless officials. In 1935 the Van Zyl Commission was appointed in response to settler dissatisfaction with the mode of administration. While not strictly in its terms of reference, the commission also considered the issue of native affairs administration and toured Ovamboland and the various native reserves. It was most impressed at what it saw in Ovamboland. The provident Ovambo were happy and contented because, so Hahn claimed, they were allowed to govern themselves. It was, the commission reported, an "excellent laboratory for the study of indirect rule" (South Africa 1936, 17). So obsessed was Hahn with preserving "traditional life" that on one occasion he turned back a shipment of plows at the border (Loeb 1962, viii). However, in the files a different picture emerges. Shiweda (2011, 79) cites a monthly report in which Hahn admits, "There is no doubt that the Ovambos are fast abandoning native customs and adopting those of Europeans. Youths and young men leave the country for the labor centers as raw savages and after a year or more amongst Europeans return to their homes as 'civilized' members of the tribe." In contrast to Hahn's almost utopian public portrayal, Eedes (1933, 60–61), the commissioner in charge of the neighboring Kavango reserve, saw his wards as "lazy, degenerate, and indolent," while women were "physically weak, filthy in their habits, lazy and can only be classed as prostitutes of the worst type." He attributed this situation to the fertile locality, which meant that the Kavango had no incentive to work.

The following year, in 1937, Hahn's opinions were greeted with acclaim at the PMC hearings, and questions pertaining to the Van Zyl Commission report were put to him. In his answers he explained that while all Ovambo had the same customs, some subgroups had more tribal laws than others and that in cases of conflict he applied European laws. He described flogging as rare and only practiced in areas where there were chiefs, but that traditional authorities were beginning to find fines more profitable. Returning Ovambo migrant contract workers were happily reabsorbed into the tribal system. He attributed the problems in the Kavango to weak chiefs and proposed importing some Ovambo chiefs to the area. When asked what his policy would be in the Police Zone, he said he would re-establish the "tribal system." According to him, the Herero were already undergoing this process, and this had made them more willing to cooperate with the administration and happier. The problem with the Nama, in turn, was that they had no hereditary chiefs, though the council system might produce results.

This mythical theme of the happy, contented Ovambo living a traditional lifestyle relatively free of "Western contamination" had considerable staying power, despite a warning expressed by Austrian anthropologist Victor Lebzelter, based on his 1927 research, that the contract labor system was undermining "traditional society": "It has been proven beyond any shadow of a doubt that blacks offer their labor to European economic interests for close to gratis and that there is nothing that could be called a gross national product of their own."[3]

Hahn's views and practices were taken to be the very model of how Lugardian "indirect rule" should be implemented, which resulted in high praise not only from PMC potentates like Sir Malcolm Hailey but also from liberal social anthropologists in South Africa, such as A. Winifred Hoernlé, who gushed after meeting him in Windhoek in 1935:

> Your policy was on the sound lines that an anthropologist would like to see laid down. It was splendid to hear you say that you would refuse to see any changes introduced into the social structure of the Ovambo, which had not been carefully considered by the organized administrative units of the people themselves. . . . I gathered you felt you were playing a lone hand with not much backing from the Administration. . . . You are the anthropologists' ideal administrator.[4]

Such was Hahn's reputation that he accompanied Premier Smuts to the inaugural meeting of the United Nations in 1945 and made a repeat visit the following year.

The other groups mentioned in *The Native Tribes* did not fare much better. Regarding the Berg Damara, Vedder concluded, "Being used to subservience the Berg Damara is happiest when under a firm hand, which rules his daily conduct and nips sudden desires for insubordination and impertinence in the bud" (Hahn, Vedder, and Fourie 1928, 77). Hottentots (Nama or Khoikhoi) were "children of the moment" who had been corrupted by the alcohol trade. While they now had many opportunities to work, they were unwilling because they were averse and unaccustomed to "continual exertion." Rhenish missionaries were trying to remedy the situation, leading Vedder to conclude, "Only we must not expect too much. A nomadic tribe cannot be changed to a civilized nation within the short period of one century full of wars. . . ." (Hahn, Vedder, and Fourie 1928, 148). Catholic missionaries are written out despite the fact that they had played an important, if failed, role as mediators in the Bondelzwarts affair. Vedder also ignored the fact that most Nama were an impoverished rural proletariat, and analyses by scholars like Hoernlé, who was soon to become a major figure in Southern African anthropology. Indeed, one must ask why Hoernlé was not invited to do that particular chapter, as her research had been sponsored by the mandatory administration.

Vedder's conclusion in his chapter on the Herero is again a striking apology for administration policy:

> If the proud Hereros can be successfully brought so far as to become reconciled to the course of historical events . . . they will certainly be called to take one of the foremost positions among the nations of South West. But if they haughtily decline the opportunities offered them for developing and working themselves up and persist in wishing to live an isolated life, . . . [they] will end in their digging their own national grave. (Hahn, Vedder, and Fourie 1928, 208)

Fourie's Bushmen, on the other hand, lived in an ahistoric never-never land of splendid isolation. They did not even have neighbors to interact with. That they had been victims of genocide barely ten years earlier is not even mentioned (Gordon 2009, 29–56). Similarly, the photographs included are telling. There are some anthropometric portraits to signal the scientific credence of the project, while Hahn's photographs seem to deliberately ignore evidence of Western commodification. Examining what was left unsaid in this handbook enables one to develop insights into the construction of local expert knowledge.

Aware of Smuts's interest and sponsorship in matters anthropological, South African scholarly entrepreneurs seized the opportunity. First into the starting gates was Dr. Louis Peringuey of the South African Museum, who managed to extract the then princely sum of £1,000 from the mandatory administration in 1920 to make models of Bushmen and have Dorothea Bleek undertake a simultaneous study of the Bushmen in the Gobabis district, all justified in the belief that they were scientifically valuable and sliding into extinction. In making this grant, Herbst also insisted:

> Up to the present few of the officials have shown any special interest in anthropological questions and those who have done so have not had the necessary guidance. Research would receive a great impetus if during your intended visit some organization or society for the study of native races and allied subjects could be inaugurated at Windhuk.[5]

Though the note was ultimately signed by Herbst, the key gatekeeper and its author was Dr. Louis Fourie, ardent Anglophile physician who had come into the territory in 1916 as part of the military forces and had stayed on as medical officer for the territory. As a senior administration official, his network and close friends tended to be of a similar background and included the trio of native affairs officials, Manning, Hahn, and Eedes. They were all English-speaking and tended toward being relatively liberal (at least in the South African context). Fourie was an active proponent of developing local expert knowledge and was instrumental in founding the South-West Africa Scientific Society and being elected its first president in 1926. A keen amateur ethnologist, Fourie was a fellow of the Royal Anthropological Institute and encouraged his friend, Cocky Hahn, to join as well. It was Fourie who persuaded the mandatory administration to produce *The Native Tribes of South West Africa*.

Undoubtedly the research visit by Hoernlé had much to do with this waning of interest. Hoernlé had done some pioneering research among the Nama before World War I and had then spent five years in the United States before returning to Johannesburg in 1920, where she had rapidly established her scholarly and liberal credentials. Invited by the mandatory administration, who provided transport and supplies, to do a restudy of the Nama (of whom the troublesome Bondelzwarts were members), she arrived in Windhoek just before Christmas and was met at the station by a delegation of noteworthy officials: A. J. Waters, crown prosecutor and acting secretary for the territory; Dr. Fourie, who was in charge of her expedition and probably the instigator of her invitation; Rupert S. Cope, the district native affairs officer; and Octavius G. Bowker, the superintendent of the Windhoek location. She spent three weeks in Windhoek and, judging from her field diaries, was given an earful by these officials. The chief difficulty lay with the Land Board, which was tasked with allocating land (to white settlers). Board members were political appointments and engaged in land-grabbing for friends. While land had been set aside for reserves, a good deal of it was "absolutely unsuitable." The Land Board and the new Afrikaner settlers were at the root of the problem, as they balked at all attempts by the Native Affairs Department to do anything for natives. Indeed, Cope had gone up-country when the Bondelzwarts Commission had visited Windhoek, because his evidence would have been critical of the mandatory administration and would thus have placed him in an intolerable position (Hoernlé 1987, 109).

In a carefully prepared twenty-five-page preliminary fieldwork report to the secretary for South-West Africa, Hoernlé drew attention to the pitiful conditions the Nama found themselves in. The situation in Windhoek was "entirely artificial," a "tragedy," with "tribal structure breaking down." She thanked the mandatory administration profusely for their assistance and hoped that they would fund a follow-up expedition so that she could complete a monograph on the Nama. After reading it, Hofmeyr noted in the margins to Herbst, "I find little results in this report from the point of view of anthropological research. Much useful time seems to have been spent in listening to . . . misgivings with administration defects, which is the function of our NA Dept [Native Affairs Department]. At the same time we should thank Mrs Hoernlé." She was thus duly thanked for "drawing attention to the complaints which were advanced by the Hottentots against the Administration, but it is assumed, of course, that your report for publication will confine itself strictly to the results of your research work."[6] To this she replied that her "preliminary report was private and gave the state of mind of the various tribes, as I thought it might be of interest, but I have no intention of going into this detail in the Monograph."[7]

Clearly the politics of embarrassment were a significant factor, especially when coupled to the changing political climate. In June 1924 the Smuts government in South Africa fell, to be replaced by a coalition between the Nationalist Party and the Labor Party. The Nationalists, who had been distinctly silent during the Labor Party evisceration of Hofmeyr, kept him on as administrator for another two years, and he oversaw the

barrage of legislation that framed segregation in the territory. They then
appointed their own man, the journalist Werth, who prioritized Afrikaner
interests, spoke only Afrikaans, and insisted that official correspondence
be written in that language. When in 1928 Werth emphasized the "great
harm . . . done to the native in the past through misguided efforts at kind-
ness" (PMC 1928, 59), he was trying not only to negate liberal arguments
internationally but also to put down the "liberals" in his administration.
Indeed, in private Fourie referred to Werth as a nationalist apostle and "an
opinionated petty Napoleon" (Wanless 2007, 69). Werth's successor as
administrator, another Nationalist hack, David G. Conradie, echoed his
predecessor by claiming that policy was "based on an unbroken experience, amplified by daily contact and intimate personal study, over a period
of 250 years in South Africa" (PMC 1935, 162).

In what was regarded as a South African coup, the Marquis Theodoli,
the PMC's long-term chair, was feted by the mandatory administration
on an all-expenses-paid "private" reconnaissance and hunting trip the next
year.[8] At the same time, the Van Zyl Commission investigating the territory's constitution was visiting the territory. While its brief was largely
concerned with the European segment, it felt obliged to note, echoing
concerns raised by the PMC, that the mandatory administration was "always disinclined to be too liberal with appropriations for services pecu-
liarly in the interests of the natives" and lacked the requisite expertise in
native affairs. It thus recommended that the South African Department
of Native Affairs take over this function (South Africa 1936, 75). This
triggered a strong denial from the then secretary for South-West Africa,
Francis P. Courtney-Clarke:

> It is well known that natives seldom make verbal protestations of gratitude and
> such feeling[,] when it is present[,] is shown then in their actions. As remarked by
> one Native Affairs officer . . . when a native expressed gratitude to him for anything
> he immediately awaited a request from him for something to which he was not
> entitled.

Successful native administration, Courtney-Clarke continued, depended
on the "personal touch," and it was obvious that the local administrator
would be better qualified than distant officials in Pretoria. Current officers
were better acquainted with local problems through long residence in the
territory and thus better able to gauge and meet the needs of natives.
It was thus "a cardinal point of wise administration to pay due regard
wherever possible to the beliefs, prejudice and established customs of the
governed." The mandate, he argued, did not require a full-time ethnologist because there were few distinct tribes and considerable "overlapping."
The suggestions of the Van Zyl Commission that more funding should
be made available for education would be disastrous because it should

follow economic rehabilitation of the native. The reserve policy was itself educational, as they were being taught that they had to build their own economic life in the reserves and that "service with Europeans and on the mines was itself a form of education." Indeed, Courtney-Clarke averred that the mines were a more important educational tool than missionaries. He posited that more expenditure for native administration and development was undesirable, since Indigenes had to be taught to realize that they must pay for their own development and that progress depended on their own efforts. He proudly claimed that revenue collection from natives more than covered the overhead cost of native administration. In short, the colonized paid the costs of their own colonization.[9]

Curtain Call?

To be sure, as a newly independent entity South Africa sought credibility in the international arena. Not only had Smuts played a key role in the founding of the League of Nations, but even his successor as prime minister, the avowedly nationalistic General J. Barry M. Hertzog, kept the portfolio of foreign affairs. One of the most important theaters where South Africa sought to maintain and retain credibility was in the protocol-bound and highly scripted formal hearings of the PMC. This was a stage on which petty politicians and officials could grandstand to impress not only the immediate audience but also those back home. In this focused interactional setting, the accredited representatives and their advisers "would come to the table" to have their annual reports examined by the PMC. It was not a situation without its challenges. Accredited representative Eric Louw, ardent antisemitic Nationalist and later longtime minister for foreign affairs, summed up his personal philosophy of diplomacy at the League of Nations: "1. There are more ways of killing a cat than drowning it. 2. The end justifies the means. 3. An Ambassador is sent to lie abroad for the good of his country" (cited in Peberdy 1996, 16). The tightly scripted ceremonial interaction in the daily life of the territory between Indigene and settler promoted the social production of ignorance. Fear of appearing to be ignorant or ridiculous led to the extended use of experts to lend credibility to claims in these hearings. Experts were an intrinsic part of the policy of display, trying to create the impression that they knew what they were doing and were not ridiculous. Yet the harder they tried, the more ridiculous they became.

The mandatory administration's claims to expertise, and their demonstration of it, were monotonously repetitive and had deep historical roots. The pre-terrain of this expertise has been well-documented in South Africa, where the ethnographic discourse of the lazy or idle native was the dominant trope among travelers and visiting scientists (Coetzee 1988). These early accounts situated "natives" within the extant discourses of wicked and lazy versus diligent and civilized and framed state policy. As George Steinmetz (2008, 25) argues, the expertise on which "native affairs" blueprints were based was to be found not so much in official ministries as in precolonial ethnographic discourses emanating from the scholar's study and the tales of adventurers. Intra-elite competition, under-girded by larger political considerations, largely ensured that accented variations on this discourse (as per Hoernlé and the other liberals) were largely rendered tone-deaf. This was facilitated by the ease in which it was possible to revert to this discourse rather than to try to develop an alternative, especially since effective sovereignty lay not with the League of Nations or even South Africa but with the proverbial "man on the spot"—for no matter how one might characterize colonialism, ultimately it amounted to decentralized despotism.

At the same time, while the South Africans were putting up smoke-screens to avoid the system of international surveillance, they were ame-nable, to paraphrase Mark Twain, to use expertise like a drunk uses a lamppost, for support rather than illumination. The emphasis on the in-strumentality of expertise diverted attention from the contradictions in-herent in it. In particular the cultural and attendant moral meanings of this expertise have been ignored. "Native" expertise was more important on a symbolic level for the settlers than a crass instrumentalist interpretation would allow. There were important contradictions between agency and structures in this process of internal pacification, not only of the colonized but, equally important, of the colonizers as well. The rhetoric inherent in expertise not only regulates sociocultural life, it represents it as well. As an ideology, "native affairs" expertise contributed to the social construction of the social world by creating images of social relationships as natural and fair to the settlers. The actions of experts can be treated as political constructions in two senses. First, their language and actions created their sense of who they were. Second, as Murray Edelman (1988) points out, they are symbols to other observers, emblemizing values, moral stances, and ideologies. What makes their performances blatantly ridiculous was that no one in the imperial old boys' club—the PMC—seriously chal-lenged their accounts. But in performing this expertise, could the experts also have been deluding themselves?

Erving Goffman (1959, 80–81) noted many years ago:

> A performer may be taken in by his own act, convinced at the moment that the impression of reality which he fosters is the one and only reality. In such cases the performer comes to be his own audience; he comes to be performer and observer of the same show. Presumably he intracepts or incorporates the standards he

attempts to maintain in the presence of others so that his conscience requires him to act in a socially proper way. It will have been necessary for the individual in his performing capacity to conceal from himself in his audience capacity the discreditable facts he has had to learn about the performance; in everyday terms, there will be things he knows, or has known, that he will not be able to tell himself.

In 1946 Hailey, erstwhile member of the PMC and author of the famed and influential *Africa Survey* (Hailey [1938] 1956), visited the territory. While his public talks were sympathetic to the South African administration—indeed, he even went so far as to declare the disputed referendum favoring incorporation into South Africa as free and fair—his report of more than 140 pages was never published and is hard to locate.[10] Yet it is clear that despite the careful diplomatic language of the era in which it was written, its suggestion that the mandatory administration was not doing enough for the Indigenes was only lightly critical of the administration's attempts at native administration. In 1949 Hailey was so horrified by the accusations against the territory's administration by Reverend Michael Scott at the UN that he wrote to the South African government urging them to publish his report, as it was more "objective."[11]

Backstage: The Politics of Homegrown Expertise

Mindful of the need to be "scientific," at least in the eyes of the League of Nations, the mandatory administration in 1920 included in its annual budget a small amount to fund basic anthropological research, which was soon used to pay for the Bushman casts by John Drury and Dorothea Bleek's Naron Bushman research, done under the aegis of the South African Museum.

From the twenties onward, a number of foreign quasi-scientific expeditions visited the territory. These received wide publicity in the local settler press, stimulating controversy and initiating arguments about the need for well-supported local institutions.[12] The 1925 Denver expedition was clearly the most important of these foreign efforts. The expedition, led by C. Ernest Cadle, a self-styled doctor with a flair for publicity, was originally meant to capture some "wild Bushmen" for American science but settled for making a movie about them. Even as the Denver expedition was making its way to SWA, Fourie was complaining that this was the final straw:

> At the present time all the material collected in this happy hunting ground finds its way to institutions either in the Union or abroad. . . . It may be said that we are not competent to make such a collection[,] to which one need only reply that museums

have in the past always been most complimentary about the completeness of the specimens sent to them from this country.[13]

Fourie touched on the sensitive nerve of incipient settler nationalism, and his proposals quickly gained settler support. A few months later the Windhoek-based *Allgemeine Zeitung* published a strong plea for a museum, arguing that the country was in danger of being denuded of its scientific treasures. Bushman skeletons, for instance, were being sought after by South African museums, having distressing implications for South-West Africa and its worldwide reputation:

> If we keep these things in the country, scientists will be forced to come to SW Africa, and carry out their studies on the spot, and this would contribute in no small degree to make the land better known. . . . The ignorance of America as to this country is shown by the fact that the scientific Denver expedition left everything in Cape Town which is regarded as essential in civilized countries and only brought to Windhoek the equipment suited to an expedition into the Sahara and the members of the expedition were astonished to find Windhoek a pretty little town with modern conveniences. We must therefore endeavor by every means in our power to make SWA known to the world. Advertisement is essential in these days. A museum would advertise us at no great cost. (*Allgemeine Zeitung*, 5 December 1925)

This strong reaction to the Denver expedition stemmed from both a desire for civic self-promotion that might, in the end, prove lucrative and the fact that within the context of the times, as Germany was being admitted to the League of Nations, the mandatory administration was debating what sort of citizenship to give the erstwhile German citizens who had not been repatriated. As a legislative assembly was being created for European settlers, the one common ground these different settlers could agree on was the interests of science.

It was in this milieu of intellectual and nationalist fervor that the South-West African Scientific Society was founded. A meeting chaired by Dr. Fourie drew some seventy citizens, who quickly agreed that the society should be autonomous, rather than a "daughter organization" to the South African Association for the Advancement of Science. The society emphasized that science would be used to bridge ethnic animosities, at least among the three European sections of Afrikaner, English, and German. United in science, people would develop a common loyalty to the country, and indeed, the society agreed to publish all its proceedings in both English and German (although financial constraints ultimately limited them to publishing papers in the language of the presenter). Its intended audience and clientele were clearly not professional scientists but amateurs, people like Fourie, who they all agreed could do a much better and more cost-effective job than many of the questionable professional experts visiting the territory.

Science and scientific associations, of course, had always been treated as ritually important by the state and its officials. Consider the visit of a contingent from the German oceanographic research vessel *Meteor* to Windhoek in 1926. Practically the whole town, led by the administrator and the mayor, waited at the railway station to officially welcome them. Both the German Pfadfinder (Pathfinders) and their South African counterparts, the Boy Scouts, were there in full force, the former waving German flags. After a march to the town hall accompanied by the ship's band and cheering along the route, the mayor, Councilor Menmuir, gave "an exceptionally eloquent speech" in which he stressed that the visit was important to the local citizenry because they could "*visualize in your presence a living link* with their old homes across the Sea, and also an actual expression of the ever-present pulsations of the civilization of their great Country." More importantly, they were welcome because they were "workers in that inscrutable and inexhaustible subject—SCIENCE." The mayor then greeted them by explaining:

> You are *missionaries of Science*, and also let me say, of Peace, engaged upon a mission of research, the results of which will no doubt be of the greatest importance and benefit to Mankind. . . . We, as Laymen . . . can only dimly appreciate the enormous physical and mental energy required from you. We are here in Windhoek, isolated many hundred miles away from the big centres of civilization in the Union, but none the less we realize the importance and seriousness of the mission you are engaged upon. (*Windhoek Advertiser*, 4 August 1926, italics added)

Within these and other public statements, the connection between science and colonization was accepted both implicitly and explicitly. This is perhaps best captured by Professor Fritz Jaeger (1934, 17) who had done research in South-West Africa:

> To colonize a country means to create a new, higher culture. This is only possible for superior cultures. Colonization is a process of cultural dissemination across the earth. Just as air flows from areas of high pressure, so culture spreads from geographical regions of high culture to those of low culture. . . . Military superiority allowed the European colonizing peoples to seize African colonies, but only their scientific and technological knowledge allowed them to develop the countries economically. It is to be hoped that they will also succeed in educating the natives to become a cultivated people.

Despite the resounding support for the SWA Scientific Society, Fourie, who was widely regarded as the driving force behind its establishment, resigned in 1929 under conditions that are as yet unclear. But two interlocking factors seem to have been crucial. Werth, the new administrator, started a policy of aggressively settling Afrikaner farmers in the territory. English speakers, let alone German-speakers, had little chance of obtaining inexpensive government-subsidized farms, and this policy marginalized anglophiles like Fourie. But it was the German-speaking sector that felt particularly threatened by this land policy. Historically, Germans in the territory had looked down upon the "Boers," who were now becoming a significant force in the territory's political life, and the situation was further exacerbated by the perceived inefficiency and disinterest of the Afrikaner-dominated administration (A. Tötemeyer 1999, 60).

Deutschtum's Worldly Provincials

The antithesis of the mandatory administration's pro-Afrikaner action was of course scientific engagement, which also emphasized the German-speaking colonists' claims to being trustworthy colonizers. Within a few years, the SWA Scientific Society had been transformed into a German cultural enclave, and English as a language of publication dropped into virtual nonuse after the third volume of its journal. This dovetailed with a number of other organizations initiated at the time. The German Pfadfinder, for example, eschewed any contact with the Boy Scouts and rapidly became a major force.[14] Avowedly nationalistic, the organization's members wore hats modeled after the Schutztruppe, emphasized veld-craft, or survival skills, and celebrated anniversaries of local triumphs of German colonialism. Science, scientific societies, and scientific institutions were among a number of different vehicles harnessed to help promote a vigorous local identity during the mandate era—an identity that was distinctly German and, ironically, increasingly tied to Bushmen.

Both the first public lecture it sponsored and the inaugural issue of the *Journal of the South-West African Scientific Society* focused on the Bushmen, and they continued to dominate the ethnological articles published in the journal right through the interwar period. The presence of living Bushmen was one of the few things that demarcated the territory from its powerful neighbor South Africa, and consequently Bushmen became a major icon for important factions within the settler community. Placing a special emphasis on the still surviving Bushmen in the territory drew legitimacy from German anthropologists' persistent emphasis on salvage anthropology, and it implicitly served as a critique of South Africa, where Bushmen were rapidly approaching extinction. Thus in many ways their focus on Bushmen enabled German settlers to recoup some national esteem after being defeated by vastly superior numbers just a few years earlier.

This emphasis was also supported and extended in the following decades by the fact that the only serious research done by metropolitan anthropologists during the interwar years in the territory, namely that by Viktor Lebzelter and Lidio Cipriani, had as its central concern Bushmen. Interestingly the findings of both were largely ignored, Cipriani's probably because they were published in Italian, but Lebzelter is an interesting case. Asked to undertake the research by Pater Wilhelm Schmidt, the founder and leader of the *Kulturkreis* school that argued for a common God for all people, Lebzelter spent a year traveling though the territory and concentrated on physical measurement, claiming to have examined some eight thousand Indigenes. Not that he did not try to do ethnology, but he found it virtually impossible: he noted that few scholars saw their informants as fellow humans but rather treated them as objects; there was much distrust; money could not buy information. He found the rules governing interracial etiquette stultifying: Indigenes were forced to squat on the ground for interviews, although some whites provided benches outside their front door for Indigenous *Honoratorien* (honoraries) to sit on. To ignore these rules would risk antagonizing Europeans, who would then withdraw their support (Lebzelter 1934, 2–3). A photograph of Lebzelter doing fieldwork has him placed sitting on the ground level with his informants. No wonder local native experts ignored Lebzelter.

Moreover, amateurs and dilettantes remained focused on Bushmen as well, further promoting their particular importance.[15] During this period a number of German missionaries wrote about the need to bring Christ to this *sterbende Volk* (dying people). Indeed, Bushmen constituted one of the most popular cover stories for the *Berichte der Rheinischen Mission*, the journal published by the Rhenish Mission for its supporters in Germany.

But how did local settlers view Bushmen and all this scientific interest in them? There was a strange duality at work in both popular conceptions of the Bushmen and popular assessments of scientists' ability to study and understand them. In a locally published book that aimed to encourage German settlers, SWA Scientific Society stalwart Paul Barth (1926, 150) proclaimed:

Like a beast of prey the Bushman quietly stalks his victims, so that they are never even aware of his presence until his poisoned arrow has hit its mark. In this manner the Bushman also catches his four-legged prey. . . . The Bushman is so exceptionally frugal that he can go days enduring hunger and thirst without letting it seem to bother him. However once he has his prey he will stuff himself as full as he possibly can, so that with his wrinkled skin, bloated stomach and sly cunning eyes, he looks like a beast of prey himself. His speech, like everything else about him is primitive, and composed mainly of consonants. . . . They seem therefore to be dying out and no one will be any worse for their loss, as they are destroyers rather than producers.

Undoubtedly Barth was echoing the dominant settler view that tended to disdain the Bushman as unproductive and deceptive; yet while many settlers regarded the Bushmen as vermin, they also thought of them as cunning— so cunning, in fact, that they could easily hoodwink naive foreign experts. Thus a 1931 article on "wild and tame Bushmen," published in a small Windhoek-based German-language magazine under the nickname Outis (Afrikaans slang for an "old hand"), described how the author encountered the Denver expedition in 1925 and recalled their Munchausenesque bragging; they claimed, for example, to have "discovered" a completely unknown tribe of Bushmen who had never seen Europeans before and were extremely pleased and proud of their film footage of wild war dances and secret religious rituals that they confidently predicted would be a smash hit. As befits an experienced "colonial," Outis was skeptical. When shown the sacred Bushman religious relic they had discovered, he dismissed it as a readily available ordinary Ovambo doll. He also claimed to have met the Denver expedition interpreter, the "Bastard" Jeremias, on one of his trips through the Etosha Game Park, at which point he asked to see these "wild Bushmen." Jeremias obliged and organized for Outis to meet them, complete with a staged mock attack. After satisfying their requests for cigarettes, the Bushmen performed their war dances, which Outis recalled was to the tune "Matiche," a Mexican song that had been popular with German troops during the 1904–7 war. Moreover, he also recognized one of the dancers as Jephter, the Bushman headman who had served as general factotum/interpreter for the same military company Outis had served in during the German era. After insisting on seeing their living quarters, Outis was first taken to a "primitive encampment," clearly constructed for tourist consumption, and then to their real abode, which consisted of tin shacks, including an old German military bed and, best of all, an old phonograph on which they played their only record, "Matiche"!

Despite the role that locals might play in such deceptions, "authentic" Bushmen and German settlers' desire to serve as spokesmen for their authenticity remained critical to their local identities, as the SWA Scientific Society's president remarked with regard to the first book they published, not surprisingly on Bushmen:

> This book [Metzger 1950] represents a most interesting and important development. The subject matter is peculiar to this Territory, the author is a member of our own community and the book was produced entirely in this country. . . . Members of the Society do not need to be told that the opportunities to record Bushman lore and other information contained in this book, are fast disappearing, and that the author has rendered a service by placing them on the record. (Watt 1951)

Clearly metropole-periphery relations in the interwar years were significant, and they served to develop a very strong sense of local Deutschtum, and thus a means of combating the allegedly seditious efforts of South Africa in the mandate, by invoking German culture for identity as both a rallying point and a tool for enforcing conformity.

Indeed, the political situation made it inevitable that reactions to outsiders would play a key role in the overt Germanization of the scientific community. As a reaction to the interloping actions of these outsiders, the SWA Scientific Society soon began informally purging its ranks until largely German science and scientists made up its community. Indeed, this was so much the case that when early English-speaking notables in the society were referred to, like H. H. G. Kreft and Clemens Gutsche, the fact that they are descended from German missionaries was conspicuously mentioned. Articles in Afrikaans were virtually nonexistent, the first (a translation by the former government ethnologist F. Rudolph Lehmann) appearing only in 1955, followed by two articles in the sixties by Johannes P. van S. Bruwer (both of whom feature later in this book). This homogenization was so extensive that in many ways the Scientific Society started to resemble the *Vereine* (associations) and *Gesellschaften* (societies) that were such an important part of the social scenery in small-town Wilhelmine Germany. They were acting like true "worldly provincials" (Penny and Bunzl 2003).

What is striking about the SWA Scientific Society is its elaborate organization, which penetrated into multiple levels of territorial society and covered a variety of scientific fields. Equally impressive is the persistence of its staunchly German character—even during the decades when many people in the world of anthropology were eagerly abandoning those things thought to be most German. World War II marked a low point for the society, and a special general meeting was held in 1947 to resurrect it. By making the SWA administrator the patron, the society secured itself a more consistent source of government funds. But apart from the administrator at the apex, the society also had a number of different kinds of members, all of whom gained some mention in the journal in the sixties, including fifteen honorary members (all German-speaking) and six corresponding members (all German, including luminaries such as Professor Eugen Fischer of "racial hygiene" fame). After this are listed the various work groups of varying duration: archaeology, botany, geology, herpetology, mineralogy, and ornithology. Later, other work groups in speleology, astronomy, and ethnology were added.

One of the problems the SWA Scientific Society continually faced was to find suitable papers for its journal; in some instances papers would be reprinted. Which papers were selected is quite telling: they were largely ethnohistorical and about Bushmen. Almost all the books and monographs the society has published until recently have been in German, and if the society has any heroes, they are German-speaking ethnologists/ethnohistorians: Heinrich Vedder, Eugen Fischer, and Martin Gusinde. They share a number of attributes: all are male German-speakers who took a special interest in Bushmen and represented ideas long abandoned in the metropole. Undoubtedly the most prominent was Vedder, the Rhenish missionary who came to Namibia in late 1903 and displayed a remarkable facility for learning Indigenous languages, claiming to be fluent in both Nama and Herero within a year. In 1912 he published some pioneering papers on Bushmen. Deported in 1919, he returned to Namibia in 1922 as head of the Augustineum, the only high school and training center for Indigenous teachers in South-West Africa. Hamburg University published his two-volume *Die Bergdama* in 1923, the draft of which he had submitted to Carl Meinhof, the foremost African linguist, in 1920. It was written based on observations he had made in Swakopmund, Karibib, Otjimbingwe, and Omaruru while serving as a missionary. Much of his eminence derived from the fact that there were no other experts. In 1924 Pretoria University even offered him the chair of Bantuistics (Baumann 1965). In 1925, facilitated in part by the intervention of Theodor Seitz, former governor of German South-West Africa and honorary president of the German Colonial Society, the University of Tübingen awarded Vedder an honorary doctorate for his research on Indigenous languages and cultures in Namibia. The Scientific Society celebrated Vedder in a number of ways: it made him an honorary member in 1937 and honored him in 1961 with the only Festschrift it ever published. In addition, the society ensured that *Das alte Südwestafrika* (Vedder 1934) and its English translation remains in print. Most of his papers dealing with Namibia were published either in the society's journal or in the *Afrikanische Heimatkalender*, the almanac of the German Evangelical Lutheran Church of South and South-West Africa.

Eugen Fischer was another notable, and notorious, celebrity. While he is largely forgotten now, Fischer was a physical anthropologist of some fame. In 1959 he was invited to reminisce in the journal to commemorate the fiftieth anniversary of his research among the Rehoboth Bastards. This research was pathbreaking in that it was the first study in biological anthropology to apply Mendelian genetics. Five years later, the society's *Mitteilungen* (newsletter) featured a special commemorative article to celebrate his ninetieth birthday ("Professor Dr. med. Dr. sc. h. c. Dr. med. h. c. Eugen Fischer" 1964). An honored Fischer donated to the society a personal copy of his recently reprinted book, *Die Rehobother Bastards*, which emerged from his Mendelian study, as well as his album of Baster photographs. Having started out as professor at Freiburg University in 1918, he became rector of Berlin University in 1933. He coauthored a best-selling text on human genetics and then became director of the Kaiser Wilhelm Institute for Anthropology, Human Genetics, Racial Hygiene, and Eugenics, where he perfected and taught, inter alia, the science of "racial hygiene." When he retired in 1942 after obtaining the highest scientific honors the Nazis could bestow, a grateful Führer allowed the institute to be renamed after him (Lösch 1997). As Franz Weidenreich (1946, 399) noted, he was among "the leading Nazi anthropologists who are morally responsible for the prosecution and extinction of the peoples and races the Nazis considered 'inferior'. . . . If anyone, he is the man who should be put on the list of war criminals."

Compared to Fischer, Pater Martin Gusinde SVD (1886–1969) was a minor academic. Gusinde was inspired to become a missionary by a traveling colonial exhibition featuring live Africans. As a seminarian he soon fell in with Pater Wilhelm Schmidt and quickly developed a lifelong interest in the origin of the concept of God and diffusionism. He was dispatched to Chile, where he made his reputation with a study of the Yahgan of Tierra del Fuego and later, like so many of Schmidt's acolytes, undertook research on the Pygmies. In 1949 he was made a visiting professor at the Catholic University in Washington, DC, and undertook his first visit to Namibia to study Bushmen. In the space of ten months, he completed three tours: one to the Etosha, another to the Kavango, and a third to the central Kalahari. His latter expedition was heralded as the "first survey ever of Bushmen," and the *Cape Argus* (12 September 1951) portrayed him as somewhat of a hero because he, along with only two "half-Bushmen," spent months alone with "wild" Bushmen and examined over two thousand of them in only four months. Two years later, in 1953, he spent the summer in Namibia traveling to places where, courtesy of the Catholics, Bushmen were congregated. On his return to Austria he gave a slide show of his Bushman research to an applauding audience of over thirteen hundred and ceded his valuable material on Bushman genitalia to his friend Professor Eugen Fischer (Bornemann 1970).

Notes

Part of this chapter was previously published as "Collecting the Gatherers," in *Worldly Provincialism: German Anthropology in the Age of Empire*, edited by H. Glenn Penny and Matti Bunzl (Ann Arbor: University of Michigan Press, 2003).

1. Even among the higher ranks there were serious problems. To quote from Gorges's letter to Smuts:

    Major Uys soon got into trouble and had to leave. Captain W—— has been too fond of the ladies and found it desirable to return to the Union. Captain M—— has been continuously drinking and disgraced himself beyond redemption on the recent Ovamboland Expedition. He was in charge of the Constabulary Transport; but between Otjiwarongo and Ondonga managed to get through eleven bottles of rum. . . . A couple of other officers have also been sailing very close to the wind in horse and cattle transactions of doubt-ful character. One R——, a Lieutenant in the Native Affairs Branch, lately embezzled £600 deferred pay of Native labourers. (Smuts 1966, 455)

2. Later, however, Vedder was to present the mandatory administration and the University of Stellenbosch a twenty-eight-volume collection of source material, much of it laboriously copied by Sister Emma Maier from the archives of the Rhenish Mission Society in Barmen, Germany.

3. The quote is cited in a memo written by government ethnologist Nicolaas J. van Warmelo in 1956: "so dass klar erwiesen ist, dass der Schwarze seine Arbietskraft fast kostenlos der Wirtschaft der Europäer zur Verfügung stellt und ein eigenes Nationalvermögung nicht gebildet wird" (N. J. van Warmelo, Memo: Oor Ovamboland, 1956, A591 van Warmelo Collection, National Archives of Namibia [hereafter cited as NAN]).

4. Letter from A. Winifred Hoernlé to Cocky Hahn, 6 September 1935, Hahn Papers, NAN.

5. Note by Louis Fourie, signed by J. F. Herbst, 15 September 1920, A198/3 Museums and Scientific Research, NAN.

6. Letter from Secretary SWA to Winifred Hoernlé, 23 May 1923, A198/3/4 Museums and Scientific Research, NAN.

7. Letter from A. Winifred Hoernlé to Secretary SWA, 30 June 1923, A198/3/4 Museums and Scientific Research, NAN. There was a shortage of professionally qualified "native experts." In 1925 the South African Department of Native Affairs appointed Gerard P. Lestrade (1897–1962) as its first government ethnologist. Lestrade was a linguist with three master's degrees, in Latin and Greek from Cape Town, Hebrew, Arabic, and Chinese from Harvard, and African languages and phonetics from London. In 1930 he accepted the chair in Bantu Studies at the University of Pretoria.

8. It was a short-lived coup for South Africa. Theodoli was forced to resign the following year when Italy was expelled from the League of Nations.

9. Francis P. Courtney-Clarke, memorandum, 12 August 1936, A427 Visits to SWA, NAN.

10. Malcolm Hailey, 1946, "A Survey of Native Affairs in South West Africa," NAN.

11. Malcolm Hailey to High Commissioner, 13 December 1949, NTS 47/378 Sir Malcolm Hailey Visit to the Union, South African National Archives (hereafter cited as SANA).

12. What is striking is how many local inhabitants had, or at least thought they had, far superior knowledge about the history and the people of Namibia than any deployed by these scientific expeditions. For example, a series of lectures originally given in Windhoek in early 1925 by Professor Griess, principal of the Deutsche Realschule, the local German school, drew the comment from the *Windhoek Advertiser* (22 April 1925) that "the paper should be printed for the benefit, not only of people of this country, but of those in the Union and overseas interested in S.W. Africa."

13. Louis Fourie, Memo, 23 September 1925, A198/3/4 Museums & Scientific Research Mrs Hoernlé. NAN.

14. By 1932 it had been taken over and renamed the Hitler Youth Movement; two years later the administration was forced to ban it. Resurrected under a slightly different format, it was again banned in 1939. Its impact was such that there are at present two private museums in Namibia devoted to Pfadfinder memorabilia.

15. This is indicated in van Warmelo's (1977) massive compendium of anthropology in periodicals for the period 1900 to 1950, where entries for his "Khoi" category vastly outnumber the combined entries labeled as "Bergdama," Herero, Ovambo, Okavango and Caprivi.

CHAPTER 2

Post–World War II Ethnological Dispositions in a Disputed Territory

With the demise of the League of Nations in 1946, South Africa saw its opportunity to achieve its long-held aspiration to incorporate the territory of South-West Africa as its fifth province by refusing to acknowledge the UN as the legal successor to the league and continuing to administer the territory as if it were still a mandate. In this operation South Africa had to invoke its credentials as a progressive colonial power, for which anthropologists played a key role in providing the veneer of enlightened administration.

Three issues dominated this effort, all with a weather eye cocked at the international arena: first, there was concern about "Bushmen dying out" and having to be saved for "science"; second, South Africa participated, albeit elliptically, in the International Africa Institute's "Ethnic Survey"; and, third, there was concern about South-West Africa's largest ethnic group, which constituted more than half the population, the Ovambo. In all three cases the initial key gatekeeper was the South African prime minister and international statesman Jan Smuts. Smuts had long championed anthropology and archeology and was instrumental in founding the School of African Life and Languages at the University of Cape Town (UCT) in the early twenties and later the state-funded Archeological Survey. He had written forewords to Monica Hunter's classic *Reaction to Conquest* and to *Realm of the Rain Queen* written by his nephew, Jack Krige, and his wife, Eileen Jensen Krige (Hunter 1936; Krige and Krige 1943; Smuts 1936, 1943). While attending the meetings in San Francisco in 1945–46 that led to the creation of the UN, he had met Edwin Meyer Loeb, a well-connected and independently wealthy ethnologist who was connected to the University of California. Smuts had invited Loeb to study the Ovambo, who, he believed, had a model-functioning traditional sociocultural system relatively untouched by "contact." Loeb even at that stage was very much a diffusionist who was to argue that there were Phoenician elements in Ovambo culture.[1] This theory fitted in well with the other person Smuts sponsored shortly thereafter to undertake rock art research in SWA, the Abbé Breuil, who was to claim that the "White Lady" rock painting in the Brandberg mountains represented a Phoenician. Obviously such diffusionist theories played well with settlers keen to justify their claims to the land.

In 1945 Smuts had also been approached by his friend, Sir (later Lord) William Hailey—author of the highly influential *Africa Survey*, former PMC commissioner, and president of the International Africa Institute—about an ethnographic survey of Africa that his institute proposed to undertake. It would be systematic and comprehensive, serving as a basis for further research and as a foundation for development schemes. Organized synoptically it would focus on a number of topics, namely the definition of tribal groups, their demography, outstanding social and cultural features, main features of economic life, and agencies of modern development.

Gordon Mears, secretary of the South African Department of Native Affairs,[2] responded enthusiastically. Apart from self-interest, South Africa could not afford to be lukewarm on this matter for reasons of prestige:

> [South Africa] is the major state in Africa, incomparably the wealthiest and most influential, and aspires to leadership in many ways. The Government has sanctioned the expenditure of thousands for propaganda publications to influence public opinion abroad. What that propaganda is designed to do amongst the general reading public, the survey will do, and with more practical effect, amongst the scientists, administrators and statesmen. It is essential for this country to participate.

But, he added, "the Department cannot contemplate allowing investigators, over whom it has no control, free access to its records. This points to an officer of the Department being in charge."[3]

Three months later the SWA administration and the South African Department of Native Affairs had been persuaded to jointly fund such a survey in the territory. The survey was to be conducted under the supervision of the department's chief ethnologist, Dr. Nicolaas J. van Warmelo. Van Warmelo was to undertake the research north of the Police Zone, namely in Ovamboland (renamed Owambo in 1982) and the Kaokoveld (later renamed Kaokoland), while a suitable ethnologist was to work in the Police Zone, the area of white settlement. Originally van Warmelo envisaged doing a survey of all sixteen magisterial districts in the Police Zone, but time, finances, and changing priorities were to restrict this vision.

Then began a search for qualified personnel. A major drawback concerned remuneration. The Public Service Commission fixed the starting salary at £250—while, in comparison, the Rhodes-Livingstone Institute in Northern Rhodesia started at £450 and South African universities at £600. This meant that van Warmelo resorted to hiring underemployed

German ethnologists, an option to which he was eminently amenable, having obtained his doctorate at Hamburg University. Moreover, the territory still had German as an official language, and much of the historical material was in German. In addition, as foreigners they made ideal servants of power, as any unsavory actions on their part could lead to withdrawal of their visas (though this was not something van Warmelo had much to worry about, as most of these ethnologists were refugees from East Germany and staunchly anti-Communist).

The first ethnologist appointed to the territory was Friedrich Rudolph Lehmann (1887–1969), an anthropologist of religion affiliated with Leipzig University. In May 1939 he went to Tanganyika, but on his way back to Germany his ship was captured by the allies in December 1939. After being interned for two years in Baviaanspoort, he was released to lecture anthropology and German at Wits on a part-time basis. In July 1946 he was hired as an assistant ethnologist and, together with van Warmelo, arrived in Windhoek in December of the same year. By August 1948 van Warmelo could report that district surveys had been completed in the Okahandja, Windhoek, and Gobabis districts, while his own work in Ovamboland and the Kaokoveld was partially finished.

Lehmann and van Warmelo soon fell out, however, and Lehmann's contract was not renewed in September 1949. The reasons were complex and resulted in lengthy correspondence. Lehmann objected to working on a district basis and being restricted from focusing on issues such as religion and race relations. He accused van Warmelo of having pedestrian interests. Van Warmelo, in turn, criticized Lehmann for producing work of poor quality and quantity. Fortunately for Lehmann, he was offered the inaugural chair in anthropology at the Potchefstroom University for Christian Higher Education, starting in January 1950, his credentials undoubtedly vouched for by some of the right-wing Afrikaner nationalists who had been his fellow internees at Baviaanspoort.[4]

A few months later van Warmelo wrote that Günter Wagner (1908–52) was going to take up the position of ethnologist in June 1950. As he informed Jos Allen, the territory's additional native commissioner specifically charged with dealing with UN issues, Wagner was "a different proposition compared with some people we know."[5] Indeed, he was. An experienced African fieldworker, his two-volume *Bantu of North Kavirondo* (Wagner 1949, 1956) was published by Oxford University Press. He had studied with some of the most prominent academics, including Franz Boas, Bronisław Malinowski, Alfred Kroeber, and Robert Lowie, not to mention Georg Thilenius in Hamburg, the *Doktervater* (doctoral advisor) of both Wagner and van Warmelo. Unable to find academic employment abroad, Wagner had returned to Germany in 1938 and became a minor functionary and member of the Nazi Party, employed in the *Antisemiti-*

sche Aktion (antisemitic action) attached to the Reich Ministry of Public Enlightenment and Propaganda. Nevertheless, he managed to have prominent English-speaking colleagues condone his activities by testifying to his "objectivity." Eking out a near-subsistence existence in Hamburg as a freelance translator, he was happy to receive van Warmelo's offer of employment at the end of 1949. He arrived in Windhoek in June 1950 and, despite lacking his own transport and having to deal with officials who objected to giving his interpreter a ride, energetically set about fieldwork, updating much of Lehmann's research and inaugurating research in the Karibib district. Like Lehmann, he focused on Herero-speakers and started learning their language. Wagner tragically died of pneumonia in June 1952 after returning from a two-month stint as visiting lecturer at Wits.

Given his previous experiences, Wagner was not afraid to ask questions and make suggestions to van Warmelo, querying the intentions of the survey and suggesting, with underlining for emphasis, that it should contain material on living standards, local observations on health, economic development especially on the reserves, attitudes to life on the reserves, interethnic relationships, and the relationship between Christianity and tradition. He also suggested listing influential natives, religious survivals, and crime and assessing economic development by inventorying modern utensils owned and used. Like Lehmann, he was concerned with how Indigenes adapted to changing circumstances and, especially, with Herero "retribalization." His major achievement was the monumental 354-page "Ethnographic Survey of the Windhoek District."[6] It provided valuable material, especially as it related to farmworkers and urban inhabitants, such as their survival strategies and the heterogeneity of urban living, which was beyond the ken of the normally minimalistic district surveys. Jan-Bart Gewald (2002) speculates that it was this debunking of ethnic primordialism, both on the farms and especially in Windhoek itself, that resulted in the report not being published, along with the fact that it never fitted the structure that van Warmelo envisaged for district surveys.

Three years later, in 1955, the ethnologist position was filled again, this time by Oswin Köhler (1911–96). A student of Dietrich Westermann in Berlin, where he completed his doctorate in African linguistics, he fled East Germany and completed his habilitation at the University of Cologne. Köhler spent from 1954 to 1957 in the territory before returning to Cologne as a *Privatdozent* (private lecturer), but he eventually worked his way up to director of the African Studies Institute there before retiring in 1977. He was to make many return visits to the territory to complete his magnum opus on the Mbarkwengo Bushmen of the Eastern Caprivi. Displaying his political nous, he volunteered to serve as an expert witness in the famous World Court case of 1962–64 to testify as to why separate development was necessary (H. Behrend, pers. comm., 2005) as well as assisting the South African Defence Force (SADF) during the so-called Border War. Displaying a remarkable work ethic, Köhler managed to edit and update four district surveys based on Wagner's work (Lehmann's research in Okahandja, Gobabis, and Windhoek not being acknowledged). In addition, he managed to produce two district studies himself. While Lehmann and Wagner, in terms of publications, focused on the Herero,[7] Köhler's intellectual passion lay with the Bushmen.

After a long hiatus, Kuno F. R. Budack (b. 1934) was appointed in 1966. Born in East Germany, he escaped after being imprisoned by the Stasi for three years, an experience that was to profoundly influence his praxis, and continued his studies in Cologne and Pretoria. Warmly welcomed and employed by van Warmelo in 1963, he completed a master's degree in 1965 with a thesis on interethnic relations in the Tses reserve in the Keetmanshoop district and later successfully submitted a doctorate on traditional Khoekhoen political leadership, both at Pretoria. Budack was to remain in government employment until his retirement in 1991, undertaking varied commissions on behalf the administration, the SADF, and, apparently, the security police. Like his forerunners, he was to display considerable linguistic skills and fluency in Indigenous languages. But, by this time, the Ethnic Survey had run its course.

A year after his appointment in 1967 he became a defense witness for Ondonga King Martin Ashikoto, whom the administration ostensibly wanted deposed for ordering a habitual thief to be blinded.[8] An infuriated administration wanted him fired, and van Warmelo was forced to intervene by personally pleading with the minister. As a compromise Budack was unofficially banned from entering Ovamboland, and eventually the department, then renamed the Department of Co-operation and Development, appointed Johan Malan as a second ethnologist with responsibility for Owambo and the Kaokoland. As was the wont of bureaucracy, after spending two and a half years doing research for his doctorate on Himba kinship while partially serving as an assistant native commissioner, Malan was then, with the logic the department was notorious for, transferred to Natal and later to the Eastern Cape before resigning to become the ethnologist at the State Museum in Windhoek. In 1978 he took a professorship at the University of the North. Left unsaid in his online autobiography accompanying his various Christian websites was that Malan continued to visit Owambo as a consultant for the SADF. In 1980 Malan wrote a short popular book, *Peoples of South West Africa/Namibia*. A revised edition was published in 1995, entitled *Peoples of Namibia*, which was translated into German (by Budack) and enjoyed extensive sales, going into an eighth impression in 2017. Centering on the "ethnic image," it provides a mosaic tour of the twelve officially classified ethnic groups. It paid minimal attention to "others," in this case coloreds, Basters, and whites, who had developed unspecified cultural features that had fueled strong sentiments to their new fatherland. The illustrations were overwhelmingly of a "traditional" nature, and the book contains rather odd assertions, such as that Hamites were probably responsible for introducing cattle from Asia Minor into the region. Malan's discussion of culture change focused on social evolution,[9] in particular the change from matrilineality to patrilineality he claimed to have occurred in Owambo. Social evolution, Malan asserted, had been accelerated by external factors such as conversion to Christianity, education, and an expanding contract labor system. He attributed the rise of the South-West Africa People's Organization (SWAPO) to social and cultural evolution in Owambo, especially the rise of neo-locality, the loss of matrilineal ties, and the rise of liberation theology. Apparently wage labor and the "modern economy" played a minimal role, while there is no mention of the role of the military or a discussion of illegitimacy that some estimates place at over 80 percent for the country (J. Malan 1995, 32–34).

Constructing the Ethnic Survey

Van Warmelo (1904–89), the long-term state ethnologist from 1930 to 1969, was a linguist turned ethnologist. His studies in Germany left two important methodological imprints. First, heavily influenced by Carl Meinhof, the pre-eminent African linguist of his era, van Warmelo was interested in classifying South African Bantu languages and the use of the vernacular on an areal basis (Pugach 2004). Second, van Warmelo was exposed to the *Fragebogen* approach—the use of detailed checklists to solicit information. In 1934 van Warmelo compiled a "Guide and Questions on History, Law and Custom" and thought it so indispensable that he brought out a revised sixty-four-page single-spaced mimeographed edition in 1969, the year that he retired. It opens with suggestions such as to use only old and reliable informants, to retain the original language or dialect of the informants, to record stories of actual events, and not to try to collect hidden information—thus, "let women collect facts about women's matters." He concluded with the admonition "Write very clearly, and on one side of the paper only" (van Warmelo 1969, n.p.). Strikingly, the guide contains almost no questions concerning culture change or development.

After the Lehmann imbroglio and in consultation with Wagner, van Warmelo constructed a list of 313 questions on which information should be sought, divided into four sections: under the general heading were 32 questions concerning demographics, ecology, and district history. The next section, "Non-Europeans on Farms," featured 42 questions on issues like interethnic relations, the role of churches, native sects, and crime.

The section on native reserves had 134 questions focusing on traditional politics and leadership and on mostly sociological and quantifiable information, such as the number of letters written and received. A final section on urban areas centered its 102 questions on social problems and activities like beer brewing, music, sport, and employment. A special section, "Bushmen Residents in the District," was also included. It ended with a directory of missionaries and officials who were considered the influential people in the district.

The reports that were compiled on the basis of this questionnaire were simply called *A Study of the . . . District*, in an unexplained break with the practice in South Africa where they were typically titled *The Tribes of the . . . District*. Van Warmelo insisted that each study be about thirty thousand words or one hundred pages double-spaced in length. The surveys are remarkable for excluding any mention of the role and position of Europeans in the local economic life. Van Warmelo demanded that the ethnologists submit their fieldwork diaries along with their surveys and that inquiries on special topics such as Herero millenarianism only be undertaken after at least half the district survey had been completed.

The empirical value of these surveys was certainly open to question. It was a struggle to do fieldwork. Lehmann had no transport and had to rely on rides with officials, who, he complained, were uncooperative and treated him like a journalist. At best he was tolerated and not allowed to interview Indigenes in the absence of an official. Similarly, Wagner had to cadge rides with officials, who objected to his bringing an interpreter along. Even van Warmelo was forced to take the bus ferrying contract workers to and from Ovamboland when he did research there, if he could not wheedle a ride in an official vehicle. In 1956 Köhler complained to van Warmelo that the Gobabis farmers thought he was collecting information for the UN and threatened him with a beating. He added that the information provided by the police did not reflect the real position of Indigenes, especially Bushmen.[10]

In prioritizing which districts should be surveyed, political and international issues featured prominently. In 1948 the Herero began to protest to the UN about their status and condition and were aided in this by an Anglican priest, Rev. Michael Scott, an early petitioner on their behalf. Allen, the additional native commissioner at the time and van Warmelo's liaison in Windhoek, was so impressed with Lehmann's work that was coming out at the time that he passed it on to the South African Department of External Affairs, since it "helps to refute the UNO [*sic*] criticisms that not enough is being done for the natives,"[11] a view Allen was to repeat later on a number of occasions. It was no accident that Lehmann's first priorities were the Okahandja and Gobabis districts, the former a major symbolic site for Herero and the latter the home of chief Hosea Kutako, the leader of the Herero petitioners and the resistance to South African over-rule. Lehmann had also done some preliminary work in Keetmanshoop in the south, where many Nama-speakers had seceded from the Rhenish Mission Church and joined the independent African Methodist Episcopal Church, an action the administration viewed as potentially dangerous.

That Scott's spectral presence continued to haunt the South Africans is clear from Lehmann's evidence as part of the delegation from Potchef-stroom University to the Commission for the Socio-Economic Develop-ment of the Bantu Areas within the Union of South Africa (commonly referred to as the Tomlinson Commission), which was to lay the ground-work for the implementation of "grand apartheid":

> Based on his three years of experience in the Territory one knows how difficult it is to get the correct relationship with the Herero especially after Michael Scott acted the way he did. For the Herero the actions of Michael Scott were so important that it greatly strengthened their national consciousness. Before this emergence of national consciousness, European culture was regarded as a tool not an aim. Their aim was never to change themselves into black Europeans. . . . As I understand it in the political arena they want political independence. That is a problem there and here. People here also want to become autonomous and thus the actions of Michael Scott have been welcomed in that he brought their political interests to an international arena.[12]

Blame outsiders for disturbing "happy and contented" natives!

Creating Ethnographic Knowledge North of the Police Zone

Immortalized, along with Hahn, as one of the "lords of the last frontier" and heralded by Hailey as a model native commissioner, Eedes had served as assistant native commissioner in Ovamboland from 1923 to 1931 and then been promoted to native commissioner in neighboring Kavango before succeeding Hahn as commissioner in 1946 (Woods 1977). Un-like Hahn, Eedes had little interest in ethnology or ethnologists. He infa-mously, and unsympathetically, dismissed Kavango inhabitants as having become immoral, improvident, and sexual perverts who practiced child prostitution. Yet his self-image on retirement was that "90 percent of the Kuanyama [Ovambo] were sorry to see him go" (cited in Cooper 2001, 249). His major interest appears to have been promoting contract labor and, after retiring in 1954, took a part-time job as adviser to the American-owned Tsumeb Mining Corporation and then became secretary to the SWA Farm Employers of Contract Workers organization, which sought to increase the flow of inexpensive contract workers to white farmers. Kavango oral historians remember Eedes for his legendary rudeness and his violent outbursts and gloss his nickname Nakare (the large one) as "let him be" (Fumanti 2016, 63). As a gatekeeper for research, Eedes played an important role and achieved a certain notoriety for kicking out Europeans who had entered Ovamboland without the requisite permits, including individuals associated with the Loeb expedition (Woods 1977, 38; Larson 2004).

The first ethnologists Eedes encountered were from the Loeb expedition in late 1947. On Eedes's suggestion, the expedition set up camp at Oshikango on the Angolan border but, also on his advice, withdrew prior to the rainy season. Returning to Windhoek, Loeb declared in the press that Ovamboland was one of the success stories of enlightened administration. The expedition returned on a follow-up visit for a few months in the next "dry season." As befits a wealthy relative of the ultra-rich Guggenheim dynasty, it was a luxuriously equipped, old-style colonial expedition, with a bevy of servants to wait upon the Loebs (Larson 2004). Eedes, however, was outraged by the behavior of the expedition members and complained to the chief native affairs commissioner:

> When Mr. Rodin [the expedition botanist] arrived here he was entertained at the Mess, and enquired whether his coloured servant could use the shower bath. I understand that Mrs. Loeb is teaching an Ovambo to type in Grootfontein, and that the instruction takes place in her bedroom at the hotel. . . . I think Dr Loeb should be summoned to Windhoek, or to Swakopmund, when he can be given advice, and instructions by a senior official as to the attitude foreign visitors are expected to adopt towards Natives in South Africa, more particularly in the Native Areas of South West Africa.[13]

Moreover, Eedes believed Mr. Camp, Jr., the son of the overall expedition leader under whose auspices the Loeb expedition fell, described as having a "long face, sickly appearance and what is described as 'an idiotic expression,'" was allegedly having an affair with Mrs. Laura Bolton, the expedition's musicologist. The consequence was a request from the administrator to the prime minister that overseas visitors to native areas be "very carefully screened because laxness in personal habits, such as some recent visitors to our Native Areas exhibited, when they seldom washed or shaved . . . may do us more harm in the eyes of the Natives than the good such visitors could do for us abroad."[14]

Just prior to the arrival of the Loeb expedition, van Warmelo made his first visit to Ovamboland in May–June 1947, spending twenty days collecting information in the company of Eedes. He was later to make a number of short-term visits. After spending March 1947 and September 1948 in the Kaokoveld, van Warmelo managed to publish his "inventory" of *Notes on the Kaokoveld* (1951, republished in 1962 probably to make the international case of how "backward" SWA natives were).

By mid-1949 van Warmelo had completed a typescript of an *Ethnic Survey of Ovamboland*, which he sent to Eedes and Allen. Allen thought that he had done an "amazing job" considering how far the Loeb report had fallen short and that the survey would be invaluable in rebutting UN criticism.[15] Eedes's response, however, was negative: he complained that there was some denigration of the administration and demanded that all reference to officials past and present be erased. He also claimed that it would take at least two years to do a proper study, as it involved collecting information from "old natives, missionaries, officials and from books and documents and then cross-checking them."[16] These criticisms so "damped" van Warmelo that he only responded eight months later. What stung, he informed Allen, was the comment that "such a hastily written report might harm the Administration," yet Eedes had provided no details on what information was incorrect. The value of the survey, van Warmelo claimed, was that it revealed lacunae in knowledge, and since he was not going to criticize the government, he foresaw no objection to it being published like the Kaokoveld report. Moreover, van Warmelo said, Eedes did not provide detailed criticism, and most of the information included about officials had already been mentioned by previous writers. Van Warmelo indicated that he still wanted to publish the survey and would revise it accordingly.[17] The survey, however, never saw the light of day, and the draft is not locatable.

By 1956 the administrative system of the territory was under considerable strain, with officials alarmed about the behavior of some Ovambo headmen, and van Warmelo was asked to advise.[18] He explained that because of the matrilineal kinship system in which the mother's senior brother played a key role, each royal family was small and did not use its own relatives to govern. The tedious environment necessitated the need for strong protection, which facilitated despotism. Chaos emerged when a king died, as the *omalenga*—commoner sub-headmen also known as the "owners," who derived their power from selling plots of arable land called *omikunda*—started assassinating one another. The local government unit was the ward, consisting typically of about twenty homesteads over which the sub-headmen practiced enlightened self-interest, doing as they pleased as long as they did not antagonize the king (or latterly the administration). Administratively, van Warmelo averred, it was a house of cards, with little internal stability. A system of control was only as good as the people who operated it. The crux of the matter was that only one sub-headman or "ward owner" had triggered complaints. What was the evidence of exploitation, van Warmelo wanted to know; all politicians had the capacity to exploit. He did not deny that population growth had led to an increase in sub-headmen, but argued that a number of part-time "old men" would be cheaper and better than having ambitious young headmen. He critiqued the administration's proposal to treat the Kavango, Ovamboland, and the Kaokoveld as a single unit under a common developmental formula, arguing that this ignored the diverse circumstances between these societies. In addition, Ovamboland was too important for the territory (especially economically) and of too much interest to the UN and to South Africa's enemies to engage in such experiments. The "matriarchy" or *epata* (matrilineal sib), where the father was simply an "alien blighter," was the swivel around which Ovambo economic, political, and social structure operated, yet this was ignored by the administration, reflected in the comment by one official—his bête noire, Eedes—that "this uncle business has got to stop." To experiment with replacing the system would lead to chaos, as the Belgians had discovered in the Congo. Van Warmelo thus doubted that reform was necessary, as no system would protect Ovambo from corruption, and the uproar this proposal had already triggered among sub-headmen would only get worse. Instead he urged that officials be freed from clerical trivialities so that they could spend more time with the inhabitants.[19]

The administrative crisis remained unresolved, and van Warmelo was instructed to further investigate the situation. Six months later he submitted a thirty-six-page memorandum that represented his most anthropological attempt at understanding the situation.[20] In the memorandum he denied that there was a crisis. He explained this by referring to the situation a year earlier: when the South African Department of Native Affairs took over from the SWA administration in 1955, it presumed that everything in the territory was quiet, remained ignorant about the importance of matrilineal kinship, and did not allow people to speak. This was wrong, as "it is an elementary principle of etiquette that the negro-race must be allowed to speak until they have nothing left to say." Van Warmelo disagreed with the view that trouble was unexpected, as Lebzelter had foreseen the situation in 1927 because of the impact of the contract labor system, and posited in contrast that Eedes was living in a "fool's paradise."

According to van Warmelo, both whites and Ovambo were confusing cause with effect. Development was inevitable, and while historically Ovambo had been traders, modern communications and migration had sped up the process of exposing Ovambo to new ideas. This had resulted in a change of values, with certainty replaced by uncertainty and the creation of a strong feeling of inferiority. Enlightened by a wider world, Ovambo were questioning the authority of chiefs and headmen and asking why matriliny was seen as ludicrous. Because headmen were not there by birthright, they followed and obeyed the native commissioner blindly to stay in his good books, going so far as to take a request for information as an instruction. Many Kuanyama wanted the kingship restored, because the last King Mandume had stopped the *omalenga* headmen from exploiting them and had not been intimidated by Europeans. However, such a move would, van Warmelo expected, lead to heavy resistance from the headmen and the ward owners (*omuene uomukunda*, also called sub-headmen). He stressed that the bought land reverted to the immediate superior on death; nevertheless this was not a commercial transaction but had wide social implications, including dispute resolution. Sub-headmen were successful because they were self-made entrepreneurs, not just "windbags at meetings."

Van Warmelo claimed that officials who were concerned about the increase in the number of sub-headmen were causing discontent. While local Ovambo might complain about individual sub-headmen, they did not oppose the overall setup. The old system was not dead, he argued, though its vitality had been robbed by imposed limitations on the punishments that headmen were allowed to execute, since "blacks cannot govern without nepotism, injustice, corruption and violence. If they could do so, they would already be truly civilized." In sum, van Warmelo advised against tinkering with the system: it was supervision by the administration that was important, and this supervision should be educational and emulative.

The memo went further. Land was so scarce that shifting agriculture could not be practiced. Overpopulation was visible and this stimulated contract labor, which had grave implications. As workers stayed away for longer and increasing periods, relatives did not know whether the worker had died, which meant that land could not be reallocated. Widows were driven away to live with their brothers, but these might be absent as well. Aggravating the situation, higher land prices meant purchasers were getting older and would then die before they had paid for the land. Economically Ovamboland was an island with few natural resources. Ovambo could not develop capital, as they had no fixed property and homes, and home improvement had no value. To be sure there were some cafés and small shops, but these were simple establishments and built largely for prestige. Van Warmelo pointed out that Lebzelter had already observed this when he noted that productive labor was being exported, while the reserve stagnated.

Van Warmelo also acknowledged the opinions and feelings of Ovambo. Historically they had accepted the roles of the headmen and kings and seen missionaries and the administration as protecting them against exploitative headmen, but contract labor had changed this. They now saw themselves as indispensable to the white economy, yet were treated like animals by whites who despised but were equally dependent upon them (echoing an observation by Albert Memmi in his 1964 classic *The Colonizer and the Colonized*). Psychologically Ovambo were used to sudden and unjustified behavior as a result of the matrilineal system. While fathers were relatively unimportant, they exerted a powerful influence on their children, especially when expressed with anger. Frequently wives would leave husbands and take the children with them, while youths were sent to stay with an uncle. Such actions led to obedience based on fear and a lack of attachment or loyalty to authority. For authority to work in such situations, subjects had to be kept in a constant state of fear. In practice this meant that chiefs could apply maximum indirect pressure, while the administration could only apply minimal indirect pressure. Van Warmelo advised, therefore, that the administration should have maximum freedom to immediately act when necessary without bureaucratic hindrances.

When Ovambo worked in the Police Zone, (unspecified) ameliorative actions by officials were sabotaged by the crass racism the Ovambo encountered when on contract. Ovambo complained about discrimination against some workers whose wages were locked into a contract while other workers' wages were not. The railways and package services that contract workers were forced to use were simply scandalous. There was huge economic frustration because the railways would constantly lose or damage luggage and packages because they had a monopoly. Van Warmelo even suggested that the administration hire a lawyer, as the railways were being deliberately malicious. Contract labor was leading to social disintegration in Ovamboland as wives were being neglected and moved to other men, and agriculture was being disrupted because more than half the productive labor force was in the Police Zone, yet the South-West Africa Native Labor Association (SWANLA), the contract recruiting organization, wanted longer contracts and was protecting weaker employers, van Warmelo claimed. Good employers wanted and needed permanent employees, and Ovambo should be allowed to bring their families with them, he argued.

Finally, van Warmelo honed in on the administration, accusing it of suffering from overcentralization and top-down management. The takeover of the administration of South-West Africa by the Department of Native Affairs in Pretoria had led to an increase in ignorance and delays in decision-making. Sometimes requests would take more than fourteen months despite follow-up requests. This was leading to a loss of legitimacy and demoralization of local officials. More officials did not necessarily lead to an increase of knowledge, while increasing centralization led to officials becoming clerks rather than being out in the field. Inspection tours of Ovamboland were so "pathetic" that they were leading to departmental self-destruction. Ovamboland should not be a punishment posting.[21]

Five years later van Warmelo was asked by the department to advise on creating an Ovambo Regional Authority, the standard building block that the government hoped would lead to independent homelands. He refused, denying that he had the requisite knowledge or expertise of either tribal or regional authorities. In his conclusion he asked whether the possibly destructive effect of the proposal on South Africa's pleadings at the ICJ had been considered.[22]

Shortly before his retirement in 1966, van Warmelo was asked by Allen to comment on a proposal by then commissioner-general Martie Olivier to create tribal councils consisting of headmen, a tribal secretary, and a small number of elected members, justified on the basis of the supposedly favorable World Court decision, the considerable economic and social development that had taken place in Ovamboland, and the need to take pre-emptive action to accommodate younger educated Ovambo. The council's main source of income would be from the sale of *omikunda*, conducted by the councils and not the headmen or sub-headmen, and the payments would be placed in tribal funds. Van Warmelo responded, without elaborating, that the proposals were "extra-ordinarily unrealistic" and on par with Eedes's celebrated dictum that "this uncle business has got to stop."[23]

Countering International Accusations

Until 1960, in complex legal maneuvering, South Africa responded to the annual reports of the UN Special Committee on South-West Africa (in its various iterations) by pointing out various alleged errors of fact (Carroll 1967, 57–71). This effort was coordinated by Jos Allen, in consultation with van Warmelo. In early 1960 van Warmelo submitted a memo entitled "The Inhabitants of SWA from an Ethnological Point of View." It was divided into three parts: the first described the different racial groups and their origins; the second discussed the progress of the various groups under the mandate; and the third responded to specific points raised in the UN Special Committee's allegations. It was to undergo several reiterations, especially concerning the first two parts, as the ICJ hearings in Ethiopia and Liberia versus South Africa took shape.

Replying to the allegations that South Africa had not administered its mandate in the best interests of the territory's Indigenous inhabitants, van Warmelo pointed out that South Africa's policy of differentiating between different races and groups was simply following the precedent set by the mandate: some rights had to be suppressed to facilitate the orderly evolution toward self-government, which had to be learned, "as with children restraint is a large part of the educative process." Residential segregation was natural "in towns, the influx of untutored peasants and cattle nomads into well-ordered centers constituting an utterly strange environment, rendered separate dwelling areas imperative and indeed they spontaneously grew as distinct areas." Restriction of movement by Kavango and Ovambo south into the Police Zone was in the best interest of the people concerned, as extended absences of large parts of the male population in particular had wide-ranging effects on biological reproduction, family stability, morality of wives, discipline of children, maintenance of dwellings, food production, and solidarity of tribe and language ties. This restriction was favored by both traditional leaders and relatives, since the longer contract workers stayed in the Police Zone, the more they tended to abandon their families, who then had to be fed by the government in times of famine. Extended contracts meant that laborers "contribute little to their home area, whilst dissipating earnings on cheap watches and useless novelties, and spending much on town women and liquor."

Concerning political organizations, van Warmelo claimed that the only existing ones were tribal or traditional in nature, which were not only recognized but fostered by the administration, but that there was no room for opposition groups within such organizations, "a concept not known and repugnant to the people's thinking." People organizing parties with no "tribal affiliation" lacked leadership status in their own tribal groups and

> are rejected by them, have made themselves unpopular at home, and are the type that disdains the routine and hard way of achieving status and becoming a public figure, preferring the role of agitator and demagogue, and seeking office and influence for themselves without any thought of rendering public service. It is to curb the activities of these self-seekers that these (legal) provisions exist.

Deportation of those characterized as "agitators" to their rural reserve was justified by van Warmelo as "the sole humane and effective method any type of administration can use in many cases which arise amongst people at this stage of political and social development." Moreover,

> the peaceful co-existence of opposing parties is neither understood nor wanted, because the accepted way of dealing with opponents is violence. . . . Courts cannot deal with troubles of this sort owing to prevailing ideas about evidence, truthfulness, oaths etc., and because an administration which permitted a solution of internal strife along traditional lines, that is by fighting and arson, would have to accommodate the losers in any case. . . . [Finally], in the case of other troublemakers . . . notably of those led by them and misled by specious arguments and appeals to emotions, is often best served by the removal of the key agitators after which grievances, if any, can be rectified without the presence of self-seekers working for their own benefit.[24]

Van Warmelo's memorandum on the people of SWA was critiqued by Bruwer, then professor of volkekunde at Stellenbosch (and the focus of the next chapter), and a second forty-eight-page draft was circulated in October 1960. Like the Odendaal Commission (about which more later), it listed twelve "racial groups," starting with the Bushmen and then moving up the ladder to end with the Basters, coloreds, and Europeans (later rebranded "whites" to remove the alien stigma). A sampling of van Warmelo's insights: Bushmen were known by various names because their own names were unpronounceable, and they had no history because they were never a large group; they were at a "very early stage of human economy, from which (they) never emerged"; left to themselves in reservations, Bushmen would stagnate; they needed to be civilized and integrated as soon as possible, this being the Christian and ethical duty of the government; their greatest obstacle, however, was their physical appearance, which proclaimed them Bushmen, inviting banter and ridicule.

The Damara, on the other hand, never had political solidarity because they had nothing to be proud of, "having always been despised and down-trodden," with no language of their own to draw them together, van Warmelo posited. They had thus benefited the most by European occupation. Herero agitation at the UN, in turn, was largely due to Chief Hosea Kutako, who owed his status to having survived so long, which his people took as proof that "he has got something" in the "magic-mystic thinking of the black man," abetted by the administration backing of his leadership. Herero "still don't like to be told" what to do, and regardless of Chief Kutako's status, Herero leaders "are as much at sea as the rank and file. Questions of finance, of grazing control and . . . of education as a long-term investment . . . prove hard to grasp and to decide on." Herero "relations with other groups have seldom been good," largely because Herero claim as theirs much more of the territory than they ever effectively occupied, omitting that others, whom they "treated like dogs," were settled there.

The Ovambo suffered from chronic tensions because of their slaving legacy, but van Warmelo reiterated his criticism of the contract labor system, which he described as

> a watertight pipeline . . . controlled solely by southern interests. . . . The export of migrant labor is paid for by imports in no way representing equivalent value. The best manpower is permanently absent, genetically speaking a long-term form of racial suicide. Much of the earnings is spent in the south, on clothing, liquor, women and cheap trash. We cannot ignore however that it is a system hard to defend against outside criticism which does not realize the practical difficulties inherent in proposed reforms and alternative systems . . . [which] would upset the whole territory, confront the Ovambo with a situation they would not know how to deal with. . . . Taking such a risk, on the ethical ground of granting greater self-determination, would be quite unjustified.[25]

Then came the coup de grâce, namely that different groups could be identified by physique and body odor:

> Some non-European manners are repulsive to Europeans, e.g. their method of blowing and cleaning their noses with their fingers, and cleaning their fingers on

the ground or anything else that comes to hand. Their practices in connection with micturition and defecation are to Europeans nauseously filthy, and though non-Europeans often wonder why Europeans don't like to shake hands with them, there are very good reasons. There is no guarantee that a well-dressed Native is not nevertheless still most primitive and loathsome in his habits. . . . The sight of a Native latrine, or a visit to a Native homestead where Nature all around serves as latrine just like with the animals, should make it clear why Europeans insist on living apart from Natives.[26]

Given such views, which might cause international embarrassment, and van Warmelo's condemnation of the contract labor system, it is not surprising that the South African legal team preparing for the upcoming World Court case decided that Bruwer should draft the ethnological background, and van Warmelo was asked to comment on it and pronounced it "exemplary for the purposes I understand it to be intended for"[27] and delegated his assistant, Dr. C. V. Bothma, to review a later version of Bruwer's "Peoples and Cultures of SWA."[28] While van Warmelo was thus being sidelined, his total contribution was recognized when he was awarded honorary doctorates from the University of South Africa in 1973 and Pretoria University in 1989 and personally presented with the Order of Merit (First Class Gold) by the South African state president in 1987.

Bushman Diversion:
Paranoia and Amateurs versus Professionals

Imbricated in the ethnological efforts to justify South African overrule was a concern about Bushmen. A report written in 1949 by Dr. Werner Kuschke, the medical officer of the Kavango region, suggested that Bushmen were becoming extinct. Kuschke pointed out that tuberculosis and venereal disease were rife among the Kavango Bushmen and that this was leading to population decline and inbreeding, since, "as the pure Bushman population decreases[,] . . . the proportion of inbreeding must increase and this (will) eventually leave its mark on the virility of the race." In addition, this would lead to Bushmen migration to the Kavango River, where they would find an easier lifestyle that would eventually "result in the disappearance of racial prejudice with familiarity" and an increase in "cross-breeding." Natural extinction would occur within six generations, he predicted. The only solution, Kuschke believed, was a complete and rigid segregation of all Bushmen in a reserve with adequate health, agricultural, and educational services.[29] Given the iconic status attributed to Bushmen, the administration acted with surprising alacrity when it appointed a Commission for the Preservation of the Bushmen within two months. It was to be chaired by Fourie of *Native Tribes of South West*

Africa fame, with Major J. Naude, former deputy commissioner of police, and volkekundige Professor P. J. Schoeman, newly appointed game
warden in the Etosha Game Reserve as members. Fear of international
embarrassment also shaped the commission. Given the disputed status
of the territory, the last thing the South Africans wanted were events that
could escalate into an international scandal, such as charges that they had
let the Bushmen die out.[30]

Before the commission commenced its activities, Fourie died, and
Schoeman was appointed chairman. By Schoeman's own account, he resigned from Stellenbosch University to become a full-time writer, but financial needs forced him to accept the offer of game warden in South-West
Africa in 1950. "These joint positions [were to provide] me with five of
the most fruitful years in my writing career," he explained later (Lategan
1979, 26).[31] Schoeman (1904–88) was not only a volkekundige but also
a major Afrikaner literary figure and an influential advocate for apartheid,
who proudly claimed that Malinowski was the intellectual who had influenced him most. During World War II he had been active in right-wing
organizations, occupying a senior position in the Ossewa-brandwag (an
ultra-Afrikaner-nationalist cultural movement). He had then resigned his
Stellenbosch professorship and, believing that he knew what "the natives"
wanted, had stood in the 1948 parliamentary elections as a candidate to
represent Cape Africans but was so badly beaten that he forfeited his deposit. He took his election loss badly and in private correspondence ranted
derogatorily about the "Kaffirs." His particular obsession appears to have
been miscegenation: he proposed giving "blacks the opportunity to regain
their lost self-respect and identity in their own areas, because only then will
they refuse to intermarry with us" (Schoeman 1941, 21–22), an ideology
that was to underpin his Bushman recommendations.[32]

The commission issued two reports, both drafted by Schoeman, a
preliminary one in September 1951[33] and a final, undated one in about
1955.[34] In 1950 the commission undertook a thirty-day journey of two
thousand miles during the winter months, traveling up the Omuramba
Eiseb to the Kavango River before making a separate trip to the Etosha
Game Reserve. What is noteworthy is that Schoeman appeared to avoid
contact with other people interested in Bushmen. Thus the archival record
suggests no contact with the newly appointed government ethnologist
Wagner. Even contact with Lorna and Laurence Kennedy Marshall, who
were to achieve fame for their Bushman studies and at this time were
undertaking expeditions to the Nyae Nyae area, was minimal and, where
it occurred, rather dismissive. This was the case despite Schoeman's claim
that three years earlier, on a visit to the United States, he had suggested to
the director of the Peabody Museum, which was to sponsor the Marshall
expeditions, the need to film Bushmen. Schoeman also ignored the veteran

Austrian ethnologist Martin Gusinde, who was undertaking Bushman research along the Kavango, leaving it to the local native commissioner to obtain Gusinde's views on how Bushmen might be preserved.[35]

Lack of transport meant that no research was undertaken in 1951, although Schoeman did manage to write and publish his popular book on Bushmen titled *Jagters van die Woestynland* (1951, translated as *Hunters of the Desert Land* [1982]). Then, in 1952, there was a flurry of activity as Schoeman organized, collected, and managed "the Bushman Exhibition," one of the most successful exhibits at the Van Riebeek Festival held in Cape Town to commemorate three hundred years of European settlement in South Africa. Building on the success of this venture, Schoeman invited Professor Jack Brock of UCT's medical school to examine Bushmen in situ. Their modus operandi was to have relevant officials gather local Bushmen in an encampment, where they were promised generous portions of tobacco, salt, and mealie meal, to be interviewed and measured. Schoeman now used two interpreters, Xameb for Heikum and Trados for Kung. These two were also the narrators of the twenty-six fables that he published in his last book (Schoeman 1984).

Schoeman took his duties seriously and wrote an undated memorandum on "the right attitude" the commission was to take:

> We as members of a more highly developed Western civilization, are, consciously and unconsciously, forever comparing and criticizing. . . . The result is a . . . strong tendency to despise them and lose patience with them. Such an attitude creates a barrier . . . and we remain forever not only strangers but hostile to each other. . . . Not to mend and change, but *to understand* must be our first and guiding principle.[36]

In the preliminary report of 1951, Schoeman explained that their policy would have to be one of *festina lente*, "or else social and moral disintegration would result (we already have this sad state of affairs in the rural and urban areas of South Africa)." In classic Malinowskian terms, he proclaimed that Bushmen were driven by two forces, hunger and sex, and from these emerged economic and social organization. He displayed a fatal ignorance of history: "It was not until the Bushmen became more accustomed to Europeans through official feeding schemes, etc., that it became apparent that disease was rife amongst them and that they were in danger of extermination."[37] Such a version of history ignores not only the long and well-established history of Bushman exploitation by both black and white settlers, but also the various petitions by the influential farming lobby to have "vagrant" Bushmen placed on reserves, where they could not cause trouble (Gordon 1992, 161).

In his memorandum on the study of the Bushmen, Schoeman addressed the "all-important question": "Can the Bushmen be civilized?"

He conjectured that they historically appeared to be incapable of such a move but considered their will to survive as very strong. Tragically, he pointed out, no government had ever given them a square deal, treating them either as a liability or ignoring them. Information was thus needed to determine whether Bushmen could settle down like the Bantu. As a long-term policy, Schoeman proposed considering integrating the Bushmen with the Ovambo because, while they were unable to settle down "as a race," they did submit to the authority of Bantu tribes. Schoeman concluded his memorandum:

> It might be worthwhile to lead the Bushmen via the Native to a stage of development where they will no longer slaughter cattle and sheep, but keep them. If we give them livestock straight away, I fear the worst!

> As an idealist I would like to see the Bushmen living their own lives in one or more reserves of their own—with a Chinese wall around them. But unless the Administration is prepared to supply them with food, they will, I fear, be a continual nuisance to both the Natives and the European farmers, then they will gradually exterminate all the big game.[38]

In the 1951 preliminary report, the commission reported being impressed by the richness and beauty of the mythology of Heikum Bushmen of Etosha and the "wonderful" way they had remembered and maintained their centuries-old tribal laws and customs, and indeed it suggested that Schoeman be asked to write a treatise on Heikum customs and usages. Such a treatise would not only be scientifically valuable, but also necessary for long-term planning.[39] The report claimed that Heikum were one of the oldest living Bushman races, as proved by their myths and folklore. Their tale, as narrated by Schoeman, saw them as the original inhabitants who were attacked by pastoralist Herero, who forced them to join the "Hottentots," with whom they intermarried. The report also "acknowledged that the Ovambos took Bushman wives but that it was prohibited for Heikum men to take Ovambo wives."[40] Heikum were supposedly on a higher civilizational level than Kung because they lived in the Etosha Game Reserve near European settlements and constantly interacted with whites: "Approximately 70 percent of [the Heikum] wore European clothing and regularly begged for tea, coffee and sugar. This recently learnt need will gradually persuade them to seek work on neighboring white farms."[41] They were reportedly good workers, indeed considered superior to Ovambo by some European farmers. The commission recommended that a reserve be created for Heikum adjacent to the Etosha Game Reserve in the north, while the Kung would be given a reserve further east near Karakuwisa. Part of the attraction of having a Bushman reserve along the Etosha Game Reserve would be that it would serve as a livestock-free zone and thus provide a bulwark against the spread of stock disease from the north to the white-owned herds within the Police Zone. In this reserve, gradual development would take place with as little outside interference as possible. Contact with other ethnic groups would be limited to so-called Bushmen guards—Bantu overseers hired by the native commissioner—and the position of these guards would be terminated once Bushmen headmen were available.

The commission was acutely aware that white farmers claimed there to be a labor shortage in the territory, but they felt that Bushmen were so attached to their desert life and so suspicious of civilization that they would not resettle on white farm areas. The commission reiterated this stance in even stronger terms in its final report: "The Commission definitely rejects the idea that whole families should be sent out to farms because it is feared that any such move may result in the deaths of whole families through acute homesickness."[42]

Mindful of the rhetoric of salvaging the last vestiges of this "dying race," the commission tried to answer the question "Are the Bushmen dying out?" It broke this down into three interrelated questions: "Is there still something like a pure race Bushman?"; "Are the Bushmen dying out as a race?"; and "To what degree have they already inter-married with Hottentot and Bantu tribes?" Proclaiming only tentative impressions, Schoeman noted the low fertility rates and the preponderance of males over females and observed that the commission did not find a single Bushman woman married to another ethnic group. They were simply concubines.

In its final report, the commission acknowledged that Bushmen were "dying out" and that Bushman reservations were necessary to stem the tide. The prime causes for the decline in Bushman numbers were syphilis and other contagious diseases. In typical functionalist vein, Schoeman ignored history[43] except for indirect inferences, as when he suggested that policemen should not wear uniforms when on patrol in Bushman areas. With no traditional chiefs, ordinary tribal government was impossible, and a commissioner should be appointed who would have to exercise personal control over Bushmen. The key framing question used by the commission was vintage Malinowski: "To what extent do the Bushmen provide their own means of livelihood? Can these Bushmen, who, in so far as it is known to anthropological science, have always been wanderers, hunters and *veldkos* [food from the veld] gatherers, be induced to lead settled life practicing agriculture and stock-breeding?"[44]

The commission's final report claimed (erroneously, see Gordon 1992) that there was no historical data with which to compare their observations and that it was thus unable to say how "racially" pure

Bushmen were, although the commission believed the Kung to be the "purer" group, while Heikum were "mixed." Contagious disease rather than colonial exploitation was confirmed as the primary cause for depopulation, although it stated that numbers in the Kavango region had declined because of "uncontrolled drift to unsuitable areas [where,] due to the extermination of game, uncontrolled bush-burnings and inevitable droughts, Bushmen have been subjected to an insufficient and unbalanced diet to such an extent that the birth rate has dropped to an alarmingly low level."[45]

In contrast to the preliminary report, the final report stated, "Nowhere did your Commission receive the impression that it would be worthwhile to preserve either the Heikum or the Barakwengo as Bushmen. In both cases, the process of assimilation has proceeded too far and these Bushmen are already abandoning their nomadic habits and are settling down amongst the neighbouring tribes to agriculture and stock breeding."[46] Contradictions and inconsistencies were brushed aside. "In actual fact, the Bushmen leading a free hunting life today is in the minority. Apart from those living in Bantu tribal areas, numbers also work for European farmers and other employers, and this has been the case for years."[47] It stipulated that 30–40 percent of Bushmen in Ovamboland practiced agriculture, and 10–15 percent owned livestock. Generally, these Heikum were healthy and well-fed. The commission gushed:

> It is amazing how far the Bushmen have advanced along the paths of civilization in the last two decades . . . thanks largely to the sympathetic treatment accorded them by the officials of the Administration. . . . Some of the so-called "wild" Bushmen in the Noma Omuramba, near Nyae Nyae, expressed concern at the fact that their relatives living on the outskirts of civilization were damaging the reputation of the tribe by killing European owned cattle, but they explained that this was largely due to lack of official guidance. The people who perpetrated these misdeeds had left their home areas with the intention of entering civilization and employment but on the very doorstep their hearts failed them and there was no one to help them to take the final plunge into an entirely foreign and, to them, hostile world. . . . This uncontrolled migration into civilisation, which was gathering pace, worried the elders who saw in it the doom of the tribe. They wanted the Government to control it.[48]

Bushmen, the commission argued, were unanimous in their desire for a piece of land with permanent water. However, it also cautioned that "rapid results are not to be expected. The Bushmen are still too primitive to adopt completely a settled life in one generation and many falterings and failures are to be expected. . . . A forced pace would result in irreparable damage." There should be no undue haste about this development, it cautioned, as it would have to keep pace with the "taming" of the Bushmen in a step-by-step manner:

First, those in the immediate neighborhood of the pans should be persuaded to settle down to farming. When they have done so, their vacated hunting grounds would attract the next lying bands. When these have moved in, they, in turn, should be similarly persuaded and so the process will continue with ever increasing momentum until all the Bushmen are settled.[49]

The major difference between the preliminary and final reports of the commission was that the proposed reserve for Heikum be dropped. No reasons were given for this change, and it is difficult to explain this volte-face except to note that Schoeman's role as chief warden of the Etosha Game Park might have played a role. Two possible factors seem to have been important: first, there was the old idea that people in parks would spoil the "natural ambiance," and second, there were the pressing labor needs of local farmers (Dieckmann 2007, 190–92).

The situation concerning this volte-face is indeed complex. In his classic *Hunters of the Desert Land* ([1951] 1982), Schoeman purports to record dialogues between himself and Xameb, his Heikum interpreter, who is certainly not shy to speak his mind. In Xameb's telling, the Heikum story was one of "great suffering . . . the story of our slow death . . . the starvation of the little, yellow children of the desert land. . . . [Impoverishment was the consequence of] you white people, and the black people [who] chased us away from the land of flowing waters." Schoeman responds by asking if the dislocation was not the consequence of killing the cattle owned by whites and blacks. Xameb's reply is poignant: "Alas . . . White Father, must you, who have seen so much of our hunger and thirst and death here in the desert land, still echo such a lie?" When Schoeman rejoins, "What is written in books, Xameb, does not suffer from a bad memory," Xameb ripostes, "Is it also written in those books of yours with their long memories who first started slaughtering the other man's cattle?" (Schoeman [1951] 1982, 11). Xameb continues describing how "our pregnant mothers gave birth to their children while they were fleeing from you . . . we had to leave our aged behind to fall prey." Bushmen were now reduced to begging for old clothes and tobacco next to the main roads (Schoeman [1951] 1982, 12–13). Xameb described how the Germans shot "many of us . . . just as people shoot wild dogs and wolves." Schoeman replied, "Only those of your people who murdered and stole cattle, Xameb. We must not cover the truth with sand" (Schoeman [1951] 1982, 206–8).

The concluding chapter is particularly wrenching. Xameb describes how, when they were "on the road," blacks would rape Bushman women. When Schoeman asks what message he should take to the great chiefs in Windhoek, Xameb replies, "Ask them to listen to the weeping of a race which is tired of running away. Give us a piece of land, too. Give us a piece of land where our women will not be taken from us. . . . If your law pro-

tects our women there, we will never leave our land . . . Bushman-land"
(Schoeman [1951] 1982, 212). Finally, as Schoeman is about to leave,
Xameb "squirmed uneasily": "The woman of the bulbs . . . wants to tell
the White Father something through my mouth. . . . She says, 'Eliob will
send the White Father a lovely young duiker-doe . . . to put wood on
the White Father's fire every night'" (Schoeman [1951] 1982, 213). So
touched was Schoeman that he was speechless and could not even look
up. He got into his truck and the book concludes:

> And I do not believe the old truck will ever really know why I suddenly pushed the
> accelerator right down. It would never be able to understand why I was driven to
> hurry to Windhoek where I was to deliver the beseeching prayer of the "Hunters
> of the Desert Land" . . . "Please give us a land of our own . . . Bushman-land."
> (Schoeman [1951] 1982, 215)

The book is important. It went into numerous editions, was translated
into a number of languages, and enjoyed captive sales by being prescribed
as a school text in all South African provinces. It was seen as an important contribution to Afrikaans literature for its humanistic portrayal of
Indigenous people. It is also important for the history of South African
anthropology for its portrayal of the anthropologist activist who is using
his literary skills to engage policy makers on behalf of "his people." And
yet, within two years Schoeman was to write the final report of the Commission for the Preservation of the Bushmen, which betrayed Xameb and
his fellow Heikom with not even the courtesy of an explanation. Indeed,
Schoeman asked that the native commissioner inform the Heikum of the
decision to force them out of Etosha, "because he [Schoeman] considers
that their removal from the Game Reserve is bound to [lead to] antagonism amongst these Bushmen, Dr Schoeman feels that he should not present the matter personally, as such antagonism may hamper his work in the
Game Reserve." Instead the task was left to Native Commissioner Eedes,
who informed Heikum residents in the Etosha Game Reserve in no uncer-
tain terms that there was "no appeal against this order." Ute Dieckmann
(2007, 193) reports:

> Whereas the police sergeants are often described in a positive way, Schoeman in
> particular does not appear to have been very popular with many of the Hai//om.
> He is thought to be responsible for the expulsion plan. It would appear that his
> attempts to avoid antagonism amongst the Bushmen by not informing them of the
> removal himself failed.

In his writing, Schoeman was to return to the Bushmen in a number of
books and articles. What is intriguing about this corpus, though, is that
he never mentions the fact that he was chairman of the Commission for

the Preservation of the Bushmen. In a popular article entitled "Die wees-kinders van Afrika" (The orphans of Africa) (1971), published twenty years later, he directly addressed the issue of Bushman population decline: they had become extinct in South Africa because of a "tragic reciprocal misunderstanding." In South-West Africa, their numbers were diminishing because of—wait for it—their lust for tobacco! Unable to restrain their craving, they would trek up to the Kavango River, where they sold their wives to black migrant workers returning from the mines for this tobacco. Schoeman believed that the migrant workers would eventually infect all Bushmen females with venereal disease, with fatal consequences. This was aggravated by the fact that Bushmen would flee rather than see a white administration doctor (Schoeman 1971)! It is striking how Schoeman's plans and hopes continually failed. An idealistic and fervent believer in apartheid, Schoeman tried to convince Africans of its merits, yet he lost his deposit in an election to be their parliamentary representative. Deeply touched by the Bushmen and their tales of suffering, he failed them as a commissioner and activist.

After Smuts lost the elections in 1948, paranoia about foreign researchers was given free rein. Only foreigners with impeccable conservative credentials were given research clearances, and then, significantly, their research was not on the larger, more politically sensitive groups or problems, but on Bushmen. The most famous research expeditions after World War II were undertaken by the Marshall family between 1950 and 1961. The Marshalls were seen by officials as relatively harmless, wealthy conservative amateurs who had some influence in the United States—as indeed they had, for the paterfamilias, Laurence Marshall, was the founding president of the Raytheon Corporation, a major manufacturer in the electronics and defense industry. But even they were not exempt from harassment: they were carefully vetted by the South African embassy in the United States, and their movements in Namibia were constantly monitored. In 1951 they were required to include Claude McIntyre, the secretary of the Commission for the Preservation of the Bushmen and later Bushman affairs commissioner, in their expedition. While guiding the Marshalls to their research site of Nyae Nyae, McIntyre used the trip to inexpensively collect data for the planned Bushman reserve (Barbash 2017, 36).

Despite these administrative precautions, rumors abounded and questions were raised in the settler-run legislative assembly. The administrator was pointedly asked a series of twelve questions, including the following: was the administration aware of social fraternization between the Europeans of this expedition and the Bushman community; were the Marshalls making films and tape recordings, and if so, were these censored before they were sent overseas; was the administration intending to establish a Bushman reserve in this area, and if so, was it the result of the influence and business of this Marshall expedition; and finally, would the needs of Europeans for land be considered before this Bushman reserve was established?[50] Despite the administrator's denials of these charges, the next year the administration banned John Marshall, the son, from entering the territory, a ban it kept up until 1978.

By allowing research on Bushmen, the South Africans could claim that they were not against research per se and moreover were doing their bit for promoting science, given the importance of Bushmen for international science. Another factor contributing to this focus was the intellectual climate at Afrikaans universities where Bushmen had a central role in the volkekunde discourse. Schoeman was followed by at least seven volkekundiges who researched Bushmen. The tone for this research of genocide denial and blaming the victim was set in P. J. Coertze's ([1959] 1964) influential introductory text, *Inleiding tot die algemene volkekunde*:

> Exaggerated conservatism as psychological phenomenon must not, however, be confused with cases where a people are undergoing change in a fixed direction subject to stimuli derived from foreign cultures. In the case of the Bushmen, we find, for example, that despite close contact with whites on the one hand and Bantu on the other, they became neither westernized nor Bantuized. Where it did occur, it only went to a certain level after which they die out and disappear. The intrinsic bondedness between their life-style on the one side and their inherited racial characteristics on the other side meant extinction for them. The challenge of new conditions of living was too big for them, not simply because they were conservative, but because they had an "inherent incapability" of meeting new challenges. (P. Coertze [1959] 1964, 47)

The extraordinary influence of Coertze's book derives from the fact that, in its various editions, it was prescribed at all the Afrikaans universities. Its role in the volkekunde gestalt is important if only because many whites who were to influence Bushman policy were trained at Afrikaans universities, and this shaped their explanations for Bushman behavior. Coertze's position is echoed by his student Budack, who, as we will remember, was to be appointed ethnologist in the territory in the sixties. In discussing the creation of a Bushman homeland, he remarked that "in the process of ethnogenesis, territoriality is a crucial element. This process only began amongst the Bushmen comparatively recently. Apart from that they have thus far not been able to compete freely with other ethnic groups" (*Die Suidwester*, 19 April 1978). Budack also wrote a series of articles on "the peoples of SWA" for a local German newspaper. A large number of them feature the Bushmen, whose problems he treated with sympathy and sensitivity, going so far as to plead that the landless Heikum in the Etosha region be given land. Overall though, these interventions were to lead to Bushmen having the rare distinction of becoming, by some accounts, the most militarized ethnic group in the world, a subject covered in a later chapter.

Paranoia about anthropologists and other researchers has a long history in the territory, going back to Lehmann and the Loebs in the late forties. In the late fifties John Marshall was banned because settler rumor had it that he slept with a Bushman and thus contravened the notorious Immorality Act, which criminalized inter-racial sex. Wade Pendleton, an American anthropologist who had studied interethnic relations in Katutura, the sprawling black township outside Windhoek, in the early 1970s, was denied a visa for eleven years. Even researchers with solid connections to nationalist politicians were placed under surveillance and harassed. Gerhard Tötemeyer recounted how, after discussing his research on elites in Ovamboland with the government ethnologist in Windhoek, the latter had traveled to Ovamboland in a government vehicle with false number plates, pretending to be a Stellenbosch professor of anthropology, to interview Tötemeyer's informants, who naturally then thought Tötemeyer was a spy (G. Tötemeyer 2015, 194–95). Suspicion was to continue until independence. In documents leaked from a top-level counterintelligence conference held in Namibia, concern was expressed about "leakages." High on the counterintelligence list of "manifestations of espionage," indeed following right after SWAPO members, were "foreign visitors such as naturalists and anthropologists" (*The Resister* 34 [October/November 1984]: 19).

The Rise of the Citizen Ethnographer

With the surprise victory of the Nationalist Party in the 1948 South African elections, its leader, Dr. D. F. Malan, pushed forward its agenda of incorporating the South-West African territory as a fifth province in South Africa by allocating five seats in the South African Parliament to whites in the territory as well as a Senate seat to an expert on SWA native affairs. Such a strategy was not just a ploy to cover his bases in the evolving situation at the UN but also an election gambit. By assiduously cultivating the German-speaking population, who felt hard done by the Smuts government, the Nationalists hoped to safeguard their slim majority. One of their prime targets was Vedder, the "Father-figure for settlers of German origin" (Sundermeier 1973), who, beginning in the interwar years and continuing through the fifties, both styled himself as and was coached into being *the* native expert. With the blessing of two honorary doctorates, his expertise was propelled into the academic sphere.

As Vedder tells it, after World War II he led a delegation to see Smuts and was singularly disappointed when told that the German *volk* had been insane to follow Hitler and that some Germans would be deported. This stood in sharp contrast to the visit by D. F. Malan, with whom Vedder had had a long friendly discussion and during which Malan assured him that no Germans would be deported. The courting of Vedder continued after the 1948 election with another visit to the territory by Malan, followed in rapid succession with visits by Interior Minister Eben Dönges and Minister of Justice C. R. Swart to Vedder's home. It climaxed with Vedder being awarded an honorary doctorate from the premier Afrikaans university, Stellenbosch, in December 1948. Shortly thereafter Malan invited Vedder to serve as senator, officially in his role as expert on native affairs but unofficially to protect German interests (Vedder [1953] 1957, 132–38). He was to serve in this capacity from 1950 until his retirement in 1958.

While many prominent German men had been interned during the war for their Nazi connections, Vedder avoided that fate: despite being labeled a "strong Nazi" by the police, he was classified as possessing an essential skill as head of the only native training school, the Augustineum, and allowed to continue.[51] Since all but one of the Lutheran pastors had been interned, Vedder was made acting Präses of the whites-only Deutsche Evangelische Synode von Südwest-Afrika, despite not being an ordained pastor. He maintained the church's *Afrikanischer Heimatkalender*, publishing many of his own articles on native life. Vedder certainly had Nazi sympathies: "I am a Nazi of Hitler's kind with all my heart," he wrote to his supervisor, missionary Johannes Olpp, in 1933 (Lau 1995, 5). He invited the rabid Nazi German consul Hermann von Oehlhafen to address the annual Rhenish missionary conference in the territory in 1935. In the same year he published an essay, "Race, Religion and Missions," that invoked Joseph A. de Gobineau to justify racism (Gockel 2010, 10). The following year he gave a speech to celebrate Hitler's birthday and in 1937 claimed he would resign rather than ordain nonwhite ministers (Sundermeier 1973, 18). He went further and criticized missionary Friedrich Rust (Jr.) for publicly criticizing the Nazi-appointed Landesprobst Andreas Wackwitz (Hellberg 1997, 204–6). Despite this, the Smuts-supporting administration acknowledged and drew on Vedder's native expertise. As late as 1947 it negotiated with him to write two sequels to his *Das alte Südwestafrika* (Vedder 1934), the first to document the territory under German rule and the second, the territory as mandate. Funding, diabetes, and Vedder's fledgling political career in the South African Senate, however, prevented these volumes from being brought to fruition.

Vedder was not exactly a gregarious participant in the Senate's activities. Indeed, he rarely spoke, and then his contributions were naively simplistic. In June 1951 Vedder delivered his maiden speech during the debate on the Bantu Authorities Bill, which was to create a new system of governance in the projected apartheid homelands. In his speech he focused on Bushmen. Vedder claimed that there were six native races in the territory: Ovambo, Herero, Nama, Damara, Basters, and Bushmen. Following the precedent set at the League of Nations and echoing his plea at the 1936 South-West Africa Commission, Vedder complained that the bill made no provision for protecting Bushmen. When South Africa occupied the territory in 1915, he stated, officials were surprised to learn that there were still surviving Bushmen. Nowadays, Vedder continued, they were so well-known that even an American professor had come to study them. Originally Bushmen had occupied the whole of southern Africa, but because they were incapable of distinguishing between livestock and game, they had been forced to retreat to the Kalahari. Here, contrary to settler belief, Bushmen could not move about freely because of their strong sense of territoriality. Territorial transgressions resulted in death, which fueled revenge, and this was why their numbers had declined. They killed one another!

Other countries would look askance if nothing was done to protect and preserve Bushmen, Vedder said, because they were the oldest people on earth and had a wonderful language: "It would be a pity for the linguists if it became a dead language." At the same time Bushmen could not count beyond three and celebrated only one festival, that of the New Year, when the veld onions ripened. At this festival a new fire is lit, which had to be kept alive the whole year or misfortune would befall the group. They were not a bad people, Vedder averred, and some farmers swore by them as laborers. If a farmer established a farm on land occupied by Bushmen, he should not chase them away but allow them three things: the right to hunt, the right to drink at their traditional waterholes, and the right to collect *veldkos* (edible wild plants). In return, farmers should insist that the young men work for them for a weekly ration of tobacco and matches. Vedder also modestly entertained the Senate with a few phrases of Bushman and Nama.[52]

Vedder's next display concerned the debate about the Orwellian named Abolition of Native Passes Bill, which, he felt, would be supported by the natives of South-West Africa because the metal pass disks that the German government obliged them to wear around their necks after the wars of 1903–8 were viewed as a protective talisman, and not as doglike humiliation. The replacement of these metal disks by passbooks, as envisaged in the new bill, would make a big impression on Indigenes, who would see it as a "Book of Protection." Natives, he explained, were insecure without passbooks or something similar, but he suggested that the passbooks might increase in value if they included a folder in which papers could be stored. Vedder wholeheartedly welcomed the suggestion that the bill be applied to the territory as well as in South Africa. When the debate resumed a few days later, Vedder argued that the natives would be happy to have a single pass and would not find it degrading to have their finger-prints on it. On the contrary, they would use their passbooks to identify strangers they encountered![53]

Two years later, in 1954, Vedder again made a speech during a motion discussing the policy of the minister of native affairs, to push for a very specific form of native education. After discussing European and early South African education, he claimed that "apartheid" was not a swear word if it was not the product of hate. He personally was apart because his whole nature was in favor of it. Natives also practiced apartheid, he maintained, citing the separation between Herero and Bushman as an example. While he supported the government's takeover of native educa-tion, he was concerned about the curriculum. This should not be the one followed by Europeans, as that would only make Indigenes aspire to be white. He was also concerned that suggested curriculum subordinated religious instruction to science and arithmetic. He warned that science was like a sharp knife: it could be a good thing, but in the wrong hands it could be dangerous, especially if there was no opportunity to put what had been learned into practice. Then, like the seed of a weed, it would spread dissatisfaction.[54]

In 1955 Vedder was to again use the metaphor of the knife to ex-plain the power of the state and to argue for the legitimacy of apartheid. Whether this knife was used for good or bad depended on morals. The state derived its power from God, but this power was exercised by the electorate. The state provided much, including protection, and natives should show gratitude for this. In the olden days, he explained, if one gave a Herero something, he would bend his knees and say, "*Okuhepa,*" meaning "This is something which I now have need for. I do not have the brains to get it and now it is there"; but, Vedder continued, the term could be ambivalent, also implying, "What we have now received is only a little. I still have a great need, very much more." Was the state really obliged to give everybody everything? Vedder asked. Natives were happy with what they had received, but should they be given items they could not appreciate? He then argued that the Bible, and especially the Mosaic laws, provided the answer: when it exhorted Jacob to refuse to take the daughters of the seven tribes for his sons, the Bible justified apartheid and more. Even Paul proclaimed that slaves could be mentally freed by the gospel. Apartheid was not based on hatred but was simply a desire "to give them the opportunity to remain what they are and to develop on their own lines." Apartheid was like a stream of cool water that divided the country, with whites on the one side and natives on the other. Both used the water to make their gardens, but bridges had to be built. The first bridge was built by the churches, the second by the economy, since neither black nor white could survive without the other. The third bridge, in turn, brought misfortune, since it created miscegenation and had to be destroyed. Vedder ended his rather rambling justification for apartheid by claiming that there were two things for which a native could never forgive a European: injustice, "even if it is a Bushman with little understanding and has no culture," and contempt.[55]

Participating in a debate on constitutional policy in 1956, Vedder distinguished between the church and the state in an effort to legitimize the apartheid state's treatment of nonwhite people. The latter was much larger and encompassed many non-Christians and could provide much. In southern Africa, states were built by whites and thus belonged to them but, nevertheless, had given much to natives: protection of life and property, facilities like the post office, and freedom of movement. He invoked the Latin expression *suum cuique* to indicate that people should not be given what they want but rather what they justly deserved.[56]

During the Senate discussion of the recommendations of the Tomlinson Commission about how to make apartheid viable, Vedder proudly claimed that apartheid was natural. The ethnic groups in SWA practiced it on their own accord; even mission services were segregated, he stated. The Germans had created various tribal reserves, which whites were prohibited from entering. The large Herero reserves were a "Kingdom in the East" where they could do as they liked. From these reserves, workers could go to white areas to earn money, and no one was dissatisfied with the arrangement, as whites "could not work without natives." He concluded:

> S.W.A. is the only country in the world where over the last fifty years apartheid has increasingly been implemented. Many of the recommendations of the Government White Paper [the Tomlinson Commission] have already been applied in S.W.A. and no one with intelligence pleads for change. So where apartheid is born, not out of racial hatred but out of necessity and benevolence, so too in the Union (of South Africa) apartheid will be a success and promote the blessings of peace and welfare of all races. This is my answer to the question of whether apartheid is desirable and possible.[57]

Yet, even while Vedder was displaying the shallowness of his opinions disguised as expertise, he was painfully oblivious to the obvious. Van Warmelo's reportage on the Ovambo contract system showed up Vedder's naiveté about happy migrant workers. As Präses of the Rhenish Mission Church, Vedder failed to anticipate his Nama-speaking congregations seceding and joining the black-run African Methodist Episcopal Church or Herero-speaking ones, forming their own Oruano church. Both breakaway movements could largely be attributed to Vedder's misunderstandings and policies. Vedder's claim that the Indigenes supported apartheid was contrary to the impressions of Mission Inspector Gustav Menzel after his 1950 visit that Indigenes were generally opposed to Malan and his policies (Gockel 2010, 43). Vedder rather attributed the revival of Herero neo-paganism in the form of the Oruano movement to the activities of the Reverend Scott, underwriting the hoary South African nationalist myth that native discontent was the result of outside agitators. He vehemently attacked the reverend for claiming that the Herero were being impoverished. According to Vedder's calculations, each native family, consisting of a husband, wife, and three children, had between twelve and fifteen head of cattle. Indeed, he claimed many Herero were twice as rich as their missionaries (Gockel 2010, 33). One would have liked hard data to support such claims.[58]

No wonder a grateful administration issued a postage stamp commemorating Vedder's work.

Vedder's successor as senator with special expertise on Indigenous affairs, the educationalist Dr. Karl Frey, was hardly an improvement. In a radio talk on the Bushmen, he argued:

> In spite of all that the Administration is doing to prevent the Bushmen from being crowded out by the ever-expanding civilisation, there is no certainty that its efforts will be successful. The reason is that the Bushmen themselves remain unapproachable and do nothing to help the white man to assist them. The character of the Bushman is the same as it was three hundred years ago. . . . Today we know that we cannot alter his character; for he shows no sign of ever submitting to the written laws of civilisation or of adapting himself to the customs of other races in the country. (Frey n.d., 14)

When in doubt, blame the victim!

Notes

Portions of this chapter were originally published as "'Tracks Which Cannot Be Covered': P. J. Schoeman and Public Intellectuals in Southern Africa," *Historia* 52 (2007): 98–126. Copyright for this article belongs to the Historical Association of South Africa.

1. In his monograph *In Feudal Africa*, Loeb (1962, 19) was to conclude that the Kuanyama were an enclave of ancient Mediterranean survivals.
2. This department underwent several changes in nomenclature. From 1911 to 1957 it was the Department of Native Affairs; from 1958 to 1977 it was known as the Department of Bantu Administration and Development (BAD); and it was changed to the Department of Plural Relations and Development in 1978. Within the same year it was changed to the Department of Co-operation and Development, a name that remained valid until 1984, when it morphed into the Ministry of Constitutional Development and Planning.
3. Gordon Mears to the prime minister, 6 September 1945, NTS 9715 807/400, SANA.
4. For details about Lehmann, see Jansen van Rensburg (2015).
5. N. J. van Warmelo to Jos Allen, 10 May 1950, A591 van Warmelo Collection, NAN.

6. Günter Wagner, "The Ethnographic Survey of the Windhoek District," 1951, BB 0320, NAN.

7. See also F. Rudolph Lehmann, "Geschichte der 'Truppenspieler' unter den Herero in Südwestafrika" (n.d., mimeograph, NAN), where he argued that the fundamental division within the Herero community revolved around differing strategies as to how best to achieve unity and reconstruct a pastoral economy.

8. An Owambo version of this story has Budack trying to smuggle Ashikoto back to Owambo, as according to customary law Ashikoto could then not be tried again, but they were caught, and the Ondonga councilors then banned Budack from re-entering Owambo (Namuhuja 1996, 52).

9. Malan argued this despite vehemently denying biological evolution as contrary to his reading of the Bible.

10. Oswin Köhler to N. J. van Warmelo, 17 June 1956, A591 van Warmelo Collection, NAN. Nevertheless, he denied that Bushmen had been dispossessed of their territory. In the northeastern farming districts, he reported (Köhler 1956, 140), "Numerous Bushman families have penetrated into the rural areas and have taken up employment on farms. These Bushmen have suffered an enormous change in their culture, and a great many of them seem to accept it and become a stable farm labour population. But those who leave the farms and go back to their relatives in the bush outside the Police Zone, are supplied with clothes, shoes, blankets etc. and will tell their brothers the great 'gospel' of the money."

11. Jos Allen to N. J. van Warmelo, 30 August 1948, A591 van Warmelo Collection, NAN.

12. Evidence before the Tomlinson Commission 1952, University of South Africa Library, 508–9.

13. Harold Eedes, 8 December 1947, A198/3 Anthropological Research University of California, NAN.

14. Harold Eedes to Administrator, 24 February 1951, A198/3 Anthropological Research University of California, NAN.

15. Jos Allen to N. J. van Warmelo, 28 July 1949, A591 van Warmelo Collection, NAN. In a later letter Allen, who was advising the South African delegation to the UN, suggested that "what we now need is a team which could meet violent criticisms on the UN's latest decisions and on its general NA [Native Administration] policy and hit back as hard as possible" (Jos Allen to N. J. van Warmelo, 2 August 1949, A591 van Warmelo Collection, NAN).

16. Harold Eedes to N. J. van Warmelo, 20 December 1950, A591 van Warmelo Collection, NAN.

17. N. J. van Warmelo to Allen, 17 August 1951, A591 van Warmelo Collection, NAN.

18. Alarm centered on several interrelated issues concerning headmen: Were they corrupt and exploiting commoners because of the "sale" of land, and was this undermining the legitimacy of the kings and the role of the native commissioner?

19. N. J. van Warmelo to the Secretary of the Native Affairs Department, "Ovamboland: Complaints about Headmen etc.," 22 May 1956, A591 van Warmelo Collection, NAN. Apparently this referred to the Hamutumbangela episode, details of which were unavailable to this researcher.

20. N. J. van Warmelo, "Memo: Oor Ovamboland," 15 December 1956, A591 van Warmelo Collection, NAN.

21. N. J. van Warmelo, "Memo: Oor Ovamboland," 15 December 1956, A591 van Warmelo Collection, NAN.

22. N. J. van Warmelo to Secretary of the Bantu Affairs Department, 21 December 1961, A591 van Warmelo Collection, NAN. Van Warmelo is a rather enigmatic figure. Already in 1952, when the Tomlinson Commission was set up to make proposals as to how homelands could be created and developed in South Africa and in contrast to other volkekundiges who submitted memoranda of over fifty pages and gave copious oral evidence, van Warmelo claimed to be unavailable, even though the hearings were in Pretoria where he was based, and his response was a contemptuous one-pager. Some of the questions he claimed not to

understand, such as what was an ethnic group, and failed to see what ethnic groups had to do with development. He saw no connection between bridewealth and livestock overstocking, as cattle were essentially the only means of capital formation, which people did not realize was a leaking bucket. On the final question of whether Bantu culture had any hope of survival within a modern development program, he was dismissive: not only had change already occurred and was continuing at an accelerating pace, but one could also expect a reaction against "westernization" as a result of emerging nationalism (Stuk 128, Tomlinson Commission Evidence, University of South Africa Library, Pretoria, South Africa).

23. N. J. van Warmelo to Jos Allen, 3 November 1966, A591 van Warmelo Collection, NAN.
24. N. J. van Warmelo, "The Inhabitants of SWA from an Ethnological Point of View," first draft, February 1960, NTS 9715 01 807/400, SANA. Also in A591 van Warmelo Collection, National Archives of Namibia.
25. N. J. van Warmelo, "The Inhabitants of SWA from an Ethnological Point of View," second draft, October 1960, NTS 9715 01 807/400, SANA.
26. Van Warmelo, "The Inhabitants of SWA," second draft, NTS 9715 01 807/400, SANA.
27. N. J. van Warmelo to Jos Allen, 11 November 1962, A591 van Warmelo Collection, NAN.
28. This was later published in Afrikaans (Bruwer 1965). It is difficult to reconcile these paragraphs with Hammond-Tooke's conclusion, based in part on personal experience, that van Warmelo had "extensive, shrewd and essentially practical knowledge of indigenous life (and was) skeptical of grand theory and ideological preoccupations" (Hammond-Tooke 1997, 114).
29. Report by Dr Werner Kuschke, regional medical officer, to Native Commissioner, Rundu, 27 August 1949, A50/67 (2) Bushman Affairs, NAN.
30. There was a history of attempts to deal constructively with Bushmen, especially immediately prior to World War II, when Donald Bain had led a campaign to improve the lot of South African Bushmen. This had led to an investigation of the status of Bushmen by a regional committee headed by Professor Isaac Schapera of UCT (Gordon 1995). During the war years there had also been sporadic meetings between senior officials about how to deal with the "Bushman problem," while ever mindful of the scientific value of those labeled Bushmen.
31. Nevertheless, Schoeman wanted to move on from these posts. In 1951, as member number 1,774 of the Afrikaner Broederbond (more on this in later chapters), he applied for a full-time position in the organization, though he was unsuccessful (1 August 1951 [33/9], 191 AB1, H. B. Thom Papers).
32. Details of Schoeman's career and romantic racism are provided in Gordon (2007).
33. Commission for the Preservation of the Bushmen, "Voorlopige verslag van die Kommissie vir die Behoud van die Boesmanbevolking in Suidwes-Afrika, 1950," [September 1951], para. 28, A50/67 Bushman Affairs, NAN.
34. Commission for the Preservation of the Bushmen, "Report of the Commission for the Preservation of Bushmen in South West Africa, 1950," circa 1955, para 57, A50/67 Bushman Affairs, NAN.
35. Questioned by the Kavango Native Commissioner, Gusinde opined:
    Their lives are so specialized that they cannot be changed . . . [but] it is impossible . . . to preserve them from contact with civilization. . . . It is my conviction that it is essential to prevent close dependency of the Bushmen on the Bantu. The natives are very clever and the Bushmen very childish and the Bushman has not enough courage to act against superiority of the native. He is too childish to go to the commissioner for help (a similar situation to Tierra del Fuego and in the Belgium Congo). To bring the natives and Bushmen into a common reserve cannot give good results. Experience in America has proved this. (Memorandum by Mr Morris, 13 January 1951, A50/67 Bushman Affairs, NAN)
36. P. J. Schoeman, "Memorandum on the Study of the Bushmen" (undated mimeo). Perused courtesy of Beryl McIntyre, daughter of Claude McIntyre, August 1987.
37. Commission for the Preservation of the Bushmen, "Voorlopige verslag van die Kommissie vir die Behoud van die Boesmanbevolking in Suidwes-Afrika, 1950," [September 1951], para. 28, A50/67 Bushman Affairs, NAN.

38. P. J. Schoeman, "Memorandum on the Study of the Bushmen" (undated mimeo). Perused courtesy of Beryl McIntyre, daughter of Claude McIntyre, August 1987.

39. Commission for the Preservation of the Bushmen, "Voorlopige verslag van die Kommissie vir die Behoud van die Boesmanbevolking in Suidwes-Afrika, 1950," [September 1951], para. 12, A50/67 Bushman Affairs, NAN.

40. Commission for the Preservation of the Bushmen, "Voorlopige verslag van die Kommissie vir die Behoud van die Boesmanbevolking in Suidwes-Afrika, 1950," [September 1951], para. 11, A50/67 Bushman Affairs, NAN.

41. Commission for the Preservation of the Bushmen, "Voorlopige verslag van die Kommissie vir die Behoud van die Boesmanbevolking in Suidwes-Afrika, 1950," [September 1951], para. 24, A50/67 Bushman Affairs, NAN.

42. Commission for the Preservation of the Bushmen, "Report of the Commission for the Preservation of Bushmen in South West Africa, 1950," circa 1955, para 57, A50/67 Bushman Affairs, NAN.

43. Schoeman did acknowledge that Bushmen originally occupied the whole of southern Africa but then claimed that they were driven into the waterless wastes of the Kalahari as a result of stock theft (see Schoeman 1984, 2).

44. Commission for the Preservation of the Bushmen, "Report of the Commission for the Preservation of Bushmen in South West Africa, 1950," circa 1955, para 32, A50/67 Bushman Affairs, NAN.

45. Commission for the Preservation of the Bushmen, "Report of the Commission for the Preservation of Bushmen in South West Africa, 1950," circa 1955, para 51, A50/67 Bushman Affairs, NAN.

46. Commission for the Preservation of the Bushmen, "Report of the Commission for the Preservation of Bushmen in South West Africa, 1950," circa 1955, para 20, A50/67 Bushman Affairs, NAN.

47. Commission for the Preservation of the Bushmen, "Report of the Commission for the Preservation of Bushmen in South West Africa, 1950," circa 1955, para 43, A50/67 Bushman Affairs, NAN.

48. Commission for the Preservation of the Bushmen, "Report of the Commission for the Preservation of Bushmen in South West Africa, 1950," circa 1955, para 42, A50/67 Bushman Affairs, NAN.

49. Commission for the Preservation of the Bushmen, "Report of the Commission for the Preservation of Bushmen in South West Africa, 1950," circa 1955, para 56, A50/67 Bushman Affairs, NAN.

50. Debates of the South-West Africa Legislative Assembly, 1957, 88–89.

51. A820/3803 Nazi Suspects: Vedder, NAN.

52. Debates of the Senate (Hansard), 1951, Fourth Session, 19 January to 22 June, Cols 5750–5755, 6 June.

53. Debates of the Senate (Hansard), 1952, Third Session, 18 January to 25 June, Cols 3595–3598, 27 May, Cols 4286, 7 June.

54. Debates of the Senate (Hansard), 1954, Second Session, 29 January to 15 June, Cols 3006–3011, 10 June. When the discussion moved onto Bantu education, Vedder asked that the act include non-Bantu like Damara and Bushmen and queried whether the proposed school councils would be under white supervision, without which "accidents" could happen, and whether white mission teaching personnel would have to resign (Debates of the Senate [Hansard], 1954, Second Session, 29 January to 15 June, Cols 3180–3181, 14 June).

55. Debates of the Senate (Hansard), 1955, Third Session, 21 January to 23 June, Cols 4208–4216, 16 June.

56. Debates of the Senate (Hansard), 1956, First Session, 13 January to 14 June, Cols 701–703, 2 February.

57. Debates of the Senate (Hansard), 1956, Third Session, 13 January to 14 June, Col 4082, 28 May. Vedder even quoted Malan in 1954 as agreeing: "Our government found in Southwest

Africa good earth. The German government had from the beginning practically implemented what was not done in South Africa, namely Apartheid" (cited in Sundermeier 1973, 213).

58. Another self-professed local expert on Namibian history in the South African Parliament was the Nationalist member of Parliament for Karas, J. S. von Moltke, who had achieved notoriety as a leader of the pre–World War II antisemitic Grey Shirts movement and in whose imagination the Bushmen were omnipresent. Addressing a motion to allow native representatives for SWA, he attacked the proposal by asking whether the proposer wanted wild Bushmen to sit next to him in Parliament and whether the member had ever seen a wild Bushman. Bushmen were so hard to find, he claimed, that the Commission for the Preservation of Bushmen established in 1950 took four years to locate them and then could not establish their age: "These primitive people do not want representation in this Parliament. It is something they cannot eat, drink or smoke thus they will not understand it. They prefer to hunt game. They prefer catching snakes, geckos and worms which they can eat. I know them. The only contented Bushman is one with a full stomach" (Debates of the House of Assembly [Hansard], 15 March 1955, Cols 2881–2885).

CHAPTER 3

Performing for All the World to See
Bruwer and the Fashioning of Modern Namibia

The Life and Endeavors of Bruwer

Johannes P. van S. "Hannes" Bruwer (1914–67) is an important figure in
the second generation of South African anthropologists, although overlooked in the history of volkekunde by his Afrikaner rivals (R. Coertze
1991). Born in the Cape Province and educated at the Wellington Teachers Training College, he spent fifteen years as a Dutch Reformed Church
missionary in Northern Rhodesia, becoming fluent in siChewa and, up
to the tragic end of his life in an air crash in 1967, remained a devout
Christian, occupying a number of important mission positions. Like most
volkekundiges he earned all his graduate degrees from a single university,
in this case the University of Pretoria, from which he graduated with a
doctorate in 1955. His thesis was on the kinship basis of social organization among matrilineal Bantu communities, with special reference to the
Kunda. The person who clearly influenced him most at the university
was Werner Eiselen, then professor of anthropology. Indeed, he dedicated
his first Afrikaans-language textbook, the popular *Die Bantoe van Suid-
Afrika* (The Bantu of South Africa) (Bruwer 1957), to Eiselen as "the
Master from whom I learnt the most." Appointed a senior lecturer in
volkekunde at the University of Stellenbosch in 1951, Bruwer was promoted to professor shortly thereafter.

Stellenbosch in those days was an intellectually exciting place. An important influence there was F. D. Holleman, a South African–born Dutch-
man who had been an Adat law judge in Indonesia and had later succeeded
the famous Adat law scholar Cornelis van Vollenhoven at Leiden University, before taking early retirement and accepting the chair of Bantu law at
Stellenbosch. Holleman brought to the discussion of apartheid a concern
for "jural communities." His 1952 mimeographed notes on *Bantoeregsge-
meenskappe* (Bantu legal communities) were still being used for teaching

in the late sixties and derived from his study of Indonesian Adat circles. Holleman also introduced his Stellenbosch colleagues to John S. Furnivall's concept of plural societies, and this probably accounts, at least in part, for the rhetoric that Bruwer was to use at the ICJ. At Stellenbosch Bruwer was also heavily involved in the South African Bureau of Racial Affairs (SABRA), founded in 1948 as an initiative by the Afrikaner Broederbond, a secret society that aimed to promote Afrikaner interests, to counter the liberal "integrationist" South African Institute of Race Relations (SAIRR) and to provide an academic justification for apartheid, which the Broederbond saw as one of the crucial mechanisms in ensuring the survival of Afrikanerdom.

Bruwer was rapidly tagged as a rising star in the Afrikaner establishment. In 1958 he was appointed to the Council of the (black) University of Fort Hare and the next year became a member of the South African Academy of Science and Art as well as chairman of the Council for the newly established (black) University of Zululand. He also became prominent in the powerful secretive Broederbond, being co-opted to serve on the executive council in 1961 and in the mid-sixties even acting as chair. He served as initial and longtime convener of the Oversight Committee on Bantu Affairs,[1] one of the committees whose recommendations to the Broederbond's executive council customarily became government policy.[2] Indeed the minister of native affairs was invariably a Broeder (brother) (Wilkins and Strydom 1978, 196–201), so one can speculate on the likely impact of the impact of the Broederbond on "native" policy. Bruwer was also heavily engaged in *volksdiens* (service to the Afrikaner nation), authoring a few high school textbooks, giving a number of radio lectures, some later published in pamphlet form (Bruwer 1961), and writing numerous popular articles. A recent history of the Broederbond lauds Bruwer for forcing the organization to seriously consider race relations as a policy issue (Ferreira 2018, 113–14).

Bruwer became enamored of South-West Africa during his first study tour in December 1954. Undoubtedly professional interests figured in its appeal for him. Its Ovambo and Kavango inhabitants were part of the so-called matrilineal (kinship) belt, which extended through Nyasaland to Mozambique and of which he had firsthand experience. Moreover, he realized the tactical importance of the territory, as it formed the vulnerable point in South Africa's attempts to legitimize apartheid internationally. Additionally, the goodwill of the Indigenous population was crucial, as the territory provided potential access to the "Communist-inspired" liberation movements sweeping down from black Africa. What he found striking on this visit was the "backward nature of indigenous society" and officials' ignorance and lack of interest in their wards. Later he made intermittent trips to the territory as a student chaperone and speaker, especially at Broederbond-instigated meetings and Day of Covenant celebrations. At the end of the academic year in December 1958, Bruwer undertook his first intensive research tour, with the purpose of establishing closer contact with Indigenous peoples. It soon became clear to him that Indigenes were shifting away from supporting the South African administration and would continue to do so unless firm action was taken to counter their increasing alienation, the activities of SWAPO (the fledgling liberation movement that would form the first government in independent Namibia in 1990), the unrelenting "interference" of the Reverend Scott, and the increasing number of petitions by local individuals to the UN. These observations, he claimed, were only the *visible* signs of deep undercurrents that were increasing in strength. Two issues were especially noteworthy in Ovamboland: the poverty and stagnation symbolized by the South African flag flying over a termite-eaten *rondavel* (circular hut) office; and the growing success of nightly meetings of which white officials were blissfully unaware, which were to lead to the creation of SWAPO. Much disturbed by what he took to be a deteriorating situation, Bruwer wrote a confidential report to various cabinet ministers, suggesting options for action.

Early in 1959, he commenced six months of fieldwork in Omedi, in the Kuanyama Tribal Area, selecting this as his field site because he assumed SWAPO agitation was greatest here. In order to "get to know the people" and assess SWAPO activities and anticipating that he could neutralize SWAPO through personal contact, Bruwer traveled extensively. These journeys took him east to the Kavango River region and west to the Kaokoveld, where he found individuals who were traveling to Botswana to meet priests, ostensibly for religious-nativistic reasons but, he believed, actually to enhance ties with Herero exiles. He determined that it was the situation in Kuanyama, the most populous area in Namibia, that required urgent attention in order to distract interest from SWAPO. To achieve this, Bruwer made two rather modest suggestions: organizing an agricultural show, which would keep people occupied and provide them with something to talk about; and bolstering the prestige of the headmen by erecting an imposing building for the Kuanyama Tribal Council. These suggestions were enacted by a sympathetic (Afrikaner) Bantu affairs commissioner. The first agricultural show was held in May 1959 and received massive publicity in government media; it was attended by some one hundred whites, including the administrator, the chief Bantu affairs commissioner, and the prominent South African author Stuart Cloete, who were entertained at a *braaivleis* (barbeque) afterwards. "As researcher I could propagate the matter objectively and it was quickly apparent that the matter had a calming influence," Bruwer reflected.[3] It took many visits to neutralize the SWAPO-inspired "under-currents," often at his own personal expense, he added, publicly justifying these visits as being part of his clan survey. In two months, he visited 333 wards and met groups representing 11,234 households. He worked an average of seventeen hours per day and claimed to have made contact with more than 25,000 people in Kuanyama, 31 percent of the total population.[4]

From September 1959 to February 1960, Bruwer was a visiting professor at the renowned School for Advanced International Studies at Johns Hopkins University in the United States, a credential South Africa later proudly displayed at the ICJ as evidence of his expertise. While only able to return to Namibia in December 1961, SWA continued to obsess him. In a Broederbond document entitled "South West Africa and the Union" (dated to approximately June 1960) that he personally sent to Prime Minister Hendrik Verwoerd,[5] he re-emphasized the gravity of the situation and proposed that four provinces or states be created in the territory to cater for Indigenes—Kaokoveld, Ovamboland, Okavango, and Hereroland—with a possible fifth, Bushmanland. These areas should eventually become autonomous and possibly form a federation. White interests would not be threatened, as they would be on separate voter rolls. The goodwill such a move would generate, Bruwer felt, would encourage local inhabitants to support South Africa in the international arena. Returning to what he felt was the crux, Bruwer re-emphasized the importance of gaining the goodwill of the Ovambo chiefs and headmen and suggested that the Government Information Service be expanded immediately from one officer to five and that chiefs and tribal secretaries be taken on a tour of the Union of South Africa. Verwoerd, however, was distrustful of what he suspected was Bruwer's liberalism and responded that a federation would lead to integration and accused Bruwer of having become liberal during his stay in the United States.[6] What Verwoerd left unsaid, however, was the fact that some of Bruwer's colleagues in both SABRA and in his own Bantoekunde department at Stellenbosch had recently publicly challenged Verwoerd on his insistence of a colored homeland and had, against Verwoerd's wishes, started roving consultations with black leaders. An agitated Bruwer responded that the American visit had not altered his views; on the contrary, it had strengthened his resolve and that the "English" press was trying to label him as a SABRA radical. He assured Verwoerd of his unswerving support and proved it shortly thereafter by assisting in the SABRA purge of the Stellenbosch colleagues who had challenged Verwoerd (Holleman 1989). Shortly thereafter Bruwer was elected to chair the SABRA executive board. A month later he urged Verwoerd to take a positive approach to the forthcoming visit by the chair of the UN's Special Committee on South-West Africa, Victor Carpio, and his deputy, Martinez d'Alva. They should be guided by competent people, he argued, so that they can see how "extremely futile" it would be to give the inhabitants self-government and added, "Let them spend as much time as possible in the isolated areas with minimal facilities so that they can feel the problems of the country."[7] This advice was heeded by the administration in arranging the itinerary for their May 1962 visit. While Bruwer's relationship to Verwoerd was to remain tinged with suspicion, the Broederbond appreciated his expertise and warnings and late in 1959 created a special nonwhite affairs work-group with Bruwer as convener and in the process appointed him to the Broederbond executive.

With special leave for a year and funding arranged by Verwoerd, Bruwer returned to Ovamboland at the end of 1961 and found that the political situation had deteriorated further. He expressed his concerns to M. C. de Wet Nel, the South African minister of Bantu administration, who had been given oversight responsibilities for South-West Africa, by repeating his apprehension of subversive undercurrents and the necessity of mobi-lizing goodwill. Bruwer reiterated his plea for a well-organized plan of development to be implemented as soon as possible, as well as for an ex-perienced anthropologist to be appointed at a senior level to liaise and co-ordinate development activities, preferably as commissioner-general.[8] The commissioner-general would promote acceptance of South African overrule by having broad and intensive contact with Indigenes. Ideally the commissioner-general would work tirelessly, know how to interact with local people, and have sufficient authority to act effectively. It was also important to attract foreign sympathizers. He concluded, "We will never satisfy the UN and the leftists, but if we can get the large majority of the population on our side, we can achieve much despite all our problems."[9]

Under pressure because of the impending visit in May 1962 of the UN's Carpio/d'Alva delegation, Bruwer returned to Ovamboland. The ostensible purpose was research, but Bruwer was specifically charged with promoting goodwill and cooperation and with inducing various Ovambo groups to accept a central tribal authority. Fear of an international outcry in the wake of the "Old Location shootings" when a number of people were shot in December 1959 while protesting the administration's efforts to move local Indigenes to a new township, Verwoerd acted with alac-rity in appointing a one-person commission of inquiry headed by his old friend, fellow Broederbonder and founding member of SABRA, Judge C. K. Hall, who unsurprisingly absolved the administration of any blame. So seriously did Verwoerd take the SWA situation that he appointed Jo-hannes G. van der Wath, leader of the (white) National Party of South-West Africa as adjunct minister for South West-African affairs, reporting directly to him.

Writing to the newly appointed adjunct minister for South-West Af-rican affairs, Bruwer elaborated on his plan. Officially he was going to do research on land tenure systems in Kaokoveld, Ovamboland, and the

Kavango: "This will properly cover my presence and mobility in all these areas and if necessary officials can be informed so that I can have at all times the necessary freedom of movement." It was also important that he keep his university affiliation as a cover:

> For practical purposes then I remain in the employ of the University and maintain thus my objectivity as researcher to the outside world. Apart for my striving for trust and goodwill and the other matters that have been given to me, the research itself will also have practical utility. Further I might be able in various regards be able to give confidential advice about affairs of the day. . . . There is only one valid consideration here—love for the case of SWA—for me it can only bring sacrifice. I have nothing to gain, possibly even much to lose.[10]

Reaching Kuanyama, Bruwer realized that SWAPO was aware of the impending UN visit and was trying to organize a fifty-thousand-person mass demonstration. His "contacts" also revealed that SWAPO was now in league with traditional authorities and that each ward had its own organizer. Desperate, he met the local SWAPO leader, Toivo ya Toivo,[11] as well as with various ward organizers, supposedly surprising them by knowing of their role. Expending over R 3,000 of his own funds, he succeeded in persuading the organizers to accept a compromise by only staging a local demonstration. Eventually, only seventy demonstrators turned up to meet the UN team. To emphasize the importance of his expert knowledge, he noted that during this episode, local white officials were unaware of what was going on.[12] Where possible, Bruwer provided advice informally to officials. Thus, he managed to dissuade BAD from introducing forty-three apartheid-style tribal authorities in Ovamboland in 1963 (on the expert advice of a volkekundige from the University of Pretoria, probably P. J. or R. D. Coertze), arguing that his research had shown that the traditional authorities wanted a centralized system.

While doing fieldwork, Bruwer was also helping to prepare the South African defense at the ICJ. His involvement goes back to at least April 1961, when it was decided that van Warmelo would provide the basic ethnological background, while Bruwer would prepare the section on history and provide the ethnological justification for apartheid. However, when van Warmelo's work was pronounced unsatisfactory, it was decided that Bruwer's research should provide the basis for the South African rejoinder.[13] For reasons already discussed, it is not hard to see why.

By January 1963 Bruwer was completing the draft of his memorandum. As he informed the South African agent coordinating the legal defense: "I am busy rewriting the ethnic exposition to *emphasize differences. I am also going to examine the violent struggles among the indigenous groups which raged until the end of the previous century in order to indicate that the groups could not live together in peace as a unit.*"[14] A few weeks later he described the structure of his memorandum: section 3 was to "show that the groups could not live in peace before the whites came," section 5 would emphasize "only basic and fundamental differences," and section 6 would analyze cultures to again "show the basic differences."[15] In February 1965 he was asked to make himself available as a possible expert witness at the ICJ.

Bruwer is more important for understanding and shaping Namibian society or the role of volkekunde in South Africa than his publication record[16] or expert witness status indicates. His significance for Namibian anthropology is to be found in a variety of achievements. He attracted and sponsored a number of students who undertook fieldwork in the densely populated northern areas, the Kavango and Ovambo regions, one serving as assistant Bantu commissioner, another as information officer, while a third completed a doctorate on the Hambukushu on the Kavango. More important is Bruwer's influence on government policy, especially through his role in the Broederbond, his activities on the Commission for South-West African Affairs (South Africa 1964), and his performance as inaugural commissioner-general for the Indigenous peoples of South-West Africa. It would not be false to claim that he played a leading role in guiding the Commission for South-West African Affairs and tried to oversee the implementation of its recommendations in his capacity as commissioner-general. Unlike most commissions, the government pledged a large sum to try to implement this one's major recommendations. South Africa tried to give grand apartheid a test run in Namibia by creating twelve separate homelands. Indeed, per capita more money was spent and more people (including whites) were forcibly removed in Namibia than in South Africa. In a large part this apartheid fantasy was given credence by experts like Bruwer. The intriguing aspect of Bruwer's career is that he resigned his commissioner-generalship after less than a year to effortlessly transition into the position of founding professor of social anthropology, and later vice-rector, at the newly created bilingual University of Port Elizabeth. The reasons for his resignation are complex, but judging from the expurgated correspondence, it seems that he was sidelined by officials who denied him access to official files and claimed that he could not publish material derived during the course of his official duties. Bruwer and van der Wath were bitter rivals, and the latter had Verwoerd's ear, facilitated by the camaraderie of being angling buddies. Van der Wath had obtained a copy of a confidential report Bruwer had written on the plight of Bushmen and alerted Verwoerd to the fact that the document was being circulated to unauthorized officials, making it likely that its confidential status would be broken. On the basis of van der Wath's accusation that if the memorandum had become public it would have destroyed South Africa's international credibility, Bruwer was disciplined. Humiliatingly he had to gather together all copies of the memorandum, including his personal copy, and hand them over to the minister for Bantu administration for destruction. Bruwer was so incensed by this censure, which he called a *verdoemende verwyt* (damnatory reproach), that he was prepared to personally pay the costs of an impartial committee to examine the condition of Bushmen.[17] Of course this might also be because Bruwer recognized Verwoerd's lingering distrust of him. The prominent American journalist Ely Kahn suggested that Bruwer and Verwoerd had a major falling out about the viability of apartheid and Bruwer's feeling that the government was less concerned about the welfare of Indigenes than their own strategic interests (Kahn 1968, 214).[18] Verwoerd was so chary of Bruwer that he appointed an old party stalwart and confidante, F. H. "Fox" Odendaal, the Transvaal administrator, as chairman of the commission that was to bear his name. Nevertheless, Bruwer remained a party and Broederbond loyalist, offering to serve as a commissioner-general among either the Venda or Shangaan "ethnic units" less than a month after being humiliated, and he later wrote to Verwoerd's successor, John Vorster, suggesting that he could serve as ambassador to Africa, pointing out that he had renewed contacts with presidents Kaunda of Zambia and Banda of Malawi, whom he had met during his missionary days.

Developing the Archive: The Odendaal Commission

Apart from Bruwer's incessant advocacy, a number of events led to Verwoerd appointing the Commission for South-West African Affairs in September 1962. In January 1961 Verwoerd had six private meetings with Dag Hammarskjöld, the UN secretary-general, concerning the abolition of apartheid. Upon Hammarskjöld's query whether apartheid could be developed as a "competitive alternative" to integration, Verwoerd put forward homelands as this alternative. The secretary-general agreed that this might be an option if adequate adjacent land was to be allocated, if it was accompanied by a published plan for economic development of the areas, and if the governmental institutions in these homelands were based on the will of the people, who could decide whether they wanted independence or not. During the Carpio/d'Alva visit, Verwoerd had also promised to speed up development. These discussions and promises were coupled with the slowly unfolding case at the World Court and the increasing international criticism of apartheid framed in the rhetoric of decolonization. The Bantustan or homeland policy was to be marketed to these audiences as a version of decolonization (Giliomee 2004, 483). These considerations helped shape the purpose of the commission, which was to enquire thoroughly into further promoting the material and moral welfare and the social progress of the inhabitants of South West Africa and more particularly its non-White inhabitants, and to submit . . . a report with recommendations on a comprehensive five-year plan for the accelerated development. . . .

The Commission is particularly directed to the task of ascertaining— while fully taking into consideration the background, traditions and habits of the Native inhabitants—how further provision should be made for their social and economic advancement. (South Africa 1964, 4)

Verwoerd originally wanted the newly appointed adjunct minister for South-West African affairs and leader of the local National Party, van der Wath, as chair of the commission but was persuaded it would be better to have technically qualified "objective" outsiders with no ostensible vested interests in the territory, as its main unstated purpose was to impress the international world. Thus, with the exception of the chair, Odendaal, all commission members were well-credentialed experts: Professor Dr. H. W. Snyman, chairman of the South African Medical Council and dean of the faculty of medicine at the University of Pretoria; Dr. J. Piet Quinn, manager of Zebedelia Estates and an agriculturalist; Dr. H. J. van Eck, economist and a major industrialist; Dr. C. J. Claassen,[19] secretary and sociologist; and Bruwer. Verwoerd attended the first meeting, informing the commission what he expected from it and that it was to work closely and continuously with van der Wath in order to ensure practicality and a favorable reception by both white and black population groups in the territory (van der Wath 1983, 154–56). Later, when releasing the report, Verwoerd admitted regularly meeting with the commission for consultations but denied influencing it. He also emphasized the nonpartisan nature of the commissioners, claiming that they were not directly involved in party politics, a rather tall story, as most were actively involved in the Broederbond and Snyman was a major Afrikaner cultural leader and the physician who attended to Verwoerd after the first assassination attempt on him (Verwoerd 2018, 287).

It was decided that Bruwer would draft a memorandum on the country and its people to serve as basis for the investigation, essentially repeating his ICJ memorandum. It was also agreed that Bruwer and the secretary would travel to South-West Africa ahead of the other members of the commission to arrange an itinerary for a visit. A later meeting resolved that in order to maintain the patina of objectivity, no officials would be present when witnesses were heard, and all evidence would be heard on camera, clearly aimed at impressing the international community. After six visits to the territory, ranging in duration from seven to twelve days, and forty-eight meetings, Bruwer handed the report over to the prime minis-

ter in December 1963. It contained numerous recommendations centered
on the notion of dividing the territory into twelve ethnic homelands.
The commission proclaimed boldly:

> The population of South West Africa is characterized by its ethnic diversity. In the
> course of many decades of the country's history various ethnic groups have settled
> as separate peoples in certain areas of the present Territory. In spite of internal
> strife and wars, which were particularly fierce in the southern part of the country
> during the previous century, the respective groups all retained their individual
> identity and as still distinguishable as such in the present population. . . . [They] are
> distinguished from one another by their different languages, cultures and physical
> appearance, and to a large extent also according to the areas in which they have
> settled and now live. (South Africa 1964, para. 104)

Whites were the heroes of the drama:

> The Whites not only put an end to the former strife and violence among the indig-
> enous peoples, but were also responsible for the development of the Territory in
> many spheres, and of the progress of the population in the social, economic and
> religious fields. As bearers of the Western civilization they were responsible for the
> introduction of services in the spheres of education, health, welfare and religion.
> Furthermore they placed the economy of the country on a sound modern basis by
> the provision of roads, railways and air transport. (South Africa 1964, para. 123)

Nevertheless:

> [These twelve different and distinct] population groups harbour strong feelings
> against other groups and would prefer to have their own homelands and communi-
> ties in which they will have and retain residential rights, political say and their own
> language, to the exclusion of other groups. (South Africa 1964, para. 187)

Commissions of inquiry are notorious "anti-politics" machines, to use
Jim Ferguson's (1994) fortuitous phrase, that systematically mis-recognize
and depoliticize understandings of the lives and problems of local people
by looking at them through the patina of objectivity and science, ostensibly for neutral and commonly agreed-upon purposes but in reality simply
a means of political bush encroachment (Pretorius 1985). The Odendaal
Commission was no exception. Adjunct Minster van der Wath read numerous drafts, ironing out differences between the Verwoerdian vision
and that of the commission to make it acceptable to Verwoerd. At one
stage it even managed to dissuade Verwoerd from one of his wilder fantasies, when he suggested that the administration of the territory be taken
over by the BAD, the ministry he had run before becoming prime minister. Odendaal responded on behalf of the commission that this was not
a good idea, as BAD officials were very unpopular in many parts of the
country, but Nama, Damara, Bushmen, Basters, and coloreds were not of-

ficially categorized as Bantu; not only would it antagonize local Indigenes but would be fatal in terms of international exposure: "The Commission is definitely of the opinion that to satisfy the natives to a degree and to create the best impression among the Western nations, we must propose something radical."[20]

Commissions are not only anti-politics machines, they are also edifices to impress audiences. Verwoerd flew to Windhoek for the official release of the report and symbolically offered it to the territory's (white) population at a large, carefully orchestrated public meeting held in the South-West Africa (rugby) Stadium. Whites had to accept it, Verwoerd claimed, before he would place it before cabinet and Parliament for action (van der Wath 1983, 154–56). The most important consequence of the report was that it discovered the enormity of "underdevelopment" and argued that the territory by itself was incapable of dealing with these problems and had to be more closely incorporated into the South African civil service, which could provide the required expertise. Thus, the rhetoric of fostering self-sufficient development promoted the incorporation of the territory into the South African sphere of influence. The first five-year plan would cost R 110 million (over a staggering R 951 billion by 2020 values), entailing mostly the acquisition of over thirty-three million hectare of land (mostly bought from some five hundred European farmers) to consolidate the proposed homelands. What this meant in practical terms was that 40 percent of the land was to be allocated as Homelands, whites would retain control of 43 percent, and the rest would be state land. One of the first recommendations the commission made was for the appointment of a commissioner-general as envisaged by Bruwer, and indeed, he was the first person to be appointed to this position. Bruwer later claimed that in this role he had been effective in the battle against the "militant Sam Nujoma" and to have weakened SWAPO's influence. Indeed, when news of his resignation became public, Bishop Leonard Auala of the Evangelical Lutheran Owambo-Kavango Church and a major figure in Owambo history wrote a heartfelt plea that Bruwer stay on because of the good way in which he had begun to lay a solid foundation for the implementation of the Odendaal plan.[21]

Selling Apartheid to the World

At the June 1960 Addis Ababa meeting of the Conference of Independent African States, Ethiopia and Liberia, both former members of the League of Nations, signaled their intention of instituting legal proceedings against South Africa for not fulfilling the mandate. They formally initiated such charges in November of that year. They demanded that the mandate awarded to South Africa by the league to administer South-West Africa be revoked on the grounds that South Africa had acted in bad faith by neglecting to fulfill Article 22 of the mandate, namely "to promote to the utmost the material and moral well-being and the social progress of the inhabitants of the territory." South Africa's rejoinder was that the ultimate end it was pursuing in the territory, apartheid, was in accordance with enlightened and liberal opinion. The South African state had anticipated this challenge, and already in February of the same year van Warmelo had written a long memorandum entitled "SWA from an Ethnological Point of View" for the Department of External Affairs. By April 1961 a special room had been set aside for all the relevant collected material, with "three men busy indexing it." Experts in native administration from the universities of Stellenbosch, Pretoria, and South Africa were called in as consultants. Writing to Jos Allen, the SWA's additional native commissioner, van Warmelo, was not optimistic: "Most of what falls in my orbit, will be brushed aside as irrelevant. It's like Eichmann's trial. You could not find impartial judges on the whole globe, the issue being already pre-judged."[22] Little did he realize that it was not only international opinion that was to find his research irrelevant but also the South African legal team.

An undated memo entitled "Re: Applicants Instituting Proceedings" is a multi-authored essay in which Eiselen, the secretary for native affairs, played a leading part. While van Warmelo was to describe the physical, cultural, and linguistic diversity and the great differences between them that allegedly existed before colonialism and that the administration had simply recognized, Eiselen's task was to make the general case for separate development, alleging that there was no such thing as a SWA nation, only a number of widely different nations and races who lived apart and preferred to live that way. He cited missionary sources from the thirties, including Joseph Oldham, secretary of the International Africa Institute, and Siegfried Knak, a major figure in German missionary circles. Eiselen then sought to justify the importance of race in the territory, thereby critiquing the famous 1950 UNESCO statement on race, by citing statements by the cross-cultural psychologist S. D. Porteus, published in the 1960 inaugural volume of *Mankind Quarterly*, a right-wing journal promoting the idea of "scientific" racism. Eiselen tempered his views, though, by claiming that black races were not permanently inferior but might be equal or even superior to Europeans in certain ways. Racial differences were inescapable; thus, while SWA was a multiracial country, it was not a multiracial community.[23]

The ICJ's highly contested verdict in 1966, decided by the court president's casting vote, that it had no grounds to hear the case was the result of a drawn-out procedure stretching over five years. The court's highly contested refusal to hear the complaint against South Africa had a major impact on the anti-apartheid struggle, defusing the situation for South Africa at the international geopolitical level for the next fifteen years (Irwin 2012). Not surprisingly it generated an exceptional amount of excitement in white southern Africa. The South African prime minister, Dr. Verwoerd, spoke in a live broadcast to the nation, and the bars in Windhoek stayed open all night. The court's decision was the result of much mental and intellectual effort and energy, at least in South Africa.

The South African government believed that Namibia was its Achilles' heel in international affairs, but it also saw the court proceedings as an important arena to justify apartheid to an increasingly skeptical international audience. In the words of one contemporary observer, the documentation that South Africa generated to "restore some objectivity" (de Villiers 1968, 13) amounted to the "most spirited defense of apartheid that the world is likely to see for generations to come" (Kahn 1968, 182). The applicants' sixty-two-page "Memorial" resulted in a ten-volume South African "Counter-Memorial," which with its supporting material required a furniture van to be delivered to the Palace of Justice in The Hague. In its text, South Africa sought to refute the allegations raised against it and demonstrate that "self-determination" was the most "practical course"; it claimed that Namibians were educationally and economically better off than residents of other African countries, that South Africa's policies enjoyed the support of the "great majority," and that existing policies did not represent expressions of racist ideology "but merely [the] practical recognition of existing differences between various groups in culture, language modes of living, outlook and stages of development." Sparing no expense, South Africa presented copious documentation to substantiate its case, justified on the grounds that the applicants' charges were broad and vague and failed to provide a background for a "proper appreciation of the issues raised." South Africa's legal volumes contain a wealth of material, not only on the territory but also on the rest of Africa. Indeed, they provide an update of Hailey's famous *An African Survey* (1957). Moreover, South Africa presented a list of thirty-eight expert witnesses who could be called to testify about the situation in the territory. In public hearings held from 1 July to 21 October 1965, thirteen of these experts gave evidence, including three anthropologists.

The three anthropological witnesses, Eiselen, Bruwer, and van Zyl (DPhil, Pretoria, 1952), all Afrikaans-speaking, identified themselves not as volkekundiges or even as ethnologists, but as social anthropologists. The first expert witness South Africa called to justify its policy of separate development or apartheid was Eiselen (DPhil, Hamburg), son of a German missionary, foundation professor of volkekunde at the universities of Stellenbosch and Pretoria, erstwhile secretary of the South African Department of Native Affairs, and widely lauded as the "architect of apartheid." Asked to apply his concept of multi-community to South-West Africa, he singled out the Bushmen:

> They have even to this day remained hunters and collectors of food; who have never settled down, who never endeavored to produce, but live merely by collecting, who are physically very different from the other people and also in their social structure, in their traditions, in their way of life. (ICJ 1966, 109)

Queried on the viability of "separate development" in the territory, Eiselen felt that the one exception that proved the rule were Bushmen: "No great strides were made in making them development-conscious and they still remain much as they have been ever since we came to know them centuries ago. They do not take kindly to leading a settled life and to becoming a productive people" (ICJ 1966, 110). Indeed, when asked how many independent ethnic states he saw emerging as a result of apartheid, he concluded that it would be "very difficult to say, some of the units are very small. Unfortunately, the smallest one of the Indigenous ones is also the most primitive, namely the Bushmen, so that it would be difficult to think in terms of such groups being viable communities if they once become independent" (ICJ 1966, 127). Ultimately, when pushed, both Eiselen and Bruwer cited Bushmen as the example of innate group difference and thus the raison d'être for apartheid.

Clearly the most important anthropological witness was Bruwer. Not only was he the state's resident ethnological expert on Namibia but also the first commissioner-general for the native peoples of South-West Africa and the moving spirit behind and member of the so-called Odendaal Commission, which developed a comprehensive plan for the socioeconomic development of the territory. Bruwer was called to provide expertise on the crucial question of differences among various Namibian population groups, their consciousness of separate identities, their wishes to maintain them, and the likely effects of removal of measures to ensure "differentiation"—in essence, the ideological justification of apartheid. Bruwer was examined and cross-examined more extensively than any of the other expert witnesses, spending six days in the witness box. Throughout the proceedings, he constantly stressed his anthropological expertise. His testimony was littered with the qualifier "As an anthropologist. . . ."

Namibia, Bruwer claimed, was divided into two main groups, the Khoisan and Bantu, who were distinguishable not only linguistically but also on "perceivable physical differences." Khoisan consisted of Bushmen and Nama, while the Bantu included the Herero, the Kaokoveld cluster, the Ovambo people, and the Kavango and Eastern Caprivi people. But this classification was befuddled by the Damara, who were linguistically Khoisan but physically negroid. And while the Bantu-speakers had preserved their oral traditions, the Khoisan had not. All these groups spoke mutually unintelligible languages (ICJ 1966, 242). In addition to linguistic differences, there were major differences in kinship: the Ovambo-Kavango cluster was matrilineal, Herero practiced double descent, and the Nama were patrilineal. In terms of subsistence, Ovambo-Kavango people were agriculturalists, Herero were cattle pastoralists, Nama were sheep pastoralists, and Bushmen and Damara were hunters. Save for a few isolated individuals among them, these diverse peoples were not inclined to form an overarching single "integrated unit." Separate development, he concluded, was the only workable policy: it represented respect for the achievements of African peoples, allowed flexibility in adaptation in an evolutionary way to changing situations, and did not necessitate abandoning people's "sacred heritage" (ICJ 1966, 263).

Showing the Furnivallian plural society influence of his Stellenbosch colleague Professor Holleman, Bruwer defined integration as "where you create a society by giving rights and privileges to members of other groups, who have already got their rights and privileges in another area." This had not occurred because people lacked political and property rights or, more precisely, legal rights (ICJ 1966, 296). Fundamental to Bruwer's view was the notion of a dual economy, a modern cash-sector controlled and dominated by whites, coexisting with the multitude of "traditional" ones found in the reserves. Conceding that the white economy was dependent upon natives, he denied that it was an "integrated one"; it was simply a "school for learning for these people," as the cash economy was "alien to these (Herero) people" because their "basic" culture was pastoralist and not "a money type of economy" (ICJ 1966, 277, 300). He denied that Namibia had an integrated economy, because all groups did not have rights and privileges connected to the economy, as for example land rights (ICJ 1966, 297). Bruwer insisted that "traditional economies" emphasized group rights and that group membership could not be lost in a lifetime, as ties of lineage and clan linked individuals to the larger group. Group rights were necessary to protect members of the group against other groups, although individual rights could be exercised within the group.

With mantra-like regularity, Bruwer reiterated his position that "differentiation" was necessary to protect a group against other stronger groups; while measures designed to preserve it imposed limitations on individual freedom, it was for the good of the group and in the interests of all the people. This, in a nutshell, was Bruwer's expert testimony.[24]

The Production and Procurement of
Namibian Ethnographic Knowledge

The South-West Africa case led directly to the government undertaking a documentation project the likes of which have never been equaled for the territory or anywhere in Africa. It created and normalized a vast amount of information that underwrote the Foucauldian capacity to govern. Preparations and research for the SWA case started in late 1960 and university academics, especially volkekundiges and experts on native administration, were brought in as consultants. Both totalizing and individualizing, the project helped constitute social categories and identities and marked off various forms of officially recognized hierarchies. Like Cohn's (1996) British in India, South African bureaucrats felt that the people they were governing could be known and represented as a series of facts and that effective administration derived from the efficient use of these facts; and, despite skepticism, they followed through on it because they believed that this was how international experts saw matters. This colonial project to describe and classify what the borders of Namibia encompassed was, in effect, a form of meta-ethnography undergirded by what passed as anthropological expertise. State making, in the final analysis, is a cultural project. The collected material was used not only for the World Court case but also for the report by the Odendaal Commission. Its principal recommendations to divide Namibia into twelve separate ethnic homelands formed a prominent part of the World Court proceedings. Legibility, as Scott (1998) argued, is basic to statecraft. The population had to be classified in ways that made state actions of taxation and control possible. These maps of legibility were to be refashioned by the force of law. What is noteworthy is that the classification system became vastly more complex. Prior to 1960 the census categories were a simple triad: white, African, and colored. Now people were classified according to twelve ethnic categories. Despite the invocation of expertise, many ordinary Namibians laughed at the prospect of having independent homelands or states with populations of less than fifty thousand. They also felt these categories to be arbitrary. For example, the language of the largest group in the Kavango homeland, Kwangari, is closer to Oshiwambo than it is to Mbukushu, the other large ethnic group residing in the same homeland. Why were whites lumped together when three official languages, English, Afrikaans, and German, were recognized and their geographic dispersal could be mapped approximately (with Swakopmund as capital of a possible German homeland)? And why were the Nama no longer administered by the BAD but by the Department of Colored Affairs? Was it because they had long insisted that they were not Bantu and felt that they would obtain more benefits being classified as coloreds? Was it because they spoke Nama (now known as

Khoekhoegowab)? Probably not, since the "negroid" Damara also spoke Nama but remained administered by the BAD. Nor could it be attributed simplistically to physiological features, since "Bushmen," who were seen to be similar to the Nama, remained within the ambit of the BAD. Even Budack, the acknowledged expert on the Nama or Khoi, wrote a confidential memorandum protesting against transferring the Nama to the Department of Colored Affairs. The commission had not given any reasons for this recommendation but simply assumed Nama were highly "westernized." On the contrary, Budack pointed out, the Nama had their own unique language, cultural practices and ceremonies relating to birth, marriage, and death as well as a political system featuring headmen and chiefs. Nama would be dominated by coloreds who looked down on them. In sum, Budack predicted a cultural disaster. Needless to say, his arguments were simply ignored.[25] These were questions asked not only by educated white elites but by ordinary Damara residents of Okombahe in the late sixties. Some played the system quite effectively. I vividly recall a conversation I had with a family of "Vaalgras Damaras." These Nama- or Khoekoegowab-speakers were originally Herero, but as a result of the wars of the late nineteenth century and labor hunger, they had wound up in the erstwhile Cape Colony and then repatriated to the Tses Reserve near Keetmanshoop. I asked them about their ethnic identity. Imagine my surprise when one pulled out an identity card claiming him to be Damara, another produced a card claiming Herero, a third had one signifying Nama, and a fourth claimed to be a colored! It was an optimal foraging strategy; they said they were able to make claims to a number of ethnic authorities. Clearly many realized that realpolitik was an important factor. All the homelands administered by the BAD were contingent and in the north. As such it would facilitate the argument, first mooted in discussions with the UN's Good Offices Committee (1958), chaired by Sir Charles Arden-Clarke, that the territory be split in two, the black-dominated north to fall under the UN, while the south would be controlled by South Africa.[26] One recommendation of the Odendaal Commission that was not acted upon was the call for the establishment of a special section for anthropological, sociological, and statistical research. As a compromise, however, a second government ethnologist, Dr. Johan Malan, was appointed to focus on the northern areas.

The assumptions underlying the Odendaal recommendations clearly do not hold empirically. The hoary myth of "incessant and inevitable ethnic violence" simply is not validated by the data provided by the administration itself.[27] This is not to ignore ethnicity as a factor in contemporary politics, if only because such a denial would entail denying that the state's policy of apartheid has had an impact. Moreover, to deny ethnicity is to deny Indigenous participation in creating ethnicity.

That those officials charged with implementing apartheid, both in South Africa and Namibia, were decidedly anti-intellectual has a long and well-documented history. This anti-intellectualism continued well into the 1970s and was probably one of the reasons for Bruwer's abrupt resignation as commissioner-general. His successor who had done his doctorate at Stellenbosch, a large tome on the native policy and administration in the territory (Olivier 1961), a fellow Broederbonder and Stellenbosch colleague, Dr. Martie Olivier, agreed with him that implementation of apartheid would make or break the Afrikaners and that the BAD officials charged with implementing the policy would be decisive for apartheid. Echoing Schapera's pre–World War II concerns, Olivier expressed horror that officials in this department were not required to have any specialist knowledge. Bantu administration was seen as simply and largely the application of rules and regulations, and the most important qualifications for promotion were in law, not in anthropology, sociology, or African languages. Indeed, there were special incentives for obtaining legal qualifications but none for anthropology or African languages. Merit rewards were based on keeping files up to date and having an accurate register. There were no rewards, indeed there were organizational disincentives, for learning about the customs or languages of local Africans. When senior officials from BAD headquarters undertook field visits, these resembled hunting or angling safaris rather than an occasion to learn about local problems. Lack of necessity of specialized knowledge was demonstrated by the fact that senior officials were appointed to the BAD from other departments like prisons, while other departments did not allow such cross-appointments. Intellectuals and anthropologists, Bruwer complained to Martie Olivier, were despised: "No person with a sense of honor can do his duty under such circumstances—we are despised but have to scratch their chestnuts out of the fire."[28] Once out of government, Bruwer went public but carefully avoided controversy. In 1966 he wrote a popular book in which he concluded that there were two major problems confronting peace in Namibia: one stemmed from the misconceptions of the "outside world" and the other from the ignorance and incompetence of officials who did not always recognize the "dignity of indigenous man, nor can they understand his problems, his way of life and his aspirations" (Bruwer 1966a, 131–32).

The fantasy world of Bruwer and officials was painfully punctured when in mid-December 1971 some 13,500 Ovambo contract workers went on strike in Windhoek and other urban areas against the contract labor system, which they called *omtete okangolo*.[29] These events shocked and surprised whites, even experts including those from the Bureau of State Security. How out of touch with reality these "native" experts were is exemplified in Peter Banghart's 1969 anthropology master's thesis on migrant labor, in which he argued that the contract labor system was more beneficial than harmful and that there is "no evidence of a disintegration of tribal life and village economy" (Banghart 1969, 144).[30] Had the ethnologists discussed the matter with others, like missionaries, instead of dismissing them as foreign agitators, a different perspective might have emerged. Rauha Voipio, a Finnish missionary with twenty-five years of experience in Owambo, had undertaken research on migrant labor at nearly the same time for presentation to the 1970 Synod of the Evangelical Lutheran Church. She received nearly one thousand responses to questionnaires she had distributed to contract workers, their wives, and church workers. Her findings revealed widespread dissatisfaction with the system and spoke so directly to the 1971 strike that they were rushed into print in an Afrikaans pamphlet *Kontrak: Soos die Owambo dit sien* (Contract: As the Owambo see it) (Voipio 1972). So desperate was the administration for informed insight that despite having been declared persona non grata in Ovamboland in 1967 because of his role in the Chief Martin Ashikoto case, Budack was asked to compile a confidential report on the Kuanyama unrest that followed the mass contract labor strike in December 1971.

This report was used by BOSS, the South African Bureau of State Security, in its investigation of the unrest. In transmitting their analysis to the secretary for Bantu administration, BOSS noted that "Mr Buddack [*sic*] of your department was very helpful and deserves praise for his thoroughness and insight. While he worked independently from us we were at all times aware of his movements and I want to again emphasize that his behavior was always correct and impeccable. We are grateful that for this purpose you placed him at our disposal."[31] The BOSS investigation claimed several factors were at work. The border fence separating Namibia from Angola and dividing the Kuanyama had been cut in more than twenty places to facilitate access to relatives and cattle posts on the other side of the border. In addition, Kuanyama objected to the weekly livestock inspections to control veterinary diseases, a long-standing source of discontent. There was dissatisfaction with many headmen, especially senior headman Kaluvi, whose homestead and son's shop were burned down because they were seen as collaborators with the South African administration, especially given their new role in labor recruitment. Finally, there was tension between Kuanyama and Tjimbundu, as a large number of Tjimbundu had settled in the Kuanyama area, especially on the Angolan side of the border, and their numbers were on the increase. This was because most of these Tjimbundu had already worked in the Police Zone and had acquired technical and mechanical skills for work on the mines. Tucked away in a paragraph, almost as an afterthought, was a note that based on his interviews and observations Budack provided the following reasons for the unrest: the ICJ's second judgment that South Africa was illegally occupying SWA; that Ovambo felt that apartheid was simply slavery and wanted nothing to do with self-government, as they were Namibians and not Ovambo. The South African government was trying to create the impression that Ovambo were satisfied with the current situation, but the protesters were trying to show the world that this was not the case. Some Ovambo were blatantly antiwhite, blaming all their ills on whites, such as the reduction in fish quantity because of dams the administration had built. Since whites came, some Ovambo averred, mice numbers had increased and grown in size, and rain had gotten scarcer. Finally, Ovambo insisted on equal pay for equal work.

Asked by the secretary for Bantu administration for his observations on the BOSS report, specifically with regard to chieftainship and the authority of headmen, Budack responded that he felt it to be absurd to comment on his own report and that "further I want to emphasize that I do not in any way want to interfere in administrative affairs of the Owambo government."[32]

Notes

1. The Broederbond committees worked in total secrecy and consisted of prominent Broeders (brothers) who "see that Broeders get effective control of key areas, check that they perform their duties properly, and advise Cabinet Ministers on policy matters" (Wilkins and Strydom 1978, 397).
2. Fellow World Court witnesses Eiselen and H. J. van Zyl were also members of this committee at one time or another. Other anthropologists who served on it included Professor E. F. Potgieter, later also a commissioner-general, and Dr. Piet Koornhof, an exception who read for his doctorate at Oxford and famously placed an embargo on it. Professor P. J. Coertze, the doyen of volkekunde, was an associate member (Wilkins and Strydom 1978, 398–99). The committee also contained a large number of senior officials from the BAD and the Institute for the Administration of Non-European Affairs, the organization representing municipal "native administrators."
3. J. P. van S. Bruwer to J. G. van der Wath, 23 February 1962, File 2/17/5, PV123 Bruwer Papers, INCH.
4. J. P. van S. Bruwer, "My Life and Striving in the Interests of South-West Africa: 1958–64," File 2/11/1, PV123 Bruwer papers, INCH.
5. Verwoerd had a long-standing interest in "native policy," having been minister of native affairs (later Bantu Administration and Development) from 1950 until becoming prime minister in 1958.
6. Hendrik Verwoerd to J. P. van S. Bruwer, July 1960, File 1/58/1/1/, PV93 Verwoerd Papers, INCH. Ironically, when the White Paper on the Odendaal Commission was discussed in Parliament in 1964, Verwoerd dismissed the opposition United Party's proposal that a federation be created as a joke that would lead to black domination (Verwoerd 2018, 338).
7. J. P. van S. Bruwer to Hendrik Verwoerd, 30 April 1961, PV123 Bruwer Papers, INCH.
8. Commissioner-generals were established under the Promotion of Bantu Self-Government Act 1959 and were largely political appointments made for the various South African ethnic groups with the ostensible purpose of providing direct links between the population groups and the South African prime minister. The ostensible purpose of their appointments was

to try to circumvent the cumbersome civil service. A surprisingly large number of these commissioner-generals consisted of volkekundiges, a tribute perhaps to Bruwer's influence.

9. J. P. van S. Bruwer to Minister of Bantu Administration M. C. de Wet Nel, 15 January 1962, PV123 Bruwer Papers, INCH.

10. J. P. van S. Bruwer to J. G. van der Wath, 23 February 1962, PV123 Bruwer Papers, INCH.

11. When I asked Toivo ya Toivo about this meeting in 2001, he denied any knowledge of meeting Bruwer.

12. For alternative accounts from a local perspective, see Ndadi (1974).

13. Letter from J. P. van S. Bruwer to Ross McGregor, 26 March 1962, PV123 Bruwer Papers, INCH.

14. J. P. van S. Bruwer to Ross McGregor, 14 January 1963, PV123 Bruwer Papers, INCH, emphasis added.

15. J. P. van S. Bruwer to Ross McGregor, 31 January 1963, PV123 Bruwer Papers, INCH.

16. Indeed, his most significant works are probably a cyclostyled study entitled *The Kuanyama of South West Africa* (Bruwer 1962) and a mimeograph entitled "Die matrilinêre orde van Kavangoland" (The matrilineal order of the Kavango) (Bruwer 1966b). He wrote a number of general articles and the popular book *South West Africa: The Disputed Land* (Bruwer 1966a), which essentially summarizes the arguments he made at the World Court.

17. J. P. van S. Bruwer to M. C. de Wet Nel, 18 February 1965, PV123 Bruwer Papers, INCH.

18. This claim could be exaggerated, as in July 1965 Bruwer wrote to Verwoerd claiming that the basic policy, including that pertaining to coloreds, was basically the only feasible and correct one but that the problem lay with the personnel charged with implementation (J. P. van S. Bruwer to HFV [Hendrik F. Verwoerd], 29 July 1965, PV123 Bruwer Papers, INCH).

19. Cornelis Johannes Claassen, a Bruwer protégé, completed a sociology dissertation at the University of Wisconsin entitled *Man on the Reservation: A Sociological Study of an American Indian Reservation* in 1967. It would be interesting to see how his experiences serving on the Odendaal Commission shaped his American research. He went on to occupy senior positions in the South African Department of Planning.

20. F. H. Odendaal to HFV (Hendrik F. Verwoerd), 24 May 1963, PV93 Verwoerd Papers, INCH.

21. Bishop Leonard Auala, letter to J. P. van S. Bruwer, October 1964, NAN. Letter courtesy of Gregor Dobler.

22. N. J. van Warmelo to Jos Allen, 17 April 1961, A591 van Warmelo Collection, NAN.

23. Ironically, if in giving evidence at the ICJ the applicants had chosen to quiz him on his views on race, his racism might have been exposed in public; but apparently, like good liberals of the era, they did not believe anyone could still subscribe to such doctrines and failed to engage him on this level.

24. Reinforcing Bruwer's evidence was Dr H. J. van Zyl, secretary for the South African Department of Bantu Education who had chaired a 1958 commission of enquiry into Indigenous education in the territory.

25. Confidential memorandum by K. Budack, 5 January 1967. BAD 18. 04 Odendaal Kommisie, Besluite van. NAN.

26. See, for example, Cockram (1976, 270–273). From this perspective the fact that a town in the south, Keetmanshoop, had a state-of-the-art hospital and airport was not due to naive pork-barrel politics but rather part of a well-thought-out strategic plan.

27. A map constructed by the SWA National Planning Office lists incidents of pre-colonial conflict. What counts as "conflict" is highly problematic and can range from full-scale warfare to what amounted to gang raids. Rather than being interethnic in nature, it is striking how most of the conflicts listed were multiethnic and cross-ethnic; some were even between members of the same group (J. van der Merwe 1983, map 31). So much for the pervasiveness of interethnic strife.

28. J. P. van S. Bruwer to Martie Olivier, 17 July 1965, 2 August 1965, PV123 Bruwer Papers, INCH.

29. *Omtete* refers to the queue, while *okangolo* denotes the identity disk each recruit had to wear.
30. The fact that Banghart's father was the former managing director of the Tsumeb mine probably factored into this conclusion.
31. BOSS to Sec, Bantu Administration and Development, 24 March 1972, BAD Box 18 File O13. Owambo: Onrus in Kuanyamagebied, NAN.
32. Budack to Sec. Bantu Affairs and Development, 23 May, 1972. BAD Box 18 File O13. Owambo: Onrus in Kuanyamagebied, NAN.

CHAPTER 4

From WHAM to Countermobilization

The failure to achieve an internationally satisfactory solution to the South-West African issue led to what was known variously as the Border War, the Bush War, or the War of Liberation in northern SWA, where this low-intensity guerrilla war lasted for twenty-two years in what was known as the Operational Area or Sector 10 (Owambo), Sector 20 (Kavango), and Sector 70 (Caprivi). In fashionable contemporary terminology it would be classed as a "small war" or a "hybrid" that combines "hard" and "soft" power. This site was important because it epitomized what Agamben (2005) termed "bare colonialism": while attempting to control the local populace, the SADF tried to get the inhabitants to like them. A key strategy in this regard was its short-lived Civic Action Program, which featured the Winning the Hearts and Minds (WHAM) initiative. Regarding gaining the trust of the local population as the modern, professional way of combating civil unrest, a special directorate focusing on WHAM was officially created in January 1978. It was run by Major General Phil Pretorius, who had been the top graduate of a special course in psychological warfare at Fort Bragg (US). Because of partisan politics, however, the directorate was disbanded again in March 1980, although WHAM-like activities continued (Grundy 1986, 61).

Faced with growing guerrilla warfare beyond the Police Zone in the densely populated north, South Africa attempted to develop a counter-insurgency strategy. Not having much firsthand experience in such situations, they had to depend on a few isolated individuals like General Charles A. "Pop" Fraser, who had served in the Malaya counterinsurgency campaign in the early fifties and visited Algeria during its civil war while serving as military attaché in Paris. More important, though, was the role of General Magnus Malan, the Nationalist wunderkind with a meteoric rise in the military, climaxing as long-term minister of defense from 1980 to 1991.[1] In his personal memoirs, Malan regarded his posting as officer commanding SWA Command from 1966 to 1968 as one of the most significant events in his life. It was here that he could start field-testing theories about counterinsurgency that he had learned while attending the regular command and general staff officer course at Fort Leavenworth in the United States in 1962–63 (coming first in the class).[2] Malan was a managerial modernizer. In charge of the Military Academy (1968–71), he proposed that candidate officers do courses in languages, ethnology, psychology, and personnel management. While chief of the army (1973–76), he created a decentralized interdepartmental counterinsurgency committee to manage the South-West African war and thus crafted the prototype of the National Security Management System.[3] A more immediate source of practical expertise was the Rhodesian war, which led to the creation of Zimbabwe. Not only were South African security forces (largely police) deployed there, but after the collapse of the white regime, a number of counterinsurgency fighters, many of them mercenaries, joined the South African forces on the SWA border. Perhaps the most notoriously effective innovation in this regard was to be the creation of the Koevoet (crowbar) police unit modeled on the Rhodesian Selous Scouts, which used local men and "turned" SWAPO members (M. Malan 2006).

Subscribing to the long-held adage that the SWA war was 80 percent civil and only 20 percent military, the military devoted considerable resources to gain the support of the local population. Broadly defined as "psyops" (psychological operations) or "comops" (communications operations), these efforts were initiated in 1972. In 1974 civic action programs were instituted in what was known as Operation "Vaskyk." Its purpose was to enable what was colloquially referred to as the "PBs" (*plaaslike bevolking*) in Afrikaans and "LPs" (local populations) in English to discover in "the South African soldier a protector, helper, teacher, ally and a true friend" (J. Visser 1984, 2). It did so by having uniformed personnel provide a host of services, such as medical, agricultural, and especially teaching. A year later the civic action programs were publicly pronounced a success. In the Kavango region, it was claimed, the military was well received wherever they went. Rural villagers were spontaneously coming forward, frequently with gifts, and even building special huts for patrols, who were entertained with *braaivleis* (barbeques) and special dances. SADF personnel were dubbed *totekela*, "the man who helps his friend out of the well." The programs were lauded with the usual bravado as the largest single bulwark against a Communist takeover (J. Visser 1984). By 1978 General Constand L. Viljoen, head of the SADF, required that all operational staff—officers and men—take a course in WHAM.

Senior SADF officers continued to see merit in the Civic Action Program despite its failure, which they attributed to the program being implemented too late and not rigorously enough (Cawthra 1986, 236). As WHAM lost its legitimacy, brilliantly analyzed by de Visser (2013), the

SADF's emphasis changed to more surreptitious activity, broadly defined as countermobilization, exemplified by various youth movements with attendant camps and the creation of front organizations. Citing an increase in reports made by the local population to the security forces about SWAPO—from 64 in 1983 to more than 2,000 in 1987—and the decline of "terrorist" acts from 620 to 483 in the same period, the South African forces claimed success of these countermobilizing initiatives (Burger 1992, 246). In these "soft power" efforts, social scientists played a significant role.

To be sure, countermobilization involved many components, including Koevoet, cross-border raids, and troops impersonating SWAPO, and there is an extensive, usually heroic, literature covering these practices (P. Els 2000, 2016). Here I want to examine efforts by social science experts to persuade the local population to accept the SADF. This is a task burdened by the difficulty in tracing the networks and affiliations of some of these experts, as they extend into the shadowy world of covert operations.

In tracing these rather opaque networks, certain experts stand out. One such personage was Dr. Louis Pasques (1925–2015) whose obituary is rather modest. Headlined "Former School Principal's Voice Becomes Silent," it mentioned that he had been head of Messina High School from 1965 to 1968, head of the Louis Trichardt High School until 1974, and had then joined the Transvaal Education Department to run their *veldskool* (field school) program that had been started in 1973 (*Zoutpansberger*, 28 August 2015). Both his postgraduate degrees, a master's in 1973 and a doctorate in 1976, concerned youth preparedness and identifying leaders. An enthusiastic Broederbonder, in 1967 Pasques was in charge of the movement's liaison program for military ballotees (Wilkins and Strydom 1978, A179).[4] A decade later, as head of the Transvaal Education Department's Youth Preparedness Program, he was forced to take to the press to deny that the field schools were used to indoctrinate white youth or that white youth were told that blacks lived only for the present and that certain numbers like seven were dangerous (*Rand Daily Mail*, 25 May 1978). These paramilitary field schools were compulsory for all white schoolchildren in government schools in the province and entailed week-long camps segregated by gender and language, run largely by right-wing instructors who emphasized the dangers of the Communist inspired "Total Onslaught" (Evans 1983, 50–67).[5]

The following year, Pasques was appointed head of educational leadership at the Pretoria Teachers College. Even the English-language press lauded this "Father of the Veld School" as "an experienced project leader in racial affairs" (*Pretoria News*, 3 July 1986). Upward mobility was rapid for Pasques, becoming adjunct director of National Education in charge of youth preparedness, but it is very possible that this was a cover, because at the same time he was signing off on classified South-West African projects as "Director: Specialist Training" in the Directorate of Special Tasks (DST), located in the larger Directorate of Military Intelligence. In 1985 President P. W. Botha seconded him to the President's Office and made him a member of the secretive State Security Council (SSC), perhaps one of the most powerful institutions in South Africa. Pasques resigned from his government posts in 1986 and formed a private consulting company called Adult Education Consultants, which served as a conduit for secret state funding to create front organizations promoting countermobilization. Over five years he was to channel more than R 160 million into such activities. Already in 1987 he was awarded one of South Africa's highest honors, the Star of South Africa, for "services to State Security" (*Weekly Mail*, 3 January 1992). It is improbable that this award was made only for his short period of service on the State Security Council; it is more likely that it speaks to his long service in the DST. He was involved in the strategic communications wing of the SSC, known as Stratcom, established in 1984 and the nexus between the SSC and various covert units. Stratcom consisted of two types: "hard" Stratcom, which included activities like assassination, sabotage, theft, and blackmail; and "soft" Stratcom, which specialized in supposedly legal activities like propaganda, disinformation, and "dirty tricks," such as the creation of front companies, trade unions, and student organizations (Sanders 2006, 230).

Pasques's countermobilization projects, in which he drew heavily on ethnologists, focused on youth and emphasized Christianity and sports. They ranged in violence and scale from the notorious Witdoeke (township vigilantes) to such innocuous-sounding institutions as the Black Crisis Center, the South African Christian Cultural Organization, and the Eastern Cape Sports Foundation. As the South African Truth and Reconciliation Commission reported:

> By around 1983 it was acknowledged that the relatively unsophisticated "hearts and minds" tactics adopted to date were not working, and that any suggestion of direct connections to the SADF was enough to guarantee the failure of projects of this nature. Far more elaborate, covert methods would have to be adopted to "counter-mobilize" the Namibian population against SWAPO.

To this end a unit code-named *Etango* was established, under the overall guidance of Dr Louis Pasques. *Etango* included many of those SADF personnel, especially those linked to Military Intelligence Communications Operations units, and to the Directorate: Covert Collection, who would later surface in South Africa under the guise of "experts" working for Adult Education Consultants (AEC) and in fronts set up by the Directorate: Covert Collection. It appears that the primary aim of *Etango* was to establish a tribally based, conservative "Owambo movement" to counter SWAPO, while a similar project code-named *Ezuva* aimed to set up a "Kavango movement." During 1985 and 1986, operatives linked to *Etango* moved into South Africa and began setting up a range of front companies in order to pursue similar objectives inside South Africa against the ANC [African National Congress] through the use of "black-on-black" violence of various kinds, the fostering of viable alternative "liberation movements," and spreading NP [National Party] propaganda through a range of "Christian cultural" organisations particularly among the coloured community in the Western Cape. (TRC 1992, vol. 2, 301ff., paras. 566–69)[6]

The Padriag O'Malley Archive cites a memorandum that by 1986 Etango and Ezuva had already grown into a "force to be reckoned with in SWA politics." "If an election is to be won in SWA, a drastic increase in countermobilization activities would be required." Control of these organizations had been transferred to the administrator-general of SWA, but the SADF still acted in an "executive capacity."[7] These countermobilization activities, run by the SSC under the aegis of Project Ancor, were concerned with national schemes that included mobilizing traditional healers in urban areas, creating pseudo trade unions, founding youth clubs, and promoting moderate black political leaders. The SSC funded Stellenbosch University scholars to undertake special studies in SWA, inter alia on Indigenous law, and supported several projects in Caprivi, Namaland, and Kaokoland. These efforts frequently concentrated on the "leadership element," developing church groups, and even a "SWA Bible School" as bulwarks against communism, all of which cost an estimated R 15 million annually.

The creation of front organizations for propaganda purposes has a long history in politics and warfare; in this case the Broederbond provided an important precedent. In 1962 the Broederbond, under the aegis of Bruwer and its secretary, the Oxford-trained social anthropologist Dr. Piet Koornhof, later a Nationalist cabinet minister, decided to create a front organization favorable to Kaiser Mathanzima, the chairman of the Transkei Territorial Council, in his efforts to have the Transkei declared an independent homeland. They did this by providing financial and organizational assistance as well as publishing pamphlets and posters. A Broederbond official, L. S. van der Walt, was dispatched to the Transkei under the guise of being a student doing cultural research. His task was to create eight tribal cultural organizations emphasizing ethnic patriotism and then to unite them into a federation. Van der Walt claimed these activities played an important and decisive role in the election of Chief Mathanzima as president of Transkei (Stals 1998, 326–27).

In examining the South-West African countermobilization projects in greater detail, it is clear that the emphasis was on identifying "the leadership element," especially of the youth, as manifested in their youth camps.

Cultural front organizations like Etango and Ezuva took on possibly added significance, as at the time Pasques, who had joined the SSC, was busily debating how to deal with urban insurrections that were engulfing South Africa. One of the conclusions they reached was that "before a riot situation can be effectively defused, the ringleaders must be selectively eliminated" (cited in Sanders 2006, 208). In these activities, piloted by Pasques, ethnologists were critical. Apart from their intelligence gathering, ethnologists were also charged with trying to improve "race relations," which they did by lecturing, writing etiquette manuals, and organizing youth camps, drawing on outside expertise as the need arose.

Youth Camps

Much of the WHAM and later the countermobilization efforts targeted youth, especially as captive audience in schools, where they were subjected to a barrage of lectures, leaflets, pamphlets, and movies. Apart from providing uniformed teachers, the SADF organized sporting events and provided children with sweets, canned food, and T-shirts. This effort was supplemented by a massive public media effort, in which the SWA Broadcasting Corporation and its Owambo and Kavango FM radio services did not even disguise their partiality. There were also underhand strategies in which youth were coerced or paid to serve as spies or, in the parlance of the SADF, as "reporters."

In SWA, as in most totalitarian regimes, youth formed a particularly important target.[8] For a variety of reasons, black youth were seen as particularly volatile, aggravated in the South-West African case by large-scale unemployment and their potential of joining SWAPO. One common strategy of neutralizing this threat and buttressing the state was through youth organizations.[9] In early 1980, Broederbond chair and administrator-general of the territory Gerrit Viljoen set up a Broederbond study group to study how to liaise with (and co-opt) militant black youth. It consisted of stalwarts from the Broederbond executive council, youth experts, and members of the intelligence services. Its intentions were, first, to develop modes of encouraging white youth to support the government and, second, to neutralize militant black youth. The latter it intended to do through a divide-and-rule strategy and by confusing blacks. This it would do not by defending Afrikanerdom but by pointing to similarities, such as a common disavowal of colonialism. At the same time the group advised that there were significant differences as well: Afrikaners had the intellectual capacity to logically analyze complicated matters, while the "thought pattern" of blacks fell prey to slogans and was influenced by concrete manifestations of power, status, symbols, and rituals and an inability to grasp the abstract. Blacks had an exaggerated sense of self-importance (Stals 1998, 561).

To encourage successful dialogue, the study group urged white youth to do more listening. By respecting black dignity, being flexible, and avoiding stereotyping and paternalism, confidence could be generated. Dialogue was an inherently fraught exercise, thus white youth leaders had to be carefully selected. Concerning youth generally, the study group urged discussions with all educational authorities, black and white, to develop that old chestnut specific youth preparedness programs and to identify the "leadership element," the best example being the Transvaal Education Department's program of youth camps, which should be extended to all population groups, but especially whites. Teacher training colleges should be urged to build modules on youth preparedness, and a new ministry of youth should be established (Stals 1998, 561–63).

The obvious person to engage in such studies and provide advice was Pasques, not only on youth field schools but on South-West Africa. Dating back to the fifties, what were known as Bantu Youth Camps were places of incarceration for delinquent youths, but in the face of the Total Onslaught they were to be given a new gloss. The first rollout of the new model was the Ekongoro[10] Youth Movement, sponsored by the regional authority of the Kavango Education Department in 1974 and set up in consultation with Pasques. It was made compulsory for all schoolchildren (Cawthra 1986, 207). Each camp was named after a recent tribal king or queen in an effort to provide it with standing. The one built on Shambyu land on the outskirts of Rundu, the capital of the Kavango region, was known officially as the Maria Mwengere Center after the local *hompa* (ruler) (Akuupa 2011, 127–34). Given its central location, it was upgraded with many facilities, including dormitories, an amphitheater, a museum, a wild animal sanctuary, and a botanical garden. It is apparently still in use, especially as a venue for *sangfeeste* (choral festivals and competitions). Ekongoro's motto encapsulated its purpose—*upampi moyirugana yaKavango* (to be hardworking and committed to the works of Kavango)—but, betraying its origins, its constitution and laws were written in Afrikaans. In an attempt to make youth nature-conscious, the camp emphasized nature conservation and had several wild animals in a camp in order to "cultivate a love of animals"; it also replanted indigenous trees to create a "sense of national pride in the pupils." Each recognized Kavango tribe had a camp that was controlled by a tribal coordinator and run by a camp secretary. These camps provided accommodation for a hundred boys and a hundred girls and had separate housing for the white youth organizer and separate facilities for the black youth leaders.

The purpose of these camps was to strengthen Kavango traditions and, of course, distract idle youths from getting involved in oppositional politics. Ekongoro was divided into three age-graded sections, a lower primary, an upper primary, and a secondary school section. While their means of engagement varied, the syllabi of the three sections followed common themes. A typical weeklong syllabus at a camp would open with ice-breakers and then include talks and discussions on topics such as "our country, our people, our language, our flag." There was a heavy emphasis on Christianity and the dangers that communism posed. Given that the territory at that stage claimed to be the African country with the highest percentage of Christians, such an emphasis made sense. Participants were taught their "cultural traditions" from "culture books," detailing the origin and history of the five Kavango tribes, supposedly researched and written by local cultural officers. However, the books were apparently largely the work of volkekundiges from Potchefstroom University, Professor Hennie Coetzee and Dr. Hendrik van der Wateren, who visited and advised the Kavango Education Department on setting up youth camps (Kleynhans n.d.). Attendees were divided into competitive groups of ten persons and encouraged to compose songs and slogans. At the conclusion of the camp, certificates and sometimes T-shirts would be handed out, and the leaders and organizers would carefully assess each participant in terms of their attitude, their leadership potential, and their sympathies toward the government.

By 1982 Ekongoro was running into some difficulties. The Kavango Ministry of Education youth organizer, Elrich Pretorius, was concerned that if local people were allowed to run the organization, as Kavango minister of education Rudolf Ngondo proposed, youth camps would soon become an incubation battery for SWAPO supporters. Addressing Pretorius's claims, a high-level meeting of South African officials and officers was critical of the administration's lack of (especially financial) control over the center and how it aggressively claimed land for agriculture without consulting the traditional authorities. More generally, it also proposed reducing the number of camps from six to four. Camps would remain under white leadership, but this would not be stated as policy, and would be managed by the Kavango Department of Education, while there would be close liaison with the SADF's Civil Affairs division in its efforts to promote "positive citizenship."

So successful were these camps deemed to be, and given the need for thorough youth resilience via veld schools, guidance counseling, and cultural promotion, that Pasques wrote to the military urging them to assist the Kavango education authorities in expanding the program by creating an additional sixteen professional officers in October 1984.[11] Michael Akuupa highlighted the importance of *sangfeeste* but suggested that by the mid-eighties these festivals were becoming politicized and unpopular because of the insertion of Ezuva, the youth movement organized by the military. At that point Pretorius resigned, he told Akuupa; he was forced out when he objected to the efforts of the SADF and the Kavango administration to promote Ezuva.[12] A few years later, in 1987, he was replaced by the ethnologist Jan Bradley, but the dynamic at the camp had changed. Singing was no longer emphasized in a context that was now dominated by members of the 202 Kavango Battalion, so that Bradley apparently promoted traditional dances and encouraged the "re-mobilization" of participants (Akuupa 2011, 134).

Youth camps were not, however, restricted to Indigenous groups. Between 1981 and 1986, the SWA Department of White Education created a division of youth leadership (*jeugleiding*), and the official charged with organizing the division sought extensive advice from Pasques.[13] The division engaged in three major activities: it created two field schools, where seventh-, ninth-, and eleventh-grade students would do weeklong courses; it developed a compulsory youth preparedness (*jeugweerbaarheids*) program, training teachers and developing course material; and, finally, it re-energized a high school cadet program in which scholars were exposed to basic military training, marching, and shooting, in collaboration with the SADF and the South-West African Territorial Forces (SWATF). The organizer believed that all three activities were successful and positively received (A. Gous email, 25 June 2018).

An indication of the content of these activities can be gleaned from the *Handleiding vir Geestesweerbaarheid* (Handbook for spiritual resilience) (Gous 1982). It proudly proclaims:

> We have a task and a calling on the southern point of Africa. The first task is to civilize a land which is characterized through the centuries by barbarism. The second task is to bring the redeeming Message of salvation to the lost heathens. The third task is to promote the Church. The fourth task is cultural—to form a people with self-pride, culture, language and heritage and to promote a love of what is our own. (Gous 1982, 94–95)

Ten units in the handbook deal with the "Peoples of SWA," based on material supplied by military ethnologist Captain Salomé Visser. The handbook avers that the chief races in the territory were the Caucasoids, the Mongoloids, the Negroids, and the Capoids and that the Bantu originated out of the mixing of Negroids with Hamites. A later unit discusses the biological concepts of race, focusing on how races are detailed in the Bible, and concludes that there is unity in diversity and that all were equal in the eyes of God. It urges reciprocal respect when dealing with blacks, but fortunately, "Blacks are well aware that Whites have a different cultural background and that their knowledge of local customs are faulty. For this reason they do not generally fault the White man if one or other etiquette rule is unknowingly broken" (Gous 1982, 164). There are also five units dealing with the "Total Onslaught," which focus on the dangers of communism and its puppet, SWAPO, and the complicity of organizations like the World Council of Churches and the Central Intelligence Agency and make the case for the necessity of having a positive image of the SADF.

The Etango and Ezuva Front Organizations

While Ekongoro focused on schoolchildren, the SADF's Directorate of Communications Operations (COMOPS) created Etango in Owambo and the Kavango clone Ezuva in 1980. Their membership was drawn largely from members of the security forces and government employees and their relatives, although the SADF formally divested from the movements in 1984 after protests by the traditional authorities concerning the role of uniformed personnel. Management was then delegated to a former army officer and teacher in collaboration with the regional government. The absence of public involvement by the SADF in these organizations led to white officials concluding that these countermobilization methods were successful and applying them in South Africa too (Burger 1992, 247–48). In a reprise of the strategy followed in Malaya and Rhodesia by counterinsurgency theorists, the South Africans believed they could neutralize SWAPO by developing a moderate multiethnic nationalist front. The goal of these organizations was twofold: to develop and reinforce an anti-SWAPO disposition among the Ovambo and Kavango people, and to get as many local people as possible involved in its anti-SWAPO activities. Specifically, it aimed to get specific target groups involved, namely those identified as opinion makers and youth.

This was when Pasques came to the rescue. To persuade the newly created ethnic regional authorities to participate, he would invite their executive committees to a weeklong tour of South Africa. In 1984 he ran at least twelve training/indoctrination courses. As military ethnologist Major Sarel Karsten admiringly wrote in a handwritten (though undated) memorandum: "Dr Pasques is totally involved with our attempt and takes every effort to seize new needs and opportunities. During 1983 and especially in 1984 he spent more time in SWA than at home. He is highly motivated and works till late at night to satisfy our needs."[14]

A typical Ezuva course, apparently the second one, ran for eight days and had fifty-one participants, drawn mostly from the 202 Kavango Battalion, with a smattering of police. They were divided into six teams of nine. Activities were designed to motivate their compatriots about the dangers of communism and its puppet, SWAPO. Akuupa's informants recalled that the daily activities at the Ezuva camp included field excursions, Bible sessions, and hide-and-seek games. Participants wore paramilitary uniforms and on the last day had to take an oath of allegiance to Ezuva before being awarded a diploma (Akuupa 2011). Pasques reported using a more sophisticated technique involving group dynamics to get the teams to compete with one another in composing and singing patriotic songs, singing being seen as an important way of motivating the participants and building team spirit, and inventing slogans that were meant to give partici-pants a sense of owning the proceedings. Course personnel were required to wear mufti and to downplay their military connections. In order to rigorously identify potential leaders, instructors would give daily assess-ments of the political orientations of the participants and their suitability for further training as instructors. Participants were also asked to fill out evaluation forms that showed, not surprisingly, that everyone was enthusi-astic about the course, the purpose of which most saw not as combatting communism and SWAPO, but as developing "leadership skills." Gradu-ates, now officially titled "communicators," were then expected to go out into the community dressed in mufti and discuss issues like capitalism, communism, and UN Resolution 435 and mobilize local people, especially the youth. Prospective leaders identified on the basis of their potential as instructors were then invited to participate in special courses, typically lim-ited to about ten trainees. Again, applying group dynamics derived from Pasques's reading of psychology, these trainees were taken on a special visit to South Africa, which concluded with the obligatory *braaivleis*. The itin-eraries of these trips suggest that these advanced courses were more about building an esprit de corps than about teaching pedagogy.

Countermobilization efforts, however, were concentrated in central Owambo, which had the heaviest population density and strong SWAPO support. In its short-lived heyday, Etango ran monthly mass courses for about one hundred novices, which took place at a specially developed facility known as Miershoop (ant heap). Located in close proximity to a prison housing SWAPO members or supporters, evidence presented at the TRC claims that many of those incarcerated there were successfully brainwashed and joined Etango. Approximately 35 percent of the mem-bers of the 101 Ovambo Battalion were former members of SWAPO, including many askaris (turned guerrillas) (Dale 2014, 99–100). By mid-1984 Pasques was claiming that more than thirteen hundred members of the security forces had attended Etango courses, approximately one hundred high-profile leaders had been identified and sent on advanced courses, and sixteen had completed a total of four courses and were being used as political commissars. Eighteen months later Etango claimed some five thousand members drawn from the security forces (*The Namibian*, 13 December 1985).

Having identified teachers and nurses as potential opinion leaders, Pasques sought to get the rising middle class and traditional leaders involved as well and offered courses tailored to their specific interests. Claiming the workshop aimed to improve nursing services, Pasques took a group of sixteen hospital matrons to an upmarket resort in the Etosha Game Park, where, in addition to lectures on nursing and daily sessions on religion—led personally by Pasques—they were subjected to daily secret leadership and political assessments. To make the matrons feel they were respected by whites, Pasques tried to follow up on some suggestions they made. He also sought to engage other women and proudly claimed to have involved over two hundred women in courses on how to be domestic workers and to have organized a street market in Oshakati for them to sell their products. He intended to create a women's organization the next year. As soon as qualified personnel could be found, Pasques planned to run business courses and create a chamber of commerce to serve as a front for anti-SWAPO activities. Teachers and youth were more problematic, so Pasques organized a weekend workshop for white teachers aimed at getting them involved in positively influencing senior black students. This resulted in 157 senior students volunteering to attend an adventure camp, and thus the groundwork was laid for an anti-SWAPO youth organization that was expected to expand into the more rural areas. Pasques ended his report by mentioning that Owambo agricultural students had been sent on a tour of the south of the territory and of South Africa.[15]

Pasques also ran special courses for headmen and senior headmen who all supposedly spontaneously joined Etango, but Pasques was so shocked at their ignorance concerning contemporary politics that he planned a follow-up course. The main purpose of these workshops was to get traditional leaders to encourage their followers to engage in anti-SWAPO activities. He was especially lauded by the ethnologist Major Sarel Karsten, who was stationed at the military headquarters in Windhoek, for developing a cell structure around them, which would consolidate their spheres of influence over their subjects. Headmen were frequently bolstered by Etango members from the security forces appointed to advise them on how to mobilize their subjects. Pasques also intended to run courses for their spouses. Finally, Pasques created an Etango Commission, consisting largely of traditional leaders, teachers, nurses, police, soldiers, and SWA Broadcasting Corporation employees, which ostensibly controlled the movement. The chairman of the commission was Kuanyama senior headman Gabriel Kautima, a prominent supporter of the Democratic Turnhalle Alliance (DTA), which was receiving much secret funding from the SADF and the National Intelligence Service (NIS). Needless to mention, Etango and Ezuva were accused in the pages of *The Namibian* of indoctrinating and intimidating the populace and of being biased toward the moderate transitional multiparty government as represented by the DTA.

By the end of 1984 Pasques had created similar organizations in the Caprivi region (called Namwi) and Kaokoland (Eyuva) and had plans to expand into Hereroland, Namaland, and Damaraland. So successful were these pseudo-cultural front organizations alleged to be that similar projects were approved by the military for implementation in South Africa to counter rising unrest in early December 1985. The bubble burst when a local muckraking newspaper, *The Namibian*, published a report entitled "A Tribal Onslaught on the People of Northern Namibia" (13 December 1985), based on a copious cache of classified vernacular literature dealing with Etango and Ezuva. It is worth quoting extensively from these documents, if only to get a feel for how the instigators went about their business.

Etango, the documents proclaimed, was a Christian (and not a fundraising) organization that aimed to "protect against SWAPO and communist influences; to help the Ovambo youth to develop their talents and use them in building their land; to help the Ovambo nation stay on their land; to help the Ovambo people so that their true friends can protect them properly; and to help the Ovambo nation to develop their good traditions." Ezuva paralleled Etango to the extent of having the same slogan, "We are fighting for true freedom," and sharing the triangular shape of its flag: "Every people has a flag. The flag is something unique to a people." Explaining the symbolism of the Ezuva flag, the documents explained that green stood for progress, orange for sovereignty, white for peace, and blue for freedom. The three corners of the triangle represented, respectively, strong administration, strong security, and the residents of the Kavango; all three stood together as one to fight the enemy. In the emblem the sun stood for "the light people need to work and the fish eagle is renowned for its sharp eyes which means that *Ezuva* identifies the problems of the country and will solve them quickly."

The Ezuva cache included several documents displaying Pasques's interest in group dynamics—"A group must have a leader and strive for a unified goal and act in unity"—and his emphasis on "identifying youth leaders preferably at an early age at school." To prevent the erosion of community, secularization should be opposed, as should city life, which leads to the disappearance of privacy and an increase in aggression. Members should be warned against subtle propaganda in the "more complicated environment," which led ordinary people to believe that they no longer had the expertise to make responsible decisions and thus placed great responsibility on leaders. Such seductive disinformation was part of the Total Onslaught, and the greatest threat posed by communism was its propaganda blitzkrieg. Ezuva recommended developing field schools to create an "island situation" where children could "reconcile nature with the Bible." The cache contained material on how these schools should be set up, generally along military lines. Documents reiterated the role of leadership, especially of headmen, and the importance of patriotism in defining leadership. Karl Marx was put down as being too lazy to work but, wanting to be rich, had developed communism to enrich himself. Communism, the tract went, sought to break down culture and tradition by encouraging revolution, which confused people and mocked government. It denied freedom of worship as well as private property. Communism was involved in promoting student unrest through, irony of irony, "front organizations." Ezuva, by contrast, was Christian, extolled free enterprise, and protected and expanded culture: "In order to achieve true freedom, a people must have a culture, it protects, it expands and develops. Groups are distinguished from one another by their various cultures." Indeed, "culture is a must, because it is an order from God. . . . Culture develops historically so that each group has its own language, building technique and general lifestyle." In truth, "God also extols workers to obey their employers because all authority comes from God." Spiritual pollution took place because youth were inclined to forget their history, culture, and traditions.

Kavango political organization was explained thus: "[The] father is the authority and leader of the family. A few families form a tribe. Each tribe has a captain with the authority. He makes the laws. A few tribes form the group. Legislative Assembly makes the laws. Executive Committee consists of a member or several members of various tribes." Ezuva was in favor of democracy, which was an "institution which makes it possible for the individual to have a say in his own affairs in a responsible manner." The advantage of democracy was that every five years the government can change, thus "democracy means true freedom" (*The Namibian*, 13 December 1985).

Playing Leporello to Pasques: Military Ethnologists

Since the early sixties, influential defense policy makers, including General Magnus Malan (later minister of defense), had argued for ethnology to be incorporated into the training regimen for officers.[16] In 1981 Brigadier F. S. Mulder, the officer commanding the Military Academy, repeated the case for ethnology because

> ethnocentrism can be regarded as one of the basic problems of white-black relations and required the correct perspective and insight into mutual cultures in multiracial situations, for example, it was essential for the incorporation of non-whites [*anderskleuriges*] into the SADF. Moreover, a study of the subject would help in making psychological warfare more effective in the African context. (G. Visser 2000, 441–42)

Nothing came of his proposal to integrate ethnology into the training of SADF staff. Yet, they did assume significant roles in other areas of the military. A striking affirmation of the high esteem in which ethnologists were held in these matters is, for example, that a Department of Plural Relations and Development ethnologist, Dr. A. O. Jackson, was a member of the Planning Secretariat of the Interdepartmental Counterinsurgency Committee from 1973 to 1978 and then served as coordinator for Community Development on that committee (van Wyk 2000, 39–40).

In 1975 General Malan established an ethnological division as a support unit within the Bureau for Military Information, part of the Department of Military Intelligence.[17] Its mission was to provide ethnological knowledge, not only for strategic and tactical operations but, more importantly, to "improve race relations," both within the defense force and between it and the black population, who suffered the brunt of military operations. Drawing on his American experiences, Malan argued that ethnologists were essential to advise on problems anticipated in the recruitment of nonwhites into the SADF. He appointed Colonel L. T. van Zyl as senior staff officer ethnology and tasked him with determining the most effective use of ethnologists, which van Zyl did by consulting with academics. A year later van Zyl and his subordinate, Commandant Pieter Möller, reported that ethnologists, especially if they were area specialists, could play a key role in the prevention and combating of insurgency or revolutionary warfare, since such wars centered on popular support from the local inhabitants. Ethnologists thus had both a training and an operational function. In the past, civilian ethnologists had occasionally given orientation lectures, but now it was proposed that all soldiers be required to attend standardized lectures in ethnology to obtain a basic knowledge of *anderskleurige* peoples and cultures, because it was assumed that such knowledge would lead to healthier relationships. The section would aggressively give lectures not only to permanent defense force personnel but also to part-time Citizen Force and Commando members as well as young people at youth preparedness camps. In addition, ethnologists would have an operational role by providing information that could be used in planning military operations, an activity that would be facilitated by developing an ethnological data bank of relevant information. It was a matter of urgency that all ethnologists be linguistically competent in one of the local Indigenous languages. In addition, it was proposed that each "homeland" have one or more military ethnologists assigned to develop in-depth cultural knowledge. Moreover, urban blacks, coloreds, and Indians should also have ethnologists assigned to study and monitor them. Van Zyl died shortly thereafter and was replaced by Möller (SO1 Burgerleiding [Civic guidance]).[18] Möller resigned in 1977 (at which point Commandant D. P. Stoffberg was appointed) but drew on his SADF experiences in a master's thesis presented to the University of Port Elizabeth (Möller 1978) on the application of ethnological knowledge in military situations. Since prevention was better than cure, Möller and van Zyl envisioned the SADF taking the initiative and playing a major role in improving race relations in South Africa. This vision was based on three observations. First, the SADF had a captive audience of thousands of young men doing their national call-up, which presented a golden opportunity to implant the idea of healthy ethnic and race relations based on reciprocal knowledge and understanding: "Ethnological knowledge should be part of the soldiers' weaponry. Peaceful co-existence can only be ensured when the cultural uniqueness of different ethnic nations [*andersvolkige landsburgers*] are considered and respected." Second, the recruitment of blacks into the SADF would result in deep cultural and racial differences within a single organization. Ill-judged actions concerning these differences would cause much friction. Third, the SADF would have to "bite the bullet" should the struggle to improve attitudes fail and a general confrontation emerged between different ethnic and racial groups (Möller 1978, 1).

In South-West Africa, the first and most influential military ethnologist was G.S. "Basjan" van Niekerk, who served from 1975 until independence in 1989. Having grown up on a farm in southern South-West Africa, he had attended Stellenbosch University as a relatively older student to study theology, intending to become a missionary in Kaokoland. Instead he switched to volkekunde. Armed with an honors degree, he was employed as a curator at the National Museum in Bloemfontein in 1974–75 and, in his own telling, asked by General Malan to give lectures to Commando units in central South-West Africa about the use of blacks in the military, since, as a South-West African, he had extensive local knowledge. The report that van Niekerk wrote on the task was passed on to Malan and, van Niekerk claimed, led (at least in Kaokoland) to the creation of the Civic Action Program. So impressed was Malan that he persuaded van Niekerk to accept a permanent post in the defense force. Appointed a major in 1977, he was placed in charge of all civic action projects in the Police Zone (P. Els 2016, 337–38). He was so successful that when the SWATF were created the following year, he was promoted to commandant by the new SADF commander, General Jannie Geldenhuys, an ardent WHAM proponent who, already in 1975 and then as director of military intelligence, had set up COMOPS to foster harmony between the SADF and the local population. Geldenhuys believed that while conventional warfare called for the exact sciences, insurgency called for the social sciences in order to gain the respect of the local population. This respect was to be achieved largely through the posting of intelligence officers to the Operational Area and engaging in what Geldenhuys termed "plow and plant" programs (Geldenhuys 2009, 88).

Organizationally the Civic Action Program and ethnologists resorted under COMOPS,[19] which was an essential feature of each command headquarters and focused on three broad areas: information gathering and interpretation; counterintelligence involving spying; and assessing its own forces and developing strategies to boost morale. Lastly, there was "communication," which entailed working with the local population in an effort to win their cooperation. A surprisingly large number of its officers were former teachers. To be admitted into COMOPS one had to take an oath swearing that one was a Christian, had never taken drugs, and was not a homosexual (Bakkes 2014, 108).

Paratus, the official SADF magazine, heralded van Niekerk's appointment with the headline "Ethnologists gain the blackman's respect," reporting that he was working on a master's thesis on Himba religion (though this was never completed). "Ethnologically speaking," van Niekerk is cited, relations between the SADF and the local population were healthy. Unless they were officially exempted, he reported, ethnologists did fieldwork in uniform. This was a research strategy he himself used: he would take medical supplies with him to show the locals that the SADF did not only kill but also healed. Van Niekerk boasted that the Himba accepted him: "I am already one of them and already belong to a descent group namely that of the *Ohorongo* (Kudu). I am classified by them as a Herero with the name of *Rubambaro*, which means long man who does not get fat." He had become a local hero when he saved a cow by stitching its torn udder and injecting antibiotics. Demonstrating his ethnological knowledge, van Niekerk claimed that Himba tolerated flies because flies were attracted by cow manure. The number of flies thus implied many cattle (D. Els 1977, 19)! Van Niekerk enjoyed rapid promotions to commandant and colonel, possibly because he was a member of the Broederbond. After Namibian independence in 1990, he became a tour guide and used his considerable raconteurial skills to impress naive international visitors and advising film crews seeking to film the "pristine Himba."

Van Niekerk managed to recruit two other ethnologists who, like him, were South-West Africans and had studied at Stellenbosch. Sarel Karsten had an honors degree and, after doing the requisite courses at the SA Intelligence School (SAINTS), was appointed in May 1978 as ethnologist in the south, headquartered in Keetmanshoop, where he did research, especially on the Nama, and developed manuals about how to work with other ethnic groups, largely in association with his colleague Salomé Visser. Transferred to headquarters in Windhoek in 1983, Karsten made a few studies of Owambo, the major operational area after the large military engagements there in 1984, including one about what the Air Force could expect on the ground and how to differentiate targets. He retired as a colonel, moved to South Africa, and opened a garage.[20]

Karsten was joined by Salomé Visser, who, after obtaining her honors degree in 1972, taught school geography until she signed up as civic affairs officer and ethnologist in 1979. *Paratus* featured her under the title "Her Love and Loyalty towards Her Country Knows No Boundaries" ("Haar liefde en lojaliteit jeens haar land ken geen grense" 1981, 50). Her job, she was cited, was to do research, which she then presented in the form of lectures and slides to national servicemen. She also lectured non-whites on the customs of whites. Asked to give an example of cultural difference, she pointed to the Bushman practice of burning down the shelter of a person who has died, drawing the conclusion that developers should not build permanent shelters. She retired in 1993 as a major and, reclaiming her Namibian citizenship, established herself as a tour guide, eventually building a luxury lodge on an island in the Caprivi, where she lived for ten years. In her memoir on her experiences there, she describes how she re-encountered a Bushman who had been her facilitator at Omega, coaching her in local etiquette and opening various social doors. Despite self-assuredly presenting herself in her memoirs as an ethnologist with knowledge of the customs and traditions of the country and the political and social milieu in the Caprivi, she failed to kneel and clap her hands in front of the chief and *khuta* (council) when she applied for a permit to build a tourist lodge (de Visser 2013, 9).

Like their ethnological colleagues in other commands, estimated at more than forty, Karsten and Visser barely met the advertised requirements for military ethnologists, which was set at a minimum of three years of university ethnology. Should more intensive specialist knowledge be required, the military could call upon a large number of professional university-based ethnologists who were members of the Citizen Force.[21] If this were not enough, it could also draw on ethnologists employed in the erstwhile BAD and other state organs like the NIS.

The activities of military ethnologists included visiting and advising defense force units, which ranged from the elite "Recces" to local Commandos (citizen militias), mostly on how to deal with Indigenes. Much effort was spent in developing and advising on programs to facilitate the incorporation of nonwhites into the defense force. Perhaps their most important task was sensitizing white troops to the local black population by providing "essential" ethnological guidance. The ethnologists would visit large employers of black labor and advise them on how to improve race relations and provide advice on matters such as kinship nomenclature (all those brothers and uncles!) and compensation for wrongful death (caused by the military). Another important activity, in which Karsten, like many of his colleagues in other commands, was heavily engaged, was helping to organize and instruct at youth camps for both whites and Indigenes.

Not all of these ethnologists were apparatchik clones. By 1988 Visser had been appointed a "civilian Bushman welfare liaison" at Omega, home of the 201 Bushman Battalion, composed of many former Angolan refugee-soldiers and a popular showpiece for SADF-squired visitors to the Operational Area. Out of frustration she complained about the serious problems in the camp to Colonel Delville Linford, the unit's founder, at the unit's fifteenth anniversary. The focus of the army was completely on the troops; families were treated as a nuisance, disabled veterans were ignored, and women and children were largely ignored. Omega was a tourist attraction—a road show—for visitors, with Bushmen being exploited to amuse visitors and politicians, Visser argued. When parties were held, more and more Bushmen came to observe whites and stare at their dancing. Bushmen were outsiders in their own camp, she concluded (Uys 1993, 203–4). The fact that Visser was willing to go outside the official lines of communication to raise this issue with a recently retired officer is indicative of her compassion and marginality, both as an ethnologist and female.

That the ethnologists were aware of their inability to fulfill their mission is clear from their 1985 proposal to recruit and train black ethnologists for the Operational Area. The problem they averred was threefold: white defense force personnel lacked linguistic, cultural, and customary knowledge of the Indigenous population; local interpreters were incapable of correct translations; and COMOPS was unable to obtain information through the interrogation of prisoners because interpreters were ignorant of ideological context. Rather, local blacks should be recruited to advise white COMOPS in the preparation of propaganda material aimed at the enemy and the local population; assist in planning COMOPS aimed at black military personnel; and help in training black communicators and generally assist in COMOPS actions aimed at local populations. To make it an attractive career, black ethnologists should receive ethnological instruction, which combined service and academic training; should be offered the opportunity to attend junior leadership courses and have a career path to at least that of major; and should be allowed to attend various COMOPS courses. Academic qualifications should include at least a year of university-level ethnology so that black ethnologists should acquire a broad knowledge of the "functions and customs of southern African people." Nothing came of this proposal, probably because of the lack of a pool of qualified recruits and possibly distrust of blacks in such a position.[22]

A Guide to Good Manners

In the SANDF archives, I managed to locate and access five roneoed and officially restricted typescripts going back to 1978 providing localized versions of how to deal with local people. Perhaps the most widely distributed one was *Die mense van SWA: 'n geo-etnologiese oorsig* (The people of SWA: A geo-ethnological overview) (S. Visser 1982), compiled by Salomé Visser, complete with an enthusiastic foreword by General Charles Lloyd, the officer commanding the SWATF, a leading WHAM proponent, and later secretary to the State Security Council. The book was largely another cookbook-style reprise of earlier manuals, which in turn were based on a template popularized by Bruwer (e.g., 1966a). It starts with the usual kaleidoscope moving up the cultural ladder from the Bushmen to coloreds—whites are not mentioned. The manual was characterized by a marked emphasis on etiquette, comportment, and clothing and advice on how to conduct interviews (key: always use interpreters). It had a section on tips for team leaders (officers and NCOs), practical tips (fifteen in number), and sixteen tips to remember (featuring advice like that blacks were never in a hurry; that for them work never ended; that they were very family bound, with many mothers and fathers; that they feared witch doctors, ancestral spirits, and other supernatural forces; and that they were not so stupid as to be unaware when lied to). The largest number of tips—some twenty-three—are admonitions about what not to do: not to use unwarranted words, drive through water sources, use a vehicle to chase livestock, drive away if one's vehicle has hit poultry or livestock, play with inflammable liquids, or overturn beer pots or litter.

The manual had a special section on how to behave toward black females. Black females, the manual informed, were regarded by locals as being of inferior status. Unless they were in a position of authority, one should not start to converse with them, as it would be taken as a sign of inferiority. If it was necessary to talk to a female, the permission of her husband had to be asked for if she was married or of her father if unmarried. Except in cases such as a serious accident or illness, one should not offer rides to women. It was unheard of among blacks for both sexes to swim together, and blacks thought bikinis ridiculous.

Ethnological Fellow Travelers

Where the military felt its expertise was lacking, it could also call on superiors from defense headquarters. The SANDF records show that Colonel Stoffberg, the officer in charge of ethnological services, made a number of research trips to South-West Africa, usually of a week or two in duration. A particular place of interest to him was the Omega base. Undoubtedly an important factor here was the international petition launched by Canadian anthropologist Richard Lee to protest the militarization of the Bushmen. Stoffberg claimed to have done research in Omega concerning their "upliftment." Acculturation had begun, he claimed, with other blacks and the Catholic mission before the SADF arrived on the scene, and he concluded that "in the present time (of) rapid development in the field of technology, it will not be possible for the Bushmen to exist in their primigenial [*sic*] state for very long and will perforce have to sacrifice their self-respect and identity in the long run."[23]

Bushmen continued to engage military ethnologists. In 1985 both Stoffberg and Commandant Ben Grobbelaar[24] made weeklong trips to the territory to respond to charges made by "leftist organizations abroad and in SA" that the SADF was a "negative change agent" preventing Bushmen from living their "national life," using them in operations in Botswana, and encouraging alcohol abuse and family disintegration among them. Both Grobbelaar and Stoffberg wore civilian clothes on these trips so as not to be associated with the military.[25] They were also asked to comment and critique John Marshall's Bushman Development Foundation, which claimed that local Ju/wasi were threatened with three alternatives: extinction, joining the military, or developing a new livestock-based subsistence economy.[26] Van Niekerk was placed on the Bushman Development Committee, created by the administrator-general to co-ordinate and integrate development in Bushmanland, distinct from the Marshall-inspired Bushman Development Foundation.

The State Security Council, however, felt that Stoffberg's work on Omega needed further study and, in late 1981, commissioned Pasques to investigate the possibility of developing a practical system of education of Bushmen at Omega, which would "realize their potential, to promote their economic growth and quality of life, to educate them politically, to open occupational possibilities and to support them in the creation of an infrastructure, which will make it possible for them to develop an autonomous viable future." It is worth discussing Pasques's report in some detail, as it is one of the few documents demonstrating his modus operandi. His research entailed reading the available literature, interviewing Europeans who worked at Omega, and questioning the "leadership element," teachers and older children through the use of interpreters. He also observed commodity purchases, games, cooking, and religious practices.

The traditional life style of Bushmen, Pasques reported, had drastically changed recently, and this caused confusion and loss of identity, resulting in numerous social and personal problems. The basic change was in the division of labor that now made men salaried workers while their wives had lots of leisure time. This led to a "spiritual decline" because, with their husbands away on six-week rotations, extramarital affairs were on the increase. Bushmen did not appreciate the value of money and wasted it on junk food. They were totally dependent upon whites, with whom they "completely identified," and if the SADF withdrew, the Bushmen would be "mercilessly exterminated." They were an obvious target for negative pro-SWAPO propaganda by Europeans, and this required urgent attention.

Since Bushmen had been placed in a Western milieu, there was a need for schooling without destroying the traditional. Bushmen had to be supported in cultural growth, but protecting what was "unique, namely their veld knowledge and their ability to stalk," and the curriculum should encourage this: "This very specialized knowledge of the Bushmen is a piece of tradition which only they possess. It will therefore be an immeasurable loss for this population group if they lose this knowledge. This loss will be extremely disadvantageous for the SADF as well because this knowledge is being very effectively used by the SADF." Moreover, urgent action was required to politicize Bushmen largely through education of children and adults because otherwise they would become a political football once they had been left by the SADF. They would be defenseless and gullible victims of neo-Marxism and communism.

To remedy the situation, Pasques urged developing and expanding field schools, utilizing the knowledge of older men. This would stimulate "a real love of nature and the soil that they can call their own. They have to learn in this field situation who their enemy are and that it includes Whites. They should also be made aware of the heroic deeds of their ancestors against the enemy in Angola who supported communism." Field schools would also facilitate identifying the

> natural leaders and the talented and place them in a 14-day veld-school which would develop their leadership, as well as increase participants' tolerance of stress, lead to improved self-knowledge, as well as positively influencing what was their own and appreciating the RSA, the Western weltanschauung, Christianity, and the free enterprise system while alerting them to the dangers of Neo-Marxism, Marxism and Communism. (Pasques 1982, 18)

Using the fashionable apartheid rhetoric of the era, Pasques concluded that the Omega Bushmen would not easily be incorporated into any of the other ethnic groups. Their future implied political self-determination, which was not possible without their own homeland. Patriotism only emerged and flourished with sovereignty over territory; Bushmen thus needed a homeland as speedily as possible. This could not be overemphasized, according to Pasques.

The major emphasis, thus, was on education aimed specifically at children and adult women, who would be taught in Afrikaans. Other recommendations slipped in, almost as an afterthought, included proclaiming Omega as a town and commercial center, to be gradually taken over by Bushmen, who would create a bus service (destinations not mentioned), all of which was meant to create employment.[27] SADF field officers engaged in passive resistance to this report, which they regarded as an outside intrusion, arguing that the recommendations should be undertaken by the educational authorities. Indeed, Pasques's recommendation that female social workers be appointed was vetoed by the SADF, who appointed a (female) ethnologist instead to serve as welfare officer.

Another ethnologist who played an influential role in the SADF deserves closer scrutiny, namely Jan Bradley. Although some of his and other ethnologists' shady activities are hard to verify, they do point to important networks of influence. Bradley (1970) did a master's thesis in anthropology at Potchefstroom University on Zulu culture. A Broederbond member since 1970, he was appointed ethnologist at the Department of Bantu Administration in Zululand (Wilkins and Strydom 1978) but soon found himself in the Kavango region advising the military on matters ethnological. He wrote the first report on the Bushman refugees at Omega in 1979. That same year, he was part of a special team sent by army headquarters to investigate the future of the (mercenary) 32 Buffalo Battalion (Nortje 2012, 326–33). In 1980 Bradley became director of the newly formed company Human and Labour Development Consultants (Pty) Ltd. "The task of this company was to help (covert operations units) with problems encountered among its various ethnic groups and to engender understanding of one another and the enemy" (P. Els 2000, 163). Known as "the man who can laugh in several languages," Bradley ran orientation courses for special forces, programs that were especially "meaningful as they stressed the significance of understanding and tolerance among the various cultural groups in Special Forces. This was particularly important in the support element as most of the problems occurred there. Women—black and white were also needed" (Els 2000, 174–75). The last sentence is tantalizingly ambiguous and open-ended.

In July 1984 Bradley proposed to General Geldenhuys, then head of the SADF, that he undertake a two-year ethnographic study of the Kavango and Owambo regions. The project would take two years because of the vastness of the territory, the ethnic and dialectical diversity encompassed, and the security situation. He would not be able to work while accompanied by soldiers, "because this will influence objectivity." Indeed, the project could not be done under the auspices of the SADF, as this would create suspicion and resistance. Bradley thus suggested that the project be camouflaged as emanating from the administrator-general, who would then allocate the "funds" to the Kavango regional government, which would provide "excellent cover." Another possibility was to have the study done under the aegis of a university, though this created a security risk. As a cover, he proposed that the projected be labeled "An Examination of the Manpower Potential of the Kavango Population with a View to Socio-economic Development with Specific Reference to Bottlenecks and Inhibiting Factors."

Three months later Bradley had a series of meetings with COMOPS and Pasques at the SWATF headquarters, where it was agreed to downscale the project for reasons of cost and to focus specifically on Owambo "tradition," especially in the most densely populated central Owambo region. Bradley agreed to prioritize the supernatural, then political organization, and finally religion (probably referring to the role of churches). Specifically, the military sought information of the role of witch doctors: their authority, who they were, their attitude toward the enemy and the government, and what symbols, rituals, and animal totems had religious value and how were they used. Concerning the churches, the military wanted to know their influence, to what degree they subscribed to the theology of revolution, what superstitions existed, and how these could be used. Concerning politics, the military wanted to know how politics was traditionally organized, who the leaders were, what authority they had, and what the relationship was between political parties and traditional authority.

Bradley undertook to complete the project within a year but finally delivered a forty-one-page report only two years later, in 1986. The scant report was not well received by SWATF headquarters. Officers complained that the report only dealt with Owambo traditional authority structures and that more than half contained material reprinted from the *Government Gazette*. There were, they diplomatically admitted, some interesting points about the tribal councils and home guard, and while the report was easy to read, the use of Owambo words was an unnecessary hindrance. Overall, they concluded that the report was disappointing, as it offered nothing concrete to act on. It identified problems that were already well-known but did not provide suggestions as to how they might be approached. Despite its cost of R 34,290, it offered no solutions or even guidelines. Moreover, the report was incomplete: sections dealing with the roles of women and witch doctors, respectively, were still outstanding. Indeed, the SWATF recommended that no further work be given to Bradley.[28] But Bradley had a knack for survival and in 1987 was placed in charge of running the Kavango Youth Movement, which was in all likelihood secretly set up by the SADF with the assistance of Pasques (Akuupa 2011, 144–45). During the UN-administered transition period leading to elections in SWA, Bradley turned up as interpreter for the Finnish battalion policing the Kavango and, with some Finns, coauthored an ethnographic pamphlet, *The Way of Life of the Mupapama River Terrace Community* (Eirola, Bradley, and Laitinen 1990), distinguished by making no reference to the recent war![29]

Other ethnologists the military could call on were those who were administration employees or former employees, like the veteran ethnologist Dr. Kuno Budack. In September 1974 he was listed as lieutenant in the South African army when he gave a lecture on ethnological aspects of the territory at a SADF-organized symposium for senior officers and officials on counterinsurgency. The speech was classified as secret.[30] In 1975 he published a guide on etiquette in the Kavango. While in German, it was given wide distribution, having originally been orally presented in 1973 (Budack 1975). Large chunks of this advice were incorporated into the military etiquette manuals (without proper acknowledgment).[31] Another source of expertise that could be drawn upon were universities. Thus the University of Stellenbosch undertook to codify the traditional laws of Owambo but apparently failed to deliver, although it was able to produce a master's thesis on Kavango law (van Rooyen 1977) and later one on community development at Omega (de Waal 1988).

Very late in the game, Johan Malan, Budack's former colleague in the BAD, was commissioned by Military Intelligence to do a survey of how the nineties' elections would turn out in Owambo. He recommended that the SADF import a *sangoma* (diviner or traditional healer) from Zimbabwe to persuade the electorate that SWAPO was the devil incarnate and that a famine would result if SWAPO won the election (Koch 1992). Malan paid intermittent visits to the area and published several papers on Owambo political attitudes and identity without mentioning the source of his funding (Malan 1982, 1990, 1995). While, as a Pentecostal Christian, he denied biological evolution, he described the changes in Owambo as being primarily a consequence of social evolution, as the kinship system moved from matriliny to patriliny as a result of the introduction of pastoralism. This had resulted in the chieftaincy losing its legitimacy, especially by being challenged by the modern elite and youth in political and religious matters. There was a large generation gap between youth and elders, exacerbated as youth became educated by teachers who were inculcating them with SWAPO ideology and slogans, while the pastors were challenging traditional leaders by incorporating politics into their activities. Apart from his simplistic model of social evolution, Malan recognized the importance of demographics, with over 60 percent of the population being under twenty-five years of age, although he ignored the fact that the military was by far the largest employer in the region.[32]

Notes

1. Malan's rise was undoubtedly helped by his father, a National Party senator with close connections to P. W. Botha, at that time minister of defense as well as a senior and influential member of the Broederbond.
2. Among Malan's rather sparse collection of papers deposited at the University of the Free State's Institute for Contemporary History are a surprising number of American roneoed tracts from the early sixties analyzing the Communist insurgency in Malaya and American ideas about counterinsurgency. Attached to several of them is a note suggesting that SADF officers study these articles. Malan appears to have been particularly impressed by Stewart Alsop's (1962) "Our New Strategy: The Alternatives to Total War."

3. Apart from Pretorius, several other officers did special courses courtesy of the US military, including the legendary Colonel Jan Breytenbach of 32 Battalion fame, who attended courses at Fort Benning from 1963 to 1964 (Dale 2014).

4. Pasques also managed to have the Messina High School renamed after Eric Louw, the rabble-rousing antisemitic minister of foreign affairs, who had no ties to the area.

5. The Total Onslaught was a rhetorical device based on the threat of the Soviet Union to South Africa, seen as the African economic and mineral powerhouse. It was intended to encourage support by Western governments and was used to repress blacks and justify regional destabilization.

6. The SADF proposed a national countermobilization project similar to Etango to the SSC, for which funding was approved three months later, in December 1985.

7. "Extension of Counter-Mobilisation Strategy" memorandum, Chief-of-Staff: Intelligence to the Head of the SADF, 29 July 1986, cited in "The National Party, Apartheid and the Anatomy of Repression in South Africa, 1948–1994," Nelson Mandela Center of Memory, O'Malley The Heart of Hope, https://www.nelsonmandela.org/omalley/index.php/site/q/03 lv02167/04lv02264/05lv02303/06lv02304/07lv02305/08lv02310.htm.

8. It was no accident that the only organization banned in the history of the territory was the German Boy Scouts movement in the thirties.

9. A lesson noted by Robert Baden-Powell, the founder of the Boy Scouts: "Scoutcraft is a means through which the veriest hooligan can be brought to higher thought and to the elements of faith in God" (www.brainyquote.com/quotes/robert_badenpowell_753097).

10. Ekongoro, a mythical snake, was the caretaker of the Kavango River.

11. Pasques was an enthusiastic proselytizer of youth camps. He so impressed the ethnologist Major Karsten at a special COMOPS course in early 1984 that the latter arranged for Pasques to visit Namaland to discuss instituting veld schools. Enthusiasm in the schools was lacking, however, and apparently nothing came of the effort. Material for this section is derived largely from the files "Burgersake 310/1/C/3/1 Jeugkampe" and "COMOPS 328/1/2," from the archive of the South African National Defence Force (hereafter cited as SANDF).

12. Pretorius's correspondence with the SADF suggests a different story, however. It suggests that he was seeking an appointment in the SADF's permanent force and collaborated closely with the security police in intelligence gathering.

13. In this they were following a Pasques-inspired South African precedent where, as Cawthra (1986, 57) reports, every summer hundreds of boys were "creamed off" for "leadership training" camps run by the SADF. There were 361 camps in 1984 alone.

14. Burgersake 310/1/C.3/1 Jeugkampe, SANDF.

15. SWA TF K O COMOPS BV 103/18/1/8/1, SANDF.

16. More details about the activities of the SADF's military ethnologists are to be found in Gordon 2017, which overlaps with this chapter but focuses on material such as the construction of etiquette manuals.

17. The SADF underwent several organizational realignments. Later, the ethnological services resorted under the Directorate Information Operations, itself part of COMOPS, a subsection of the SA Army Intelligence Corps. Here these services were code-named "Dribble," while "Eel" designated scientific research, "Harp" referred to archival services, and "Kidney" denoted current affairs.

18. Möller wrote a two-part article in the official SADF magazine, *Paratus*, making the case that "ethnology is a powerful weapon" (Möller 1975). The article attempted to legitimate the ethnology section: knowledge of the enemy's lifestyle was important, and ethnology studied how modes of living occurred within *volksverband* (one of those untranslatable Afrikaans words referring to national or ethnic allegiance). He then proceeded to discuss the Kenyan Mau-Mau movement, which he attributed to accelerated acculturation coupled with isolated and weak administration as well as a lack of information networks and knowledge of local languages. The second part, under the Afrikaans heading "What sort of people belong to which tribe and what do the ancestor spirits say?," focused on Rhodesia. He argued that

most of the LPs were neutral and that knowledgeable district commissioners, with their experience and knowledge of the spirit mediums, were effective in neutralizing the guerrilla tactics.

19. COMOPS, which resorted under the Department of Military Intelligence, also featured STRATCOM, which aimed to discredit the enemy, neutralize anti–South African propaganda, and boost anti-Marxist organizations. It operated both internally and abroad. Part of its covert operations remit was creating youth clubs, community organizations, women's clubs, and rural development and boosting traditional authorities. It was also responsible for the Civic Action Program, which entailed placing uniformed personnel as teachers, medics, vets, agriculturalists, and the like, who were expected to serve as informants on local developments (Mortimer and SANDF Nodal Point [1996]).

20. Information courtesy of Lieneke de Visser, who interviewed him 30 August 2014.

21. Intriguingly the SANDF Archives appear to have been purged of many of the files pertaining to the ethnological section.

22. SWA TF K O COMOPS BV 103/18/1/8/1, 30 March 1985, SANDF.

23. D. P. Stoffberg, letter to Robert J. Gordon, 20 November 1981.

24. Commandant Grobelaar was formerly an ethnologist at the State Museum in Windhoek. He completed a master's degree at Pretoria University on Kung Bushman technology before lecturing at the (Bantu) University of the North and later joining the SADF.

25. KOMOPS BV 103/18/1/8, SANDF.

26. AMI/MIB/328/2, undated, SANDF.

27. "Omega verslag Dr Pasques" (typescript), AMI (Group SWA) 175 161 8/10 Omega verslag Dr Pasques. SANDF.

28. KOMOPS 103/18/1/8 Top Secret, SANDF.

29. There are unconfirmed reports that Bradley was involved in Natal in advising and recruiting "turned" ANC soldiers or askari who were used in covert operations against the ANC. There is some suspicion that he was a member of the DST and that his longevity might be a result of that.

30. A611 Teen-Insurgensie Symposium, NAN.

31. Except for his service on the commission to inquire into the boundary dispute between the BaSubyia and MaFwe in the Eastern Caprivi in 1982, Budack's government and military services are glossed over in tributes to his contribution to Namibian science (von Schumann 2011).

32. Perhaps a more bizarre account features the notorious Civilian Cooperation Bureau, which regularly consulted with ethnologists and, on the advice of an unnamed ethnologist, attempted to intimidate Archbishop Tutu in 1989 by placing a baboon fetus in his garden. The ethnologist's claim was that by invoking Tutu's so-called tribal roots, he would believe that he was being bewitched (IOL 2000).

CHAPTER 5

Bringing Bonn Back In

Moritz Bonn had a keen appreciation for the incongruities of the human situation that led to his denunciation of colonialism. He realized that the raison d'être of colonialism, while decked in the rhetoric of gain and profit, lay largely in vanity or prestige. It is no accident that some of the greatest classics in the social sciences are based on this sense of incongruity. Consider Thorsten Veblen's mockery in *The Theory of Leisure Class* (1900), Goffman's wry humor as he dug through the absurd and dehumanizing dimensions of asylums (*Asylums* 1961), and C. Wright Mills's satirical gaze upon the power elite (*The Power Elite* 1956). But it is not enough to dismiss the work of these volkekundiges, or ethnologists, as simply ridiculous or as a pipe dream, as this underestimates the deep anxieties and insecurities that drove their praxis. The question must be addressed: How could these volkekundiges not see the obvious, or was it simply a case of aphasia—that they knew about it but could not express it? Was it because the form of knowledge they were practicing was what Christopher Hope recently labeled "voodoo ethnology"? By laying claim to historical, biological, or cultural facts, these ethnologists identified the enemy, despite the lack of agreement as to what constituted these "facts" (Hope 2018, 39). The net effect of their vocabulary, a pastiche of clichés and standardized modes of elliptical expression was, in essence, a simulacrum of scholarship. As Hannah Arendt (1981, 20) famously pointed out, such simulacra protect people from reality by discouraging critical questions or thinking about events and facts and mask political reality with empty language. These clichéd discourses also provided lenses through which descriptive confrontations with the realities of the process of colonization could be avoided. Of course clichés are essential, and we all use them, but their impact depends on the context in which they are used. Put differently, their expert knowledge was a form of capital of which the common currency was the "potted fact" (Fallon 2019). The *Oxford English Dictionary* (*OED*) defines "potted" as "a piece of information put into a short and easily recognizable form: condensed, summarized, abridged." The other meanings the *OED* provides add value to the term in this context: "preserved in a closed pot or other vehicle" and "under the influence of marijuana." Over time the ethnographic fairy tales volke-kundiges spun fashioned the actor orientation of different actors in what Ole Sending (2001) calls knowledge regimes, most importantly by crys-tallizing or inventing social categories that become the elementary units in the structure of internal pacification or colonial domination. By provid-ing ritual or symbolic imprimaturs to government policy in the form of shadow knowledge, volkekundiges helped fetter the colonial imagination that would otherwise have been subject to wild, undisciplined fantasies (Gordon 2014). In this they were ably assisted by their auxiliaries, the citizen scientists grouped around the SWA Scientific Society and their peculiar fixation on Bushmen.

Ethnology did not enlighten its audience but merely gave rise to a new form of domination, abetted through social scientific endeavor that pro-vided an authoritative voice that marshaled energy to be gainfully em-ployed constructing all sorts of sandcastles. At the same time local whites, the subalterns of settlerdom, were enabled to doubt the credibility and quality of knowledge that the "outside," international world was using to deny white settlers their claims to hegemony.

The lack of credibility of ethnologists reached its apex in the response by soldiers, field officers, and conscripts to the SADF ethnologists. One of the ethnologists' major activities was the production of etiquette manuals, which had two purposes: to avoid acrimony and to facilitate the collection of information by developing what Goffman called situational propriety. The manuals dealt with "asymmetrical rules of conduct" (Goffman 1967, 52) but, in their cookbook style, glossed over the intricacies of etiquette that, as Goffman points out, were not only linguistic but gestural, spatial, and task embedded. Etiquette is enacted through deference, a symbolic confirmation of a certain type of relationship with a client. In the SADF case, soldiers were called upon to engage in behavior toward blacks that was generally honorific, politely toned, and that displayed an apprecia-tion of the recipient that was supposedly more complementary than the soldier's true sentiments (Goffman 1967, 60). However, while etiquette could provide a gloss of order and predictability, it was inherently unstable because, consisting of a mix of avoidance and presentational rituals, there was a dialectical tension between the rituals that, somehow, had to be held apart from one another yet be realized together in the same encounter. This is where etiquette became interesting, because in the manuals white superiors were supposed to defer to black subordinates, yet the *routine* was channeled by historical expectations of racism and exploitation. Encounters were occasions of ambiguity, especially amplified by its sporadic nature, since,

> by easily showing a regard that he does not have, the actor can feel that he is pre-serving a kind of inner autonomy, holding off the ceremonial order by the very act of upholding it. And of course in scrupulously observing the proper forms he may find that he is free to insinuate all kinds of disregard by carefully modifying intona-tion, pronunciation, pacing, and so forth. (Goffman 1967, 58)

These ceremonial rules brought out the Janus-like character of etiquette: its Machiavellian face emphasizing performance and manipulation, while the other face was distinctly Durkheimian, celebrating the wider social values underlying the encounter (exploitative as they might have been). Etiquette masked high ideological stakes, since participants did not neces-sarily accept the values on which it was based. As Goffman points out in his classic *The Presentation of Self in Everyday Life*, in this kind of interac-tional *modus vivendi*,

> together the participants contribute to a single over-all definition of the situation which involves not so much a real agreement as to what exists but rather a real agreement as whose claims concerning what issues will be temporarily honored. Real agreement will also exist concerning the desirability of avoiding an open con-flict. . . . I will refer to this level of agreement as a working consensus. (Goffman 1959, 9–10)

Blacks were certainly not taken in. In a study of a Namibian mine com-pound, black mine workers were found to be actively manipulating eti-quette to protect their "back regions," areas of social interaction to which they did not want whites to be a party. A major source of black prestige was to outsmart whites in the game of etiquette, usually by way of credible, or at least acceptable, excuses for a range of acts ranging from inefficient work, truculence, "accidental" theft, and interrupted routines (Gordon 1977, 120–42). Given the power differential, something that the manuals largely ignore, blacks had to be sensitive observers of white ritual nuances.

Like their colleagues in the world of South African capitalist industry, the SADF ethnologists, like Bruwer, suffered the delusion that simply by changing interpersonal interaction, all their problems would vanish, while ignoring structural inequalities.[1] At the same time the etiquette manuals created the self-sustaining illusion that whites were civilized, fair, and just. In the final analysis, these manuals did not produce social order. Rather, they exhibited and reinforced the racial order, and their purpose was not so much social control of white soldiers as their internal pacification.

In the copious and growing memoir literature on the Border War, al-most without exception, issues even vaguely related to the Civic Action

Program or interaction with the local populations are largely unmentioned.[2] This silence has been attributed to censorship, possible public stigma, and a sense of loyalty soldiers had to each other (Baines 2015). Another factor was simply racism. Eugene de Kock, the notorious apartheid assassin who served in Koevoet in the Operational Area in 1978, recalled how virtually every white person in the security forces "completely disregarded the Ovambo people and their culture" despite serving in the same unit and undertaking joint patrols (Jansen 2015, 74). Interviews I conducted with former national servicemen did not recall these lectures on etiquette except for occasional talks by the base chaplain exhorting soldiers not to mutilate dead bodies. Mostly servicemen were ordered to avoid contact with local people, who were seen as potential security risks. Several former officers claimed the manuals and the lectures were so simplistic that they lacked all credibility. One commandant on the Kavango complained to John Seiler, a visiting American scholar, "All ethnologists are soft in the head—living up in the clouds. There is nothing you can do with their information." Ethnologists were believed to be too theoretical and not practical enough. Dr. Maria Fisch,[3] the government ethnologist and SADF collaborator stationed on the Kavango, was derisively dismissed as "a walking encyclopedia on the Kavango as it was 30 years ago not as it is here now" (Seiler 1988. Field officers derogatorily referred to ethnologists as *gatkruipers* (ass lickers), not of whites but of blacks (Bakkes 2014, 113–14).

Indeed, as described in the previous chapter, the absurdities abound concerning advice proffered by ethnologists. But perhaps the most dismissive of ethnologists was Colonel Jan Breytenbach, charismatic founder of 32 Buffalo Battalion, long-term West Caprivi resident, and ardent romantic Bushmanophile. He rejected the do-gooder and all-knowing theorists, "so-called ethnologists with degrees in ethnology from Pretoria"[4] who, "ensconced in claustrophobic offices in Pretoria," were concerned with "upliftment." He continued, this "clutch of ethnologists, none of whom had ever clapped eyes on a real Bushman but all of whom were instant experts. . . . One ethnologist, who ruled the roost, became as persistent as a housefly around a dog's faeces" (Breytenbach [1997] 2015, 103). Breytenbach refused to have anything to do with him and ordered him never to set foot in Buffalo camp. Then came the denouement:

> Upliftment was complete. The out of touch theorists from Pretoria proudly showed parties of important persons around the various establishments such as the modern hospital, the Church, messes, modern *kimbos*, home crafts shop and so on. The visitors admired the neatly dressed but somehow remote little bushmen soldiers and referred to them as South Africa's own Gurkha troops—the terror of SWAPO which, sadly, they were not.

Visitors always spent a delightful evening and night in the bosom of the battalion with lots to eat and drink, romantic wooden huts to sleep in and the beating drums from the bushman *kimbo* to remind them that they were in "deepest" Africa. They returned to the Republic with nothing but praise for the battalion and a wildly superficial impression of the bushman soldiers and the bushmen families.

The tragedy is that in this process of being uplifted, the Bushmen lost all their empathy for the African bush and its creatures. They also lost respect for their former culture. Inadvertently, perhaps, they have been taught to view their former existence, as hunter-gatherers, with distaste and even shame.

Our ethnologist from Pretoria, and his colleagues had done the job so well that in a few short years they totally destroyed an innocent, environment oriented primitive culture and offered in its place the cynical, greedy selfish culture of Western man.

Today the Caprivi Bushmen find themselves in the same sorry state as many of the Australian aborigines. They lounge around drunk, listless, quarrelsome and utterly incapable of competing economically with the blacks or whites of southern Africa. They are helplessly caught in the web of a world they cannot understand, and which is sucking their ancient spirit out of them like an insatiable spider. (Breytenbach [1997] 2015, 106–7)

With his romantic primordialism and by deliberately ignoring the wider socioeconomic context, Breytenbach exaggerated the culpability of ethnologists but highlighted the tension, indeed conflict, between line and staff officers. From the onset, says Annette Seegers, debates in the SADF "held that military experience counted for more than intellectual or staff ability. Staff courses and later joint staff courses at the Defense College favored those with operational experience. . . . Even for its elite, the SADF thought theory best ignored" (Seegers 1996, 141). As she noted, the SADF was not particularly hospitable to research-oriented graduates. Indeed, just over 16 percent of officers had university degrees, so that most officers with degrees in the social sciences found themselves shifted from operational or line duties to staff functions in Military Intelligence, NIS, or SSC (Seegers 1990, 210). This situation was exacerbated by the rapid expansion of Military Intelligence. An officer explained to Steven Ellis (1998, 278):

Most of them are civilians, you see. They get a degree, and so on, and he joins the Defence Force and he puts on a uniform and now he's a colonel, or he's a major, or he's a brigadier, or he's a corporal, or whatever. But now he's get status. But he's not a fighter . . . CSI [Chief of Staff, Intelligence] is Intelligence, and being Intelligence they are always secret. And when you are secret you can do all sorts of weird and wonderful things without anybody knowing what you are doing.

Clearly ethnologists suffered from a lack not only of good or even bad ideas but of credibility. Unlike the audience for World War II guidebooks,

SADF personnel grew up with firsthand experience of blacks. It was a common refrain, uttered not only by ordinary whites but even in the hallowed halls at the League of Nations that South Africans did not need anthropological expertise because they had over 250 years of practical experience dealing with blacks. The manuals, in effect, sanctioned certain types of behavior and censored other forms. This had two consequences: soldiers felt that they were being misled, and more subtly, the manuals/ lectures that the ethnologists gave made soldiers aware that they did not know what they did not know, as they had not heard about alternatives. The trouble was that neither had the military ethnologists, who ended up as much victims as the soldiers.

But perhaps the critics had a point: military ethnologists' work was overwhelmingly static, even ludicrous, with no sense of history. They had unrealistic notions of what motivated the lives of others and how those lives changed. Their presentation of culture was of a one-dimensional, internally harmonious, clearly bounded unit. Modern influences were benign if they derived from the SADF and malignant if derived from sources critical of South Africa (Seiler 1988).[5]

Even with the aid of these manuals, interaction with blacks was still a structured ambiguity, which meant that soldiers could never be certain about blacks nor blacks of soldiers. Appearances were deceptive. In the early seventies, Theodore Schwartz (1973, 153–74) suggested that in threatening environments, in situations of extreme uncertainty, and where social and political life was under threat, a paranoid ethos characterized by suspicion and sensitivity to others' motives is likely to emerge, and malice is thought to be omnipresent. In such situations, even the colonizers' best intentions are subject to doubt, with ulterior motives being ascribed. This is why efforts at proper etiquette and WHAM were structurally bound to fail. On the other hand, the settler *Umwelt*, the social space from which signs for alarm can come, created the dominant ethos in settler colonies, which Agamben (2005) called *état de siège*, or besiegement. In the Operational Area, *Umwelt* was reality magnified. Ethnological concerns as epitomized in the manuals, and especially in intelligence gathering operations, were not so much involved with appreciating cultural diversity or Indigenous ingenuity as with "undercurrents" and uncovering the "secrets of the 'Native.'" Like the officers in Jaroslav Hašek's classic anti-war novel *The Good Soldier Švejk* ([1923] 1974), settlers, soldiers, and the ethnologists could not decide whether Indigenes were stupid or having them on. At best Indigenes were *draadsitters* (fence-sitters).

Military ethnologists were schooled in *volksuniversiteite*, which stressed reverential acceptance of professorial authority. To challenge or query Bruwer's imaginings and ordering of Namibian cultures would have been seen as seditious by superiors. The rhetoric of volkekunde was exhortatory in style, intended to reinforce the convictions of the audience rather than to convince opponents (who hardly read Afrikaans anyway). A super-organic version of culture framed their activities, and thus enculturation had to be taken seriously, so seriously in fact that a prominent and influential volkekunde professor went so far as to make a strong plea that whites should not leave their children in the care of black servants, as this would lead to children becoming spiritually twisted and mentally "bantuized" (Gordon 1991, 87)! In their review of volkekunde, Jansen van Rensburg and van der Waal (1999, 50) note the near-absolute fixation with primordialism and the incommensurable gap between white and black cultures, so much so that as late as 1980 one volkekundige wrote a book arguing that a single society in South Africa was impossible (Mönnig 1980). At Pretoria, the leading Afrikaans university and purveyor of military ethnologists, rote learning was the staple, and to obtain a degree one had to answer that separate development was the only realistic solution to South Africa's ethnic problems (Swanepoel 1997, 37). The dominant analytical framework they used was that of acculturation (Els 1992), which, while still popular among cross-cultural psychologists, has long been dismissed by anthropologists for its inherent ethnocentrism and its mechanistic, unilineal, and assimilationist assumptions (e.g., Harris 1969). Undoubtedly acculturation sat well with a primordialist weltanschauung. Jansen van Rensburg and van der Waal suspect a link between the primordialist position and the authority of the (male) ethnologist that prevented too close an association with informants. Indeed, the relationship between ethnologist and informants was mostly of a formal nature, and they cite the advice of R. D. Coertze, the leading volkekundige, to end the relationship if participation is likely to occur. The danger of too close a relationship was real, and thus females should be interviewed only by female research assistants. Significantly, Coertze wrote not of participant observation, which was dismissed because participant observers engaged without knowing what they were observing, but of "interrogation in depth." Informants, he claimed, should be engaged with permission from the relevant authorities and were thus (hopefully) chosen for their expertise (Jansen van Rensburg and van der Waal 1999, 50). From this perspective, then, the various ethnology manuals with their emphasis on rigid etiquette and reliance on interpreters make sense because, in the final analysis, while ostensibly designed to facilitate information gathering, they served as a prophylactic to understanding and comprehension.

As in Orwell's classic tale of shooting an elephant, even if the ethnologists wanted to take a liberal line, their audience compelled them to adhere to the racist doctrine. In such a racist situation it was no use urinating into the wind (to use a common army expression). They were very much a product of a larger, highly racist situation. In the seventies, the SADF was not especially unique. Liberal capitalism promoted similar strategies when large industry and the Chamber of Mines, concerned about spiraling wages and the acute shortage of white skilled labor, discovered the importance of encouraging black labor. There was also concern about labor unrest, and as a result, large corporations started hiring anthropologists to advise them. In fact, that was how I got hired by a large mining corporation (Gordon 1977).

For all the vaunted claims of success for WHAM and countermobilization projects, there was perhaps a simpler explanation for their supposed success that these boosters overlooked, namely employment. In 1988 the military employed more than a third of the total formal workforce in the Operational Area as soldiers or as laborers. Moreover, the wages they paid were considerably higher than the average earned in other occupations or through contract labor, and these earnings had a considerable multiplier effect, especially in the burgeoning informal economy epitomized by some twelve thousand "cuca shops" (unlicensed establishments selling beer) (I. van der Merwe 1990, 5–6).

These SADF journeyman ethnologists, who mostly had an honors degree or four years of anthropology, were not expected to do extended fieldwork. Usually fieldwork was carried out for a few days or weeks, and then they were usually compelled to wear a uniform. The linguistic competence of these ethnologists was also limited. Ethnological research appears to have consisted largely of trawling the existing literature for insights and data, thus building on antiquated notions from the past. Moreover, the theses that these ethnologists consulted must be considered suspect. Consider the cases of two of Bruwer's master's students: J. C. "Boet" Kotzé who was later to courageously step away from the volkekunde paradigm, did a thesis on Kuanyama (Ovambo) values based on fieldwork in 1966–67. The major impediment to research, he claimed, was the heavy sand that limited mobility (Kotzé 1968). Left unsaid was that he was employed as an assistant native commissioner at the border post of Oshikango and that his office was attacked and burned down by SWAPO, resulting in the loss of his fieldnotes. Another student, Walter Louw, wrote on the traditional political structure of the Ngandjera and paid periodic visits to their area while employed as an information officer in 1965–66. The only informants mentioned were Chief Ushona Shiimi (later assassinated), the chief's personal advisers, and the tribal secretary (Louw 1967).

Judging from his master's thesis, though, Jan Bradley was perhaps the most delusional. During his five-month Zulu fieldwork, he resided in the home of the commissioner-general, Evert Potgieter, a volkekundige and prominent Broeder. Bradley used seven male informants and claimed that because of his "reasonable knowledge of Zulu customs," he had no trouble in obtaining the trust of informants (Bradley 1970). Trust, as Katherine Verdery noted, is essential for establishing rapport and underpins the ethnographer's relationship to their informants, and while it is possible to gain insights without it, the best ethnographies depend upon it. In a milieu of gross inequality and enhanced surveillance as in a war zone, there is a constant undercurrent of mistrust and doubt (Verdery 2012, 21). The work of scholarship, as David Graeber (2012) says, is interpretive labor that requires the ability to empathize with the subjects studied. In an increasingly hierarchical society, while the people at the bottom can imagine themselves in the place of those in power, it becomes increasingly difficult for the elite to imagine themselves as the poor and the downtrodden.

Schoeman's Bushman Haunts

The genealogy of these shortcomings can be traced directly back to Bruwer and Schoeman, who, despite his reputation in Afrikaans literary circles as a legendary fieldworker, never trusted the "natives." "If you offer them a finger they grab the hand," he complained to the minister of native affairs in a letter seeking employment.[6] In retrospect, Bushmen were well advised to reciprocate and not trust Schoeman.

Bushmen have played many roles in the settler imagination. If there is one ethnic group that has been commodified, scientifically and commercially, it was that labeled variously as Bushmen or San. Their spectral presence was the bedrock in justifying the difference between "us" (meaning Europeans) and "them." They have been used with formulaic regularity by experts in justifying difference in a legacy stretching back to the German era, enjoying prominence in the hallowed halls of Geneva and continuing in the ICJ presentations to the present.[7] Bushmen represent the negative inversion of bureaucratic rationality and the Enlightenment of which settlers imagined they were the proud possessors. Schoeman, especially in his popular writings, played off and shaped the "Bushman image," yet his praxis was rife with contradictions.

The role and place of dissonance—moral, academic, and intellectual— and even absurdity in the intellectual history of apartheid has not been given much attention, but is illustrated in the careers of the ethnologists highlighted in this book. How does one deal with Schoeman's awareness of his chief informant Xameb's description of suffering in *Hunters of the Desert Land* yet his failure to mention these atrocities in his official reports? Again, Schoeman was not unique in this. Bruwer and military ethnologists faced similar dilemmas.

One strategy was intellectual compartmentalization, which in Schoeman's case was a direct consequence of his interpretation of Malinowskian theory. Apart from the Malinowskian notion of the tribe or group as an isolate, there was Malinowski's notion of the primary drives of food and sex, especially the latter, in creating culture. This concept is observable throughout Schoeman's writings. In his early clarion call for "total segregation" in South Africa (Schoeman 1941), he argued for the necessity of strict physical segregation, with black women especially well removed from white contact, and the need to develop black pride, as only then would blacks be dissuaded from wanting to intermarry with Afrikaners. Also recall how Schoeman's explanations of Bushman population decline concerned miscegenation and, horror of horrors, how, as he was about to take his leave of Xameb, the spirit Eliob wanted to send him a beautiful female duiker to throw wood on his fire every night! This curious obsession with sex and especially miscegenation is reminiscent of the attitudes of other apartheid theoreticians such as Geoff Cronje. Miscegenation, they believed, would destroy the group as a cultural isolate. As J. M. Coetzee noted, such ideologues justified apartheid in terms of the long-term interests of whites, but "what animated these worthies may have been, not the altruism they claimed, but on the contrary the crassest absorption in their own passions and appetites, and that their justificatory utterances may have been no more than a cover for the deepest indifference to the fate of their descendants" (Coetzee 1996, 164). The SADF ethnologists engaged in epistemological mimicry of Schoeman, and the obsessive concern with miscegenation was carried over into their etiquette manuals, which urged avoidance of women. While there were many reasons why countermobilization failed, perhaps one of the major ones was that it overlooked women. Women were to be avoided and ignored, despite the crucial role they played in the war, not necessarily as combatants but as supporters of combatants.

Schoeman's literary meanderings met a receptive readership among the settlers, as epitomized by the activities of the SWA Scientific Society. In dealing with this curious obsession with the Bushmen by the local notables of science, one could consider the dominant role of the natural sciences in the listing of work groups of the society and the powerful impact of the Pfadfinder on German cultural life in Namibia to note that the largely mythical pristine Bushman is the Pfadfinder and natural scientist *par excellence*. Among the most popular books the society sells, with translations into English and Afrikaans, is Peter Stark's *Der Weisse Buschmann*, which details his adventures first as a poacher and then his redemption as a game warden, when he used his Bushman knowledge to combat poachers. Henno Martin's *Wenn es Krieg gibt, gehen wir in die Wüste: Eine Robinsonade in der Namib* (also available in English as *The Sheltering Desert* and in Afrikaans) is of greater vintage. It chronicles the adventures of a young German geologist who, in order to escape intern-

ment during World War II, escaped for two years into the Namib Desert
with a colleague and a dog—proof that scientific knowledge can help one
triumph over the harshest adversity. That the Bushman mystique spoke to
a broader settler audience is obvious by the huge success of the "live Bushman exhibit," even visited by the governor-general, for which Schoeman
was the impresario as part of the SWA contribution to the Van Riebeeck
Festival held in Cape Town in 1952 to celebrate three hundred years of
colonialism (Gordon, Rassool, and Witz 1996). Perhaps such fantasies are
the stuff science is propelled by?

Clearly the society, while promoting science, was also associating it
with Germanness. It facilitated Deutschtum by subscribing to the ostensible universal appreciation of good science.[8] And good science in turn
provided an important moral argument for the Herrenvolk to have their
colonies returned to them—as any casual perusal of the pages of the *Koloniale Rundschau* from the interwar years attests.

Rituals perform, and in this case helped freeze in time, some ideas of
German ethnology from the late nineteenth century. What emerged from
this complex interplay with metropolitan science was a way of conceptualiz-
ing problems, with its own specialized vocabulary. The result was a colonial
science that prided itself on its practical applications. It was a "derivative,"
inventorying science done by lesser minds working on problems set by
savants in Germany—or South Africa. As befits "low science," it was identified with fact gathering done by amateurs, while the theoretical synthesis
was still expected to take place in the metropole, either preferably Germany,
or South Africa (Gill 1926/27; MacLeod 1987)—and it was not difficult to
find savants to underwrite this particular stance. Thus, what was absorbed
was a biological science, one with a dark variation that fitted in rather well
with the emerging policy of apartheid. And it is in this context that one
must understand the survival of the Peter Pan–like representations of Bushmen. The focus on Bushmen was fundamental to the activities of the SWA
Scientific Society, and this brought to the fore a tension: while Bushmen
were the object of rather typical colonial abjection, they were also the main
vehicle for the bestowal of respectability for the society insofar as reifica-
tion of Bushmen provided an important basis for the society's claim to be
engaged in metropolitan science. Bushmen provided an important example
of how the metropole can define the value of scientific artifacts. Locally,
most settlers thought of them as a nuisance, indeed as vermin, and actively
wanted to get rid of them (Gordon 2009). Yet, since the metropole defined
them as important scientific commodities, this led to local ideological re-
appreciation of their role and place in society. Not only were they used as
the measure from which colonial progress could be favorably and proudly
gauged, but Bushmen also served as a key validation for the development of
museums in Namibia to serve as repositories of what later became known

as the "national heritage." All museums in Namibia had prominent Bush-man displays of some kind or another. This fixation, indeed scholarly love, of Bushmen served to destabilize black claims to legitimacy because it was simply assumed that blacks exterminated Bushmen. But it is also shadow knowledge par excellence because Bushmen are seen in an essentialized, timeless, and decontextualized society in which colonial brutality is conveniently ignored. This shadow knowledge served to propel further studies of Bushmen as salvage. Moreover, and this should not be overlooked, these objects/artifacts that are taken to be representations of the other were selected by (quasi) scientists and not by the Indigenes themselves and, as such, served to legitimize settlers' positions of power and privilege. The ideological importance, indeed fossilization, of the notion of pristine Bush-men was underlined in dramatic fashion at the ICJ in The Hague, where Bushmen were used as the example of innate group difference and thus the raison d'être for apartheid.

These imported discourses also provided lenses through which descriptive confrontations with the realities of the process of colonization could be avoided. Science provided the means to fantasize about the nature of the colonial world. The image of scientific knowledge as portrayed by the SWA Scientific Society—objective, fair, and discerning—serves as an important counterpoint to the image of "the native"—impulsive, irrational, and undiscerning. In an astonishing act of self-imagining, seen most prominently with the arrival of the crew of the good ship *Meteor*, and in the pages of their *Mitteilungen*, they saw themselves as part of a cosmopolitan world of science, as intellectual kin to the von Humboldt brothers and European scientists rather than individuals involved in the local instrumentalities of colonial oppression. Their imagined community was one based on the Renaissance. Their scientific selves helped them to evade Namibia's colonial realities. The discourse of science helped them evade reality and construct a sense of self and other as part of the development of civilization. Such was the ideological hegemony of the pristine Bush-men that it was only in the late eighties that alternative representations of Bushmen as victims of genocide, as the most victimized of all Southern Africa's bloody victims, started to challenge this representation.

Ethnography as Divination: The Centrifugal Pull of Bruwer

Undoubtedly Bruwer was the fulcrum around which later "native expertise" (r)evolved. Not only could he claim the most extensive fieldwork experience, but he was also the most well-connected to the upper echelons of the state and played an important role in trying to imagine and implement apartheid. A consideration of Bruwer raises the question of how scholars naively believed that the objects of their studies were going to accept that they were being objective or that Bruwer's cover of studying land tenure systems was going to be credible. How could Bruwer make serious statements that are, in retrospect, laughable? In the context of expert knowledge concerning Namibia, was he wrong, wrong-headed, or simply refusing to see reality, or all three? Was Bruwer simply cynically manipulating the intellectual preferences of the international world? Could his praxis have had some ritual value?

While the sanitation-conscious van Warmelo was obsessed with private toilet practices and deceptive dress, much of Bruwer's ethnography was propelled by a concern for discerning *undercurrents*. What motivated most Namibian volkekundige ethnography was a concern not for pattern or customs but for uncovering secrets. Patterns or customs were incidental to discerning truth or truth beneath appearances. In many ways Bruwer's praxis mirrored that of divination. As in witchcraft beliefs, whites believed blacks to be a potential source of disorder capable of destroying "normality." Divination is an attempt to see underneath appearances. It is an effort to uncover what is perceived to be the infrastructure, that is, the circulation, valorization, and revelation of what is believed to be protected or secret knowledge. Divination or ethnographic research is an "evidentiary proxy" that "gives material shape to, and thereby reproduces as social reality, the ideologies of invisible essences and agencies on which they are based" (Palmié 2007, 207). The metaphor can perhaps be extended to see apartheid as a form of magical practice: if certain actions were enacted they would create a condition for the human good, but it was magical in that the requisite ends-means relationship and the essential causal circuitry are taken on faith rather than by empirical verification. Such an analogy is heuristically useful, as it draws attention to similarities across what were treated separately as different and makes the strange familiar.

A key to the ethnographic enterprise, especially divination, are conspiracy theories that are generally harmless, but in Bruwer's case they had important ripple effects impacting the lives of many and stretching to the Border War. The extensive psychological literature on conspiracy theories (see, for example, Douglas, Sutton, and Cichocka 2017; Lantian et al. 2017) suggests a number of implications for understanding conspiracy theory practitioners. While sometimes conspiracies can be real, they are generally false because their purveyors are either self-defined as outsiders with no political power trying to impose a narrative on the world they do not understand or they are insiders with power who propound them to deflect blame for their own inefficiencies or ineptitude by blaming malicious external forces, in effect absolving themselves from responsibility for the situation. Such theorists depend on pattern recognition emerging when something is suspected of being out of place. Humans do not like unanticipated or abnormal happenings, and thus these theories facilitate making sense of the world when people are anxious or feel powerless when they perceive their world as out of control and their normal lifestyle is threatened. Such people tend to exaggerate threats, and this serves as a coping mechanism, helping them explain or justify their anxieties. At the same time, it allows one to explain events without challenging ones' own worldview. Moreover, a conspiracy theory offers the opportunity to proclaim hidden, important, and immediate knowledge so that the believer can become an expert, possessing knowledge not even held by other so-called experts, and thus achieve a certain level of uniqueness. To be sure, some conspiracy theories might be factually wrong, but many contain elements of truth and need to be seen as meaningful responses to social, political, and cultural conditions. Sometimes conspiracies can be proved, and indeed I develop some conspiracy theories of my own that need to be falsified. It should be noted, of course, that conspiracy theories are not a unique right-wing activity but are almost as common among people who define themselves as liberal or progressive.

Conspiracy theories are the conjoined twin to pseudoscience, famously defined by Popper (1963) as dealing with complex problems without a hint of uncertainty, hesitancy, or doubt and presenting largely circular arguments presenting a mass of material to support their arguments but ignoring material that contradicts their conclusions. Proper science, Popper maintained, can be proved wrong or is falsifiable.[9]

Debunking conspiracy theories is often difficult, as such theories have a self-insulating quality and, in extreme cases, are impervious to contrary evidence. Richard Hofstadter, in his famous essay "The Paranoid Style in American Politics," understood that the paranoid style was directed against a nation or a way of life, whose fate affected not only the spokespersons but multitudes of others, insofar as spokespersons did not usually see themselves singled out as the individual victim of a personal conspiracy but as somewhat more rational and more disinterested. Characteristically such spokespeople saw their political passions as unselfish and patriotic, and this intensified their feelings of righteousness and moral indignation (Hofstadter 1964).

The Janis Face of Ethnology: The Broederbond and "Groupthink"

Hermann Giliomee, the foremost chronicler of Afrikaner history, dismisses as a peculiarity the myth of the Broederbond as a powerful all-present organization that is especially believed by its most biased opponents. The Broederbond, he claims, was largely used as a sounding board for government policy, except in the sixties when Verwoerd's power was at its peak, a period during which it played the role of ideological policeman (Giliomee 2004, 373). While there is much merit in his conclusion, it ignores the sociological and psychological significance and dynamics of secret societies. Groupthink is defined by Yale psychologist Irving Janis (1982, 9) as "a mode of thinking that people engage in when they are deeply involved in a cohesive in-group, when the members' strivings for unanimity override their motivation to realistically appraise alternative courses of action." It is exemplified by excessive concurrence-seeking among members of prestigious tight-knit groups formulating policy who place such an optimal value on their membership that they "suppress personal doubts, silence dissenters, and follow the leader's suggestions." Ideologically it had a strong belief in the inherent morality of the group, while their opponents were defined as decidedly evil. In combination these deficiencies made such groups "vulnerable to initiate or sustain projects that turn out to be policy fiascos" (Hart 1991, 247). This is further enhanced by the fact that Broederbonders had access to secret information, which promoted what Travers calls the "secrecy heuristic" in which people believe secret documents to be of higher quality than public ones and regard decisions based on secret information more favorably than those grounded in public information (Travers, van Boven, and Judd 2014).

What were the social features that created this Hofstadterian self-insulating mode of thinking and action? It is almost a sociological truism that organizations, especially secret ones like the Broederbond, that "immense informal network of influence" of upwardly mobile Afrikaner men (O'Meara 1983, 64), develop groupthink, the collective mindset that served to inoculate the group against uncomfortable truths and disconfirming information. Sociologically, the Broederbond would be classified as a "greedy institution," an organization that "seek[s] exclusive and undivided loyalty and . . . attempt[s] to reduce the claims of competing roles and status positions on those they wish to encompass within their boundaries. Their demands on the person are omnivorous" (Coser 1974, 4). As an institution, the Broederbond formally sought formal voluntary compliance for its almost unlimited claim to the individual's cathexical (mental and emotional) energy. Members of the Broederbond were enmeshed in a web of inter- and cross-locking group affiliations in several public front organizations such as the Rapportryers and the Federasie vir Afrikaanse Kultuur (FAK) to which Broeders invariably belonged. At the same time, membership of potential rival organizations, such as the Freemasons or the Rotarians, was strictly prohibited or discouraged. Assent to abiding by its rules was maximized by appearing as highly desirable to members through the offer of exclusive benefits, such as insight and participation in the making of history, access to "backstage truth," and a strong elitist sense of belonging to an exclusive cadre. Stan Cohen, in his classic *States of Denial,* emphasizes some of the organizational consequences when the organization sees itself

as invulnerable and unanimous; personal doubts are suppressed, incoming information is screened and accounts are circulated to bolster the members' sense that whatever they do must be justified; unspoken arrangements allow for concerted ignorance, thus insulating individuals from culpability or even knowledge about what the rest of the organization is doing; and even strategic myths are crafted about the organization's high morality. Members gradually come to disavow what they once knew—all along denying the influence of any group pressure. (Cohen 2001, 66–67)

In secret societies these characteristics are amplified. Paranoia and secrecy reciprocally fed off each other. Randall Collins (1998, 2004) argued that this reciprocal relationship was the consequence of the interaction ritual chains in which Bruwer and others were enmeshed. Social life, writes Collins, consists of strings or chains of situations that are the starting point for sociological analysis. A situation turns into a ritual encounter when those present focus their attention on people, objects, or symbols and are thus constituted as a distinct group with boundaries. Rituals amplify emotions and show not only respect for sacred objects but constitute objects as sacred. "Once an object or an idea (a 'symbol' for short) is 'charged' by rituals, it can serve to temporarily reinforce the identities of group members and motivate them to act in accordance with what they take to be the group's values . . . even when the group is not gathered together" (Marquez 2013). Rituals without co-presence are unlikely to succeed because sociality is embodied in the present and generates emotional energy, as when one gets stimulated emotionally. Rituals then create and sustain solidarity within groups. This is why ritual is important for shaping both individual character and stratified group boundaries, and ritual further provides "emotional energy" that pushes the participants to new intellectual and emotional insights. Compare participating in a face to-face-seminar to following a Zoom seminar or even attending a live concert to listening to a recording.

Collins takes the situation rather than the individual as starting point and suggests that, initially, ideology is relatively unimportant. People most commonly join social movements before they acquire clear beliefs about issues. However, they subsequently provide post facto rationalizations when challenged on their membership, "and when a particular belief becomes entangled with an identity—when it becomes, in other words, a focus in some chain of successful interaction rituals circulating as a marker of membership in some group—it becomes more or less immune to rational argument," Marquez (2013) observes. Likewise, charismatic personality cults can be seen in terms of interaction ritual chains.[10] Verwoerd was a master of ritual manipulation. Having served at the Broederbond's highest executive level (described below) from 1940 to 1950 when he was appointed minister of native affairs, Verwoerd kept in close touch with the Broederbond, missing only two of fifty-three meetings of the executive council while he served on it (Wilkins and Strydom 1978, 3), and became the first and only prime minister to address the annual general meeting. He continued to use the Broederbond to manipulate people and silence in-house opposition.[11] Verwoerd was a master of the craft of ritual manipulation, whose modus operandi was to deal with people in face-to-face situations.[12] This tight-knit social network and the norms, sanctions, and resultant trust governed the Broederbond's character and generated a huge stock of social capital that could be used to facilitate individual and group action.

In *The Sociology of Philosophies* (1998), an earlier work, Collins demonstrated how schools of philosophy developed out of the interaction ritual chain networks philosophers were involved in and how individuals in these networks obtained their intellectual and emotional energy from their face-to-face interactions with fellow network members in secretive seminar-style situations. Until the mid-sixties Afrikaner ethnologists felt efforts to dialogue with liberal English-speaking colleagues was a futile exercise and increasingly withdrew to the security of their intellectual and emotional lager. They became increasingly encapsulated, courtesy of the Broederbond, SABRA, and various other Afrikaner civic organizations.[13]

Secret societies, as Simmel (1906) noted, increase the emotional intensity of such seminar-like small-group discussions because they strive to create a species of "life-totality," since they call on reciprocal confidence that is essential to preserve silence to the outside world and thus their invisibility. Conflict has to be minimized, as it creates the possibility of betrayal, and thus they exert a highly efficient disciplinary influence upon the moral accountability of their members. Rituals stressing fictive kinship, secret handshakes, and special secret songs serve to create a oneness for the group. Simmel noted the particular intimacy of association within a secret society. By linking inductees to a direct long tradition, individual instruction, and setting norms for the individual, they merged the inductee into an "environing living group" (Simmel 1906, 376). Here rituals are important not merely for the precision with which they are practiced, but also for the anxiety with which they were guarded. At the same time members were expected to abide by certain norms and rules, more accurately taboos, such as not sending their children to English-medium schools or not having any business dealings with Asians. Such prohibitions on commensality and connubium place limitations on socializing but generate important social capital that is reflected in generalized reciprocity (Hawley 2012, 19).

Empirical evidence bears out these sociological conclusions. Administratively, the Broederbond was composed of small cells numbering between five and twenty members. Membership was exclusive and limited to men, and new members were recruited on a personal basis. The names of potential members were circulated nationally for screening, where one well-motivated objection could disqualify a potential member. Membership demanded high cultural, family, religious, moral, and political standards: membership of the National Party and one of the Afrikaans churches, attendance at an Afrikaans school, and marriage to an Afrikaans-speaking spouse were essential. After 1930 all the Broederbond's chairmen have been people who either were professors or held doctorates, suggesting its emphasis on *geleerdheid* (education) and the need for knowledge as a mode of promoting Afrikaner welfare. But it had to be *geleerdheid* that was politically correct. Gerd Schuler, under whom I studied at Stellenbosch, recalled that when he was interviewed for the position of junior lecturer in 1947, he was not asked about his technical knowledge but about his views concerning race relations.

Organizationally the Broederbond retained its members through its elaborate structure of interlocking roles not only externally in an array of front organizations, but internally as well. A number of cells created a division or branch (*afdeling*) and formed a central committee consisting of a representative of each cell in a town or city. All central committees were grouped together as a regional council (*streekraad*). The bond council (*bondsraad*) was the highest authority of the organization and met biennially. It consisted of a member from each cell, the chairs of the regional councils, and the serving executive council (*uitvoerende raad*). The last had the highest executive authority and was made up of a chairman and nine members, who were elected at the bond council meeting. The executive council then chose a vice-chairman and co-opted an additional five members and also appointed an administrative committee (*dagbestuur*), normally including the chair and vice-chair and responsible for the organization's day-to-day management (Pelzer 1979).

Monthly meetings were held in great secrecy at a member's house. Members would share rides so as not to attract attention by having a large number of cars parked outside the house. Wives were banished to the kitchen and not allowed to serve coffee or refreshments. Meetings focused on two things: discussing documents from head office, usually circulars and study documents, and local issues. In a memoir of his Broederbond days, theologian Professor Nico Smith (2009) recalled being chuffed with the honor his membership brought him. His cell consisted of prominent local citizens, and they would discuss government policy, frequently with the local member of Parliament in attendance. Cabinet ministers and sometimes the prime minister himself regularly updated the Stellenbosch

Broeders of developments. This created the feeling that members were doing important work discussing and analyzing government policy before implementation. Secrecy and the small cell structure generated a warm camaraderie. Indeed, this close and heartfelt friendship was the main reason why members simply did not leave the Broederbond. It was liminal, as "everyone was of one heart and mind" and outside status did not count. Smith was deeply impressed by the feeling of co-responsibility concerning the way matters were developing. Hennie van Deventer (2003, 158–65), a prominent journalist who, having served his apprenticeship in the Ruiterwag, the junior Bond, became a proud long-standing Broeder and fondly recalled the ritual bonding sessions at Broederbond-owned hideaways like the Hartebeespoort Youth Center and the annual "grape festival" on Minister Hendrik Schoeman's model farm. Van Deventer emphasized the importance of the camaraderie of those serving on the executive and how this network could be and was used for special favors. There was unanimity about current affairs, especially political matters. Smith, however, with his missionary background, developed a distinct uneasiness about how the practical realities of apartheid and the situation of blacks were ignored. Study pieces sent by the head office were seldom seriously critiqued by the cell and instead taken as pointers as to how Broeders should think, engaging in anticipatory compliance. There was no criticism of apartheid, least of all that formulated by Verwoerd, since "Verwoerd knew what he was doing. We as Broederbond members just had to trust him and cooperate" (Smith 2009, 118). Like sects, the Broederbond viewed outsiders as ignorant of the "obvious truth" of their subcultural worldview and so dismissed it. Leon Festinger's (1954) well-known notion of cognitive dissonance is pertinent: one avoids information that contradicts previously held views and in which one has a stake. A common strategy in this regard is to categorize the bearers of dissonance as discreditable—as Communists, atheists, or "liberals."

Internal dissent was a different matter, and especially when members resigned because of ideological disagreements, they were heavily ostracized as traitors, even if they had not held senior positions in the Broederbond. When Brian du Toit, the son of a Broederbonder, newly minted anthropology PhD, and junior lecturer at Stellenbosch, wrote a book in Afrikaans that compared the Broederbond to other "primitive" secret societies (du Toit 1965), the university authorities (the rector being chairman of the Broederbond at the time) exerted such pressure on him that he had to find a job somewhere else. Later in the seventies Smith found du Toit's material "surprisingly correct" (Smith 2009, 61).[14] What this type of social situation promotes is not inductive or deductive reasoning, or even what Peirce famously termed abductive reasoning, but *seductive* reasoning.[15]

Just before he was assassinated, Verwoerd complained to the Broederbond's executive council that with continued growth the "the tremendous feeling of unanimity and support was being undermined," yet it was precisely Verwoerd's "solid grip on practically every facet of public life which led some to be peevish about being labeled deviant and liberal." Bruwer responded and complained that a situation had been reached where people were not willing to think more than four or five years ahead, and he said he was willing to say things if they were important for the future of the volk (Stals 2008, 405). Unfortunately, Bruwer died before this apparent opposition could be publicly articulated, so one will never know if this is true or not.

SABRA was another source of inspiration for Bruwer and other volkekundiges. Under the dynamic leadership of its vice-chairman, Bruwer's erstwhile Stellenbosch colleague Nic Olivier, it expanded rapidly and by 1956 could boast some three thousand ordinary members, with seventy municipalities and ninety-nine Dutch Reformed churches being corporate members, and with a not insubstantial budget of US$28,000. Organizationally SABRA's seat of power was located in the tea-room of the Bantoekunde Department at Stellenbosch, where Olivier, executive stalwart Banie van Eeden, treasurer Gerd Schuler, and Bruwer, salaried part-time editor for SABRA publications, were colleagues (Munger 1956). SABRA provided important technical support to the Tomlinson Commission (Pretorius 1985), and its annual congresses drew attendance from across the white political spectrum, including the SAIRR. Already in 1956 it was debating whether to invite blacks to the annual conference. The 1958 conference attracted some 339 delegates, approved a motion that SABRA visit black leaders and engage them in dialogue, and expressed reservations about separate universities for blacks. This infuriated then minister of native affairs Verwoerd, who resigned from the organization, ostensibly because SABRA and the SAIRR had collaborated on an urban adult education project. Shortly thereafter, Verwoerd refused to see a SABRA delegation if Nic Olivier was a member. When Verwoerd became prime minister later in 1958, he launched a concerted effort via the Broederbond to "purify" SABRA. With the rise of the personality cult around Verwoerd,[16] surrounded by cultish true believers and his brutal intolerance of disagreement, let alone dissent within the ranks of the faithful, ideas and discussion of the "Native Question" became increasingly facile, as Bruwer realized when his erstwhile Stellenbosch colleagues were purged from SABRA and marginalized in Afrikaner academia. As a longtime observer of Afrikanerdom put it:

> Discipline is strong. Afrikaner *eenheid* (unity) exacts a high price. One of the
> SABRA leaders paying heavily for disturbing it, is Professor L. J. du Plessis of

Potchefstroom. He has already been forced out as Vice-Chairman of the local National Party and as Board Chairman of *Dagbreek*, the leading Afrikaans Sunday paper. The technique is sometimes crude and often subtle, but Afrikaners know it and fear it. . . . Martyrdom is seldom popular in any country. (Munger 1959, 20)[17]

Bruwer was deeply involved emotionally in the Broederbond. Writing from the field to H. B. Thom, rector of Stellenbosch University and Broederbond chair, he said he regularly thought of the Broederbond and missed his close friends (Broeders) and even apologized for having to use the English letterhead of the Bantu Studies Department.[18] While Bruwer impressed Ned Munger, an American geographer, with his liberal inclinations by arguing that racial policies should be based on the scientific finding that all people have the same potential, in a private letter from Washington, DC, to Thom, Bruwer wrote that his children were attending a school "fortunately without too many Negroes."[19] When the chips were down Bruwer and his junior colleague and successor as commissioner-general, Martie Olivier (no relation to Nic Olivier),[20] demonstrated their Broederbond bona fides by publishing an article in SABRA's *Journal for Racial Affairs* claiming that the United States–South Africa Leadership Exchange Program (USSALEP), in which Nic Olivier had been heavily involved, was part of a conspiratorial alliance between Communists and liberalists seducing South Africa onto the "road of integration" as part of their strategy to gain world domination. USSALEP was subtly trying to influence Afrikaner leaders—clergy, politicians, cultural and educational— in order to create confusion and uncertainty among the masses concerning the moral justification for apartheid. Such clergy thus became the unwitting tools to replace white rule with black government that would be better suited to Communist aims (Bruwer and Olivier 1964). Conversation must have been strained in the departmental tearoom, and Bruwer, and later Martie Olivier, escaped to jobs elsewhere.

Organizational structures, thus, served to encourage a high level of focused local emotional energy. Volkekunde, whose professors were invariably Broeders, many of whom occupied senior positions in the organization, increasingly operated in a closed hierarchical network, and while they did on occasion interact with English-speaking social anthropologists, this was mostly of a ceremonious rather than a ritual nature. The emotional energy that propelled volkekundige theoretical praxis was derived increasingly from the Broederbond and SABRA, which promoted a tight-knit network with close links to the government. As Collins noted:

Groups with high network density and strong barriers to outsiders generate localistic standards of morality: defend the group and its symbols, exercise righteous anger (including ritualized punishments) against outsiders who threaten the group.

This is the morality of isolated tribes, and also of modern groups which have mobilized with strong local ties and strong barriers. (as paraphrased by Baehr 2005)

While some Afrikaner historians have recently claimed the role of the Broederbond has been exaggerated, the one arena that can be empirically demonstrated to have been profoundly influenced by it was in academic appointments and in general propaganda among the volk (Smith 2009). This obviously created a situation rife with the possibilities of nepotism, and one dared not challenge those higher up in the hierarchy. In addition, Verwoerd, as long-serving member of the Broederbond's executive committee, leader of the National Party, and ideologue-in-chief, would not tolerate dissension within the ranks of the faithful, as was demonstrated forcefully in the SABRA purge of 1961, with the dissenters swiftly marginalized in Afrikaner academia. Purgatory was such that those purged were publicly shunned. Moreover, the strong residue of patriarchy in Afrikaans-language universities created an environment where submissiveness to superiors was the norm. Obsequiousness reached an extreme form in the erstwhile Ethnology Division of the SADF, where superior officers could plagiarize their subordinates' work without consequence.

The impressive unanimity of the Broederbond, as Verwoerd proudly put it (Stals 2008, 405), was lost after his assassination, undoubtedly abetted by the organization's rapid expansion, growing from some eight thousand members in 1968 to approximately twenty thousand by the late eighties, making tight control over them more problematic. Nevertheless, the Broederbond continued to play an important role in SWA, characterized in the post-Verwoerd era by pragmatic modernizing racial domination (Adam 1971). The strategy then became one of buying time in the international arena to allow for the development of a meta-policy of internal co-optation by developing a black middle class. In the effort to create a black middle class in the territory, held to be the key to neutralizing SWAPO by way of development parastatals and educational facilities such as a proto-university, the Academy for Tertiary Education, the spectral presence of the Broederbond was ever present. If there was one thing that almost all the post–World War II key policy makers had in common, it was their membership in the Broederbond. From the mid-fifties all the administrators and later administrator-generals of SWA were Broeders with one exception, the first administrator-general, Judge M. J. Steyn, and even he was surrounded by Broeders.[21] They were not ordinary members of the Broederbond but senior and respected Broeders, most having served on the Broederbond's executive council and having been circulated into highly influential positions in government, usually being promoted to cabinet ministers. According to Stephen Ellis, in the six-month run-up to the elections that were held under the supervision of the United Nations

Transition Assistance Group (UNTAG), South Africa launched a massive coordinated covert effort, ranging from physical violence and the intimidation of voters to the funding of opposition parties, coupled to a massive propaganda effort involving faux media organizations and fake news. This succeeded in shaving the SWAPO share of the vote from about 70 percent to 55 percent over the six months. Many South African government strategists believed that similar techniques could be effective in South Africa in creating multiracial alliances with conservative anti-ANC organizations, especially Inkatha and traditional leaders, if given enough time. Decidedly influential in this regard was Steyn's successor as administrator-general, the chair of the Broederbond Gerrit Viljoen, who later became South Africa's minister for constitutional development. In March 1990, after admitting that apartheid was not working, Viljoen said:

> And that is why we went to the electorate and said: "We want to change our approach completely. We want to include blacks as fellow citizens. . . ." The whole approach of the government is to shift the emphasis from race to quality of government and the broadening of democracy, in spite of the risks. (Cited in S. Ellis 1998, 283)

Notes

1. See self-help books with catchy titles like *Understanding and Motivating the Bantu Worker* (Silberbauer 1968), *Motivating Black Workers* (Backer 1973), *Personeelbestuur en die swart werker* (Personnel management and the black worker) (Raubenheimer and Kotzé 1984), and *Bridging the Communication Gap between Black and White* (Tiley 1974). A few random assertions from the last include the following: black workers are lazy because they find manual work below their dignity because it is "traditionally" women's work; black women are sociologically better able to adapt to urban situations than men; and "sex is of greater importance to the Black than to the European" (Tiley 1974, 86). Intellectually, then, they were soul mates to the SADF etiquette manuals.
2. This is not to deny a sense of loyalty toward blacks in some elite units like the 32 Battalion (the Buffalo Battalion), something that is clear from the reaction by white officers at the unit's disbandment (P. Els 2000).
3. A German missionary medical doctor with twenty years of experience on the Kavango who spoke Mbukushu, Fisch was hired by the South African government in 1978 to research Kavango laws, despite only having studied some ethnology by correspondence.
4. The reference to "so-called ethnologists" was in Breytenbach's manuscript but exorcised from the published book.
5. The lesson seems to have been ignored. The US Army's 2007 *Counterinsurgency Field Manual* has been subjected to the same criticism (González 2018).
6. P. J. Schoeman, letter to Jansen, 28 January 1949, PV 94 1/38/1/4, INCH.
7. Even today, by far the largest number of Namibian ethnographies focus on "Bushmen," followed by the other so-called "pristine people," the pastoral Himba of Kaokoland.
8. As Afrikaner nationalism consolidated itself in Namibia and Nationalists made a ploy to control the State Museum and related activities in the mid-sixties, one of the most damning accusations they made was that the Scientific Society and its members were freely sending

artifacts abroad and thus, by implication, were not loyal "South Westers." As late as the mid-sixties the Scientific Society was accused of exporting "most valuable materials" without proper consultation or permission (A. Tötemeyer 1999, 61).

9. This discussion is based on Bjerg and Presskorn-Thygesen (2017).

10. As Marquez (2013) elaborated in his blog:

    The charismatic leader is the person who both becomes emotionally energized by being the focus of attention in successful rituals, and is in turn charged as a sacred object by ritual participants. Thus, though some people will of course be more skillful than others at using ritual situations to amplify collective emotion (and hence will be more likely to be considered "charismatic" leaders), the mere *fact* that someone can compel attention may often be sufficient to produce an aura of charisma, especially if the rituals are otherwise successful (one thinks here of in retrospect fairly *uncharismatic* leaders like Stalin or Kim Jong-il). I suspect that more skillful producers of charisma are precisely the people who seem to have the knack for putting together already charged symbols produced in everyday interaction rituals into larger narratives and symbols leading *to* them.

11. Verwoerd also used the security police. H. B. Thom, rector of Stellenbosch University and Broederbond chair, noted on an aerogram he received from Bruwer while in America that it had been opened by the South African police (J. P. van S. Bruwer to H. B. Thom, 6 June 1959, 171AB, Thom papers). The following is illustrative of Verwoerd's modus operandi: responding to the Broederbond's congratulatory letter on winning the referendum for creating a republic in 1960, he deeply appreciated the offer of future cooperation before, in the very second paragraph, launching a scathing attack on Nic Olivier and SABRA concerning their stance on the colored franchise. Sections of this were crossed out in pen but still readable. "The incalculable (*onberekenbare*) Prof. Olivier and his friends whose continuing control of SABRA and their influence on the new chairman, Dr Geyer were creating a dangerous situation":

    They were arguing for political representation in Parliament for and by coloreds and acknowledge that this was the first step to integration and immediately accept the consequences of full social and economic integration and even biological assimilation. Some also immediately accept the same with regard to Asians in South Africa. In other words they want to persuade us from within to the first step on the political terrain knowing that it will be the end of a White South Africa. . . . I will most strongly have to fight this because otherwise our victory means nothing. Since some of these deviations come from your circle, I trust you will unambiguously support me, because the clash over these affairs will become unnecessarily serious. (Letter by Hendrik Verwoerd to van der Spuy, 31 October 1960, 191AB, Thom Papers)

    The Broeders took the hint and, via Broeders serving on the SABRA council, managed to postpone the April 1961 SABRA congress, which was to focus on the theme of "coloreds," to September with a new theme. At this later conference Olivier and his supporters were voted out of office.

12. Verwoerd's style can be garnered from his response to a rather obsequious letter from Bruwer: Many thanks for your friendly letter of 23 January 1961. I was happy to hear from you in this spirit because to be honest I must say that I was starting to worry about the ideas which you uttered in the United States according to a report of your speech which was sent to me. While I always attached much value to you as someone who judges and feels about our Colour policy precisely as we do, that report created the impression that you, under pressure of circumstances or whatever, also now began doubting [*tussenweë soek*]. I, inter alia, got the same impression from your piece about South West Africa. I would have been very disappointed in view of our identical views in the past, especially now that the [Nic] Oliviers and company have gotten their way to cause a ruckus amongst a number of our people [*op hol jag*; presumably to have dialogues with African leaders]. Perhaps we can discuss this one day. (Hendrik Verwoerd to J. P. van S. Bruwer, 25 January 1961, PV123 Bruwer Papers, INCH)

13. In the seventies they launched a last-ditch effort by creating their own professional association, VAV (Vereeniging vir Afrikaanse Volkekunde: Association for Afrikaans Ethnology), glossed rather misleadingly in English as the Society for South African Ethnology.

14. When J. C. "Boet" Kotzé, by then a Broederbonder and professor of volkekunde at the Rand Afrikaans University on the Witwatersrand started displaying deviationist tendencies, fellow volkekunde Broeders in the area had a special volkekunde discussion group that tried to dissuade Kotzé. They failed and he resigned from VAV in 1983 and from the Broederbond a few years later (Cees van der Waal, pers. comm., March 2019).

15. Even without secrecy the Broederbond was an organization ripe for creating what Alvesson and Spicer (2016) call "functional stupidity" or "self-reinforcing stupidity." While recruiting talented and intelligent people, its organizational culture directly and indirectly discouraged members from thinking or from raising concerns and reflecting, since the established framework was accepted uncritically.

16. Such was the adoration of Verwoerd, enhanced undoubtedly by surviving an assassination attempt in April 1960, that a special play, *Skepper van ons toekoms* (Creator of our future), directed by Anna Neethling-Pohl, the doyenne of Afrikaans theatre, was performed for his sixty-first birthday in 1962 to an audience that contained representatives of every major Afrikaner organization.

17. Of course the fact that Olivier had divorced his Afrikaans wife and remarried a Jewish divorcee made him persona non grata in the Broederbond. A case in point concerns the leading Dutch Reformed clergyman Beyers Naude, who, in the early sixties, tried to elicit support from his fellow clergy and Broeders to discuss apartheid, but they responded:

    We are not prepared to jeopardize our loyalty to and membership of the Broederbond in any way. And if you are going to do so yourself then we wish to warn that you can expect nothing other than misery and calamity. We are sorry, but in such circumstances there will be a parting of the way between us. (Cited in Hugo 1998, 33)

18. J. P. van S. Bruwer to H. B. Thom, 6 June 1959, 191K.B.149, Thom Papers.

19. J. P. van S. Bruwer to H. B. Thom, 10 October 1959, 191K.B.149, Thom Papers.

20. As a young student Martinus Johannes Olivier had been SABRA secretary from 1953 to 1955 when he joined the South African Department of Bantu Administration in Windhoek, which had just taken over native administration from the SWA administration. He completed his doctorate on native administration in SWA (Olivier 1961) under the aegis of Nic Olivier, with Bruwer and Eiselen as co-promotors. Thereafter he joined the Bantoekunde Department until appointed commissioner-general in 1964. In 1970 he became a researcher at the Africa Institute before founding the Department of Development Studies at the Rand Afrikaans University, both institutions said to have been largely originated by the Broederbond.

21. While not a Broeder himself, Steyn was the grandson of the last president of the Orange Free State and the son of Dr. Colin Steyn who had served in Smuts's cabinet. Three months after relinquishing the administrator-generalship, Steyn was appointed to head a commission of enquiry into the relationship between the press and the security forces, in which he was accused of being highly partisan.

Conclusion: "Have We Met the Enemy and (S)He Is Us?" (Pogo)?

Given the emphasis volkekundiges placed on difference and their attempts to make a difference, this book might have been titled *Making the Difference: How Ethnologists Fashioned Namibia*. Even when the SADF's journeyman ethnologists failed to convince soldiers, they were still reinforcing *difference*. This reached its apogee in perhaps one of the most famous, or infamous, speeches in South African history, the so-called Rubicon speech delivered by President P. W. Botha in August 1985. The speech was in response to increasing resistance in South Africa and pressure from the major Western powers to release Nelson Mandela and to negotiate with the ANC about abolishing apartheid. But instead of offering concessions, as was expected in the lead-up to the speech, Botha dug in his heels. A recently discovered unedited transcript of a daylong meeting of the extended cabinet less than two weeks before the Rubicon speech suggests why it took the form it did. The transcript shows that from the start Botha set the parameters: he was not in favor of a unitary state or a federation but would only support a confederacy allowing for power sharing with coloreds and Asians but not with blacks. Black traditional leadership structures were undemocratic, he asserted and elaborated, "Most black communities are attached to witch-doctors." He quoted a *sangoma* (traditional diviner) to the effect that "one man, one vote is one of the biggest delusions in the world. It does not exist, has never existed and will never exist. Every country in Africa, since independence, has always become a one-party state with hundreds of intimidated people becoming just voting cattle." Botha then asked, "Have we explored [the influence of *sangomas*] and how we can exploit them to achieve peace?" He regarded foreign countries as "uninformed, unreasonable . . . and stupid. . . . The Lord knows how we are going to live in this world. We will have to make our Defence and Police Force as strong as possible because eventually if they want to oppress us, we will have to fight as any self-respecting nation would" (Cloete 2018).

Maybe it is time to take a different tack? In 1949 anthropologist Max Gluckman gave his inaugural lecture in Manchester on the seemingly exotic subject "Social Beliefs and Individual Thinking in Tribal Society." He sought to demonstrate how the mechanisms of "social thinking" were similar in both "tribal" and "Western society." Social thinking, Gluckman lectured, was based on collective representations that existed independently of the individual, thus deducing individual thinking from the social beliefs of a society was impossible because beliefs were highly flexible. Which beliefs were cited in accounting for particular acts depended on the particular social situation. It was the premises upon which such beliefs were based that were problematic and could coexist with contrary beliefs. Witchcraft and, more especially, divination, said Gluckman, were based on a theory of causation and an explanation of causal links. Where divination and science were concerned with transcendent non-observable facts and where they confronted reality, explanations tended to be vague. The social situation defined the relevant "causes," but the ostensible causes were constrained by closed systems of thought. Individual skeptics, claimed Gluckman, rarely questioned the whole system of collective representation, only parts of it. Should lightning strike one's house despite the fact that it had a lightning conductor, one blamed poor installation or faulty material and did not present a paper to the Royal Society debunking theories of lightning.

Toward the end of his lecture Gluckman applied the Durkheimian notion of collective representations to understanding contemporary capitalist society by citing two illustrations. First, he explained that to claim that someone was a "decent Jew" or a "decent black" would, by implication, strengthen the belief that Jews and blacks were people who, as a class, were not decent. Second, he drew on the example of how Nazis republished books of anti-Hitler cartoons from all over the world, not to demonstrate tolerance but to show how Germany was encircled by communistic capitalist Jews. Based on these examples, he argued, "The moral of propaganda is clear: direct assault on a closed system of ideas is immensely difficult, since the system absorbs the attacks and converts them to strengthen itself" (Gluckman 1949, 96). This was possible because all systems of beliefs about social relations were

> inchoate, inconsistent, malleable, flexible, fluctuating, variable—capable of absorbing the evidence that seems to contradict the system within the system as to strengthen it, yet nevertheless logical and reasonable. . . . Ultimately faith in certain ideals and confidence in certain moral rules which arise from social relations dominate over empirical observations and scientific skepticism about social behavior. (Gluckman 1949, 96–97)

Confronting closed systems of thought was challenging, and Gluckman concluded:

If we can be made aware of the distorting structure of our systems of ideas, we are greatly helped not only to more objective observations of social behavior, but also to mutual understanding. However, this examination may make us politically impotent. We must remember that the structure of a social situation presents a moral choice between limited ends and values with all the disadvantages that choice may entail. (Gluckman 1949, 98)

Throughout his career Gluckman was obsessed with what constituted a "social fact": how observations were given meaning by both informants and anthropologists. Émile Durkheim famously regarded social facts as "things," which were whatever resists one's wishes and imposes itself upon one, whether one likes it or not. "Objectivity" is likely, Berger and Zijderveld (2009, 65) argue, when "an observer is compelled by the evidence to make statements about facts which are contrary to the observers' interests or prejudices." In this regard Gluckman relied on Durkheim's concept of collective representation and his own notion of closed systems of thought. In Gluckman's view, a closed system resembled what later became known as *schemas*. Schemas slotted into *collective representations*: the ideas, beliefs, and values elaborated by a collectivity and that were not reducible to individual constituents. They were central to Durkheim's search for the sources of social solidarity. These representations were created through the intense interaction of religious rituals and, being richer than individual activities, came to be autonomous of the group from which they emerged. Collective representations helped to order and make sense of the world but also expressed, symbolized, and interpreted social relationships. Collective representations inhibited and stimulated social action. Their force or authority came from their being within all individuals and yet also external to the person. People generally do not think logically, relying instead on stereotypical generalizations, fitting experience into preordained categories. Anthropologists borrowed the concept of schema from cognitive psychologists in an effort to understand how thoughts about culture were organized within one's mind and how they played into post hoc justifications. Schemas provide people with simplified models of what their world is like and how one ought to act, feel, and think. Whenever one remembers something, it is literally reconstructed by grabbing tiny bits of imagery and information that interconnect in a vast and complex web. Schemas can obviously lead to frequent misinterpretations. Information is now largely accepted because it feels right and slots conveniently into pre-existing schemas that people have. Psychologists call this "confirmation bias," where stories, facts, and ideas that do not agree with one's beliefs are blocked out. Schemas are kindred to what economics Nobel laureate Herbert Simon called "bounded rationality," where "broadly stated, the task is to replace the global rationality of economic man with a kind of rational behavior that is compatible with the access to information and the computational capacities that are actually possessed by organisms, including man, in the kinds of environments in which such organisms exist" (Simon 1955, 99).

In short, schemas are about how one is influenced by emotions, stereotypes, and what one thinks one knows but does not really know. Given the information bombardment courtesy of the internet, the proverbial gaze has become a glaze. Ostensible authorities and ordinary people can get away with making assertions that are often fantasy, because it takes too much effort for most people to fact-check claims for accuracy. Perhaps the most important factor in seducing one into accepting a certain new item or story, I would argue, is peer belief and the desire to be accepted by one's peer group, factors that loomed large in the Broederbond and in the SADF. Recent psychological research has provided strong evidence that people from higher classes tend to have a more inflated sense of their own skills. They have a strong tendency to "overconfidence" in their own judgment and skills, and this self-confidence was misinterpreted by strangers as competence (Belmi et al. 2019). Add racism to the mix and the likelihood of living in a fantasy world is even higher. To escape this delusionary trap requires *critical self-reflection and humility*, since, as Katherine Hawley (2012, 51) points out, "the worse people are at telling truth from lies, the more confident they are that they're getting it right—self-confidence is highest amongst those who are worst at judging truth from lies. . . . So a first step towards becoming a better lie-detector is learning to question your own judgement on the matter." This means returning continually to earlier ideas in an effort to move deeper into the problem that animated their original research question.[1]

Closed systems of thought or bounded rationality and schemas thus provide a useful scaffolding from which to examine how Bruwer, his colleagues, and their intellectual progeny were constricted. But it also has relevance in dealing with the critical contemporary issue of "fake news." Typically, the explanation goes, people examine the evidence supporting a new claim, and if it fits into their existing knowledge regime by being logically consistent and meshing into their existing knowledge, they accept it. With information overload and other priorities requiring attention, however, people tend to accept stories without examining them critically and simply slot them into preordained schemas or categories.

Fake news mimics reliable reportage and is thus often difficult to identify, but recently researchers have subjected verified fake news to linguistic analysis and found that in contrast to proper reportage, they tend to use overly emotional language and words that exaggerate, typically superlatives like "greatest" or "worst," subjectives such as "terrible," and emphatics like "really" and "most" while displaying a fondness for abstract generalities (Shariatmadari, 2019), eerily echoing the "potted knowledge" this book has sought to identify and analyze.

Complicating the issue, however, conspiracy theories have undergone a transformation. Whereas historically they were based on an attempt to substantiate a causal theory, now fueled by the revolution in mass communication a new conspiracism has emerged that, write Muirhead and Rosenblum (2019), in contrast to older conspiracies that relied on theories and on facts withheld by those in power, is characterized as being devoid of theory and based on insinuation. While conspiracy theories have core empirical and normative claims, new conspiracism is eclectic. Its modus operandi is well captured in the title of Muirhead and Rosenblum's book, based on a famous Trumpian phrase, *A Lot of People Are Saying*. This conspiracism derives its authority/credibility through repetitive assertion, not presentation of facts hidden by the powers that be. It is also convenient for the claim maker, as "bare assertions, ominous questions, and innuendo" are elastic and can be pulled in every direction depending on the situation, while purporting to be merely asking questions "evades ownership of the claim" (Muirhead and Rosenblum 2019, 39). New conspiracists tend to simply deny others' standing on an ad hominem basis while simultaneously distorting the very knowledge criteria that has underpinned our societies. It targets not only knowledge-producing institutions but also political parties and makes it almost impossible to argue with its proponents, let alone persuade, negotiate, or compromise, the very basis of democracy.

It is a truism that truth and reality are explicitly interpreted through the lens of power and privilege. Stanley Cohen (2001) describes the dilemma: no absolute moral imperatives can be drawn from particular bodies of information (or text) because morality and values are relativistic and culturally specific. Every text is the product of some form of narrative, and since all narratives reflect some form of self-interest, many postmodern theorists assert that there can be no way to distinguish factual, historical information from situated stories or multiple narratives that compete equally and openly in indeterminate searches for the truth. Epistemology is therefore relative—it depends on who is deconstructing which historical record. Given the intermeshing of those social constructions known as truth and belief, how is one to respond? Cohen (2001, 265) suggests striving to create a culture of acknowledgment by enabling these closed-systems adherents to see themselves as "part of common humanity." Peter Berger and Anton Zijderveld (2009, 127) argue that the one overriding universal value that everyone should be able to agree upon is a concern for human dignity. One cannot claim to infringe upon this in the name of the Lord, Allah, the Law, or the People.

One could start by encouraging people to be sensitive to the language used in the narratives that justify South Africa's defense of Western civilization against communism. Perhaps the most moving stories of epiphanies of South African servicemen occurred when they discovered Bibles in the pockets of dead guerrillas. Gluckman argued that one has a moral obligation to believe responsibly only that for which one has sufficient evidence and that which one has diligently investigated. Rather than simply uncovering more evidence of lack of insight, the focus should be on discovering the social conditions under which lack of insight and fake news are produced. Joining Gluckman in returning to the intellectual roots of Western liberalism in the tradition of George Orwell and Noam Chomsky, Cohen (2001, 286) argues that "the intellectual responsibility of the writer as a moral agent is obvious: to try to find out and tell the truth as best one can about matters of human significance to the right audience— that is, an audience that can do something about them." For Cohen, the social significance of truth-telling should not be underestimated. Quoting Marx, he suggests that "shame is a revolutionary emotion." The solutions in dealing with closed systems of thought thus lie in establishing circumstances that elicit more altruism and in strategies that encourage *curiosity*. Should anthropologists, to paraphrase Jessica Mitford, while "*not . . . able to change the world, . . . at least . . . embarrass the guilty*" (cited in J. Collins 2016, emphasis added)?

How does one deal with looking but not seeing and more broadly with the dangers of fake news? Simply providing more information, as Gluckman argued and numerous later studies confirm, can boomerang, reinforcing and entrenching existing views, especially among those who consider themselves well educated. Commenting on this situation, an expert in science communication at the Massachusetts Institute of Technology, Dan Kahan, suggested a means of overcoming this polarization: while neither scientific knowledge nor reasoning is associated with objectivity, scientific curiosity is:

> Experimental data suggest why. Afforded a choice, low-curiosity individuals opt for familiar evidence consistent with what they already believe; high-curiosity citizens, in contrast, prefer to explore novel findings, even if that information implies that their group's position is wrong. Consuming a richer diet of information, high-curiosity citizens predictably form less one-sided and hence less polarized views. (Kahan 2018)

How to promote intellectual curiosity? The first step would be to encourage *doubt*. Sincere and consistent doubt is the source of tolerance and the hallmark of democracy. Doubt is intrinsic to the Socratic method, in which, by asking questions, doubt is raised, which eventually demolishes preconceived and fashionable beliefs. Of course there are many kinds of doubt, ranging from apostasy to cynical doubt. But there is also playful doubt that is usually ironical, best exemplified by Desiderius Erasmus's famous *In Praise of Folly*, in which, when looking into the mirror, Wisdom sees Folly, but when Folly peers into the mirror, Wisdom is reflected (Berger and Zijderveld 2009, 105). This is where anthropology can play a crucial role. There is nothing more irritating to me than reading authors' blurbs proclaiming they are keen amateur anthropologists. This is a measure that no one really takes anthropology seriously in the current sociopolitical milieu, which means anthropologists are largely seen as nonthreatening. This could be turned into a strength. Leszek Kolakowski, the Marxist humanist, divided people of knowledge into two categories: priests and jesters. The former are guardians of tradition, characterized by a belief in absolute knowledge, facts, finality, and eschatology, while jesters are simply impertinent and questioning, even questioning their own questioning: the jester "doubts all that appears self-evident." For the jester, knowledge always rejects whatever the current absolute is. The jester's maxim is raising doubt (Kolakowski 1968, 15–36). It is no accident that nowadays the most insightful political commentary is done not by political scientists or policy wonks but by comedians. One explanation for this is that a joke's punch line has to be unexpected, which means the comedian has to be able to think beyond convention or outside the box; or, as Arthur Koestler (1964) put it, "it is the sudden clash between two mutually exclusive codes of rules—or associative contexts—which produce the comic effect." He went further and noted that "dictators fear laughter more than bombs." Anthropologists could function as the jesters (yes, we are privileged members in the Court of Neo-liberalism). The metaphor of the anthropologist as court jester opens up many rich interpretations. By looking at the foibles and follies of others, we recognize our own. But being a jester is a role filled with fragility. While the jester is allowed to show up power for what it is, the critical iconoclastic impulse prevents the jester from exercising power. Crossing this intellectual River Styx contaminates the jester's praxis. Rather than teach our students the dangers of fieldwork, says Köpping (2002, 203), we should teach them about the dangerous dirt in the corridors of power. The anthropologist as jester is well placed to speak the proverbial "truth to power" by innocently and humorously pointing to alternative perspectives, by asking closed-systems thinkers how people in other cultures or social situations would respond. Anthropologists, indeed all critical thinkers, need to puncture the certainty of absoluteness epitomized by Dr. Hendrik Verwoerd, meta-architect of apartheid, who claimed that he never allowed himself the luxury of wondering whether he was wrong (Moodie 2017, 154). It was this utter certainty, so characteristic of gurus, that brought him disciples. Of course raising doubt should be done with critical self-reflection and humility, for without these qualities, the jester risks becoming a buffoon, like some of the SADF ethnologists. But be forewarned, it is dangerous work. Liesl Schillinger's (2019) conclusion is applicable here as well: "Comedians who twit presidents or kings [and one could add, academics] are in the firing line because they are the front line. They are the advance guard against those who treat human beings like cartoons."

Redeeming Bruwer?

A year before his death, as acting chair of the Broederbond, Bruwer sent out a confidential mimeographed memorandum entitled "Volkere-aangeleenthede" (People's affairs, 3 March 1966), in which he warned that time was running out for apartheid. People were "walking with their heads in the clouds." If there was not a change of direction, Afrikanerdom was doomed, he prophesied. He was raising these questions, Bruwer wrote, because he had no clarity in his own conscience. While he found the eventual establishment of a community of peoples attractive, it would not succeed unless there was equality. He had frequently raised these issues at the highest level (i.e., with Verwoerd) but had never received an answer.[2] The memorandum is quite lengthy, but to focus on Namibia: Bruwer criticized his friend and successor as commissioner-general, Martie Olivier, for not understanding the broader context and being too busy holding parties for whites to know and appreciate the Ovambo. SWAPO, Bruwer feared, was going to resurrect itself. But perhaps the most remarkable of Bruwer's paragraphs involves Bushmen. If the outside world had the information he had concerning Bushmen,

> South Africa's name would literally and figuratively be besmirched. What happened to them and is still happening I regard as a blot on our people, who will be held responsible (even if I am now labeled as a liberal!). It eats into my Christian conscience because I know the Father we worship will not let such affairs go unpunished and *our* children will have to suffer. (Bruwer 1966c, 19)[3]

Clearly Bruwer was beginning to doubt. He had also started to make public statements critical of apartheid.[4] This was enough for his family to believe that the airplane in which he was flying on 13 March 1967 was deliberately sabotaged to kill him. They cite several unanswered questions around the official inquiry into the airplane crash, but their efforts to have the inquiry reopened have to date been unsuccessful (Harvey 2019). In some circumstances the price of doubt can be unbelievably high.

Notes

1. As Szakolczai and Thomassen (2019, 8–9) point out, to teach students to be "self-critical" risks producing a split mind, as it is nigh impossible to make a statement and be critical at the same time.
2. Bruwer might, however, have had some impact. The speech Verwoerd was preparing to give when he was assassinated on 6 September 1966 was said by Paul Heylin of Verwoerd's secret research committee to have heralded a major departure from orthodox apartheid by proposing a federal model (Sanders 2006, 26). Alas, we will never know the verity of this claim, as the briefcase containing the speech went missing in the hurly-burly of the assassination, providing much fodder for conspiracy theories.
3. Undoubtedly this must have been a humiliating experience for Bruwer, as discussed in chapter 3. Van der Wath, who saw a copy of this memorandum, claimed that it would have been dynamite if it had been leaked to the international press. Bruwer was personally instructed by Verwoerd to collect all twelve copies he had made, including his personal one, and return them to the minister of Bantu affairs, who would destroy them.
4. He had also started to step out of the intellectual laager and, to the ire of his colleagues who later formed the exclusivist Vereeniging van Afrikaanse Volkekundiges (Society for Afrikaans Ethnologists), had initiated discussions with social anthropologists at liberal English-language universities to create an annual conference, the first of which occurred shortly after his death in 1967.

References

Newspapers, Magazines

Allgemeine Zeitung
Cape Argus
Cape Times
IOL (Independent OnLine)
The Nambian
Paratus
Pretoria News
Rand Daily Mail
The Resister
Die Suidwester
Sunday Times
Weekly Mail
Windhoek Advertiser

Historical Texts

Nachlass Moritz Bonn N.1082, Bundesarchiv Koblenz, Germany (NMB)

- Bonn, Moritz Julius. n.d.a. "The Economic Basis of Imperialism."
- Bonn, Moritz Julius. n.d.b. "The Twilight of Economics."

H. B. Thom Papers, Stellenbosch University, Stellenbosch, South Africa (Thom Papers)

- 1919AB
- 191AB
- 191AB1
- 191K.B.149

Institute for Contemporary History (now Archive for Contemporary Affairs), University of the Free State, Bloemfontein, South Africa (INCH)

- PV123 Bruwer Papers
- PV94 Jansen Papers
- PV93 Verwoerd Papers

John Seiler interviews, conducted during 1983 in northern Namibia, edited audiocassettes, Sterling Library, Yale University, New Haven.

National Archives of Namibia, Windhoek, Namibia (NAN)

- A50/60
- A50/67 Bushman Affairs
- A50/67(2) Bushman Affairs
- A50/217 Survey of African People
- A591 van Warmelo Collection
- A198/3/1 Anthropological Research University of California
- A198/3 Museums and Scientific Research, 1916–49
- A198/3/4 Museums & Scientific Research Mrs Hoernlé
- A427 Visits to SWA
- A427/34 Lord Hailey's visit to SWA
- A591 van Warmelo Collection
- A611 Teen-Insurgensie Symposium, donated by B.J. van Zyl
- A820/3803 Nazi Suspects: Vedder
- A450 CHL Hahn Papers
- BB 0320

South African National Archives, Pretoria, South Africa (SANA)

- NTS 9715 807/400
- NTS 47/378 "Sir Malcolm Hailey Visit to the Union"

South African National Defence Force Documentation Centre, Pretoria, South Africa (SANDF)

- AMI/MIB/328/2
- AMI (Group SWA) 175 161 8/10 Omega verslag Dr Pasques
- Burgersake 310/1/C/3/1 Jeugkampe
- COMOPS 328/1/2
- KOMOPS 103/18/1/8
- SWA TF K O COMOPS BV 103/18/1/8/1

South Africa. 1951–56. *Hansard Reports of Senate Debates.* Pretoria: Government Printer.

- Debates of the House of Assembly (Hansard). 1955. 15 March.
- Debates of the Senate (Hansard). 1951. Fourth Session, 19 January to 22 June.
- Debates of the Senate (Hansard). 1952. Third Session, 18 January to 25 June.
- Debates of the Senate (Hansard). 1954. Second Session, 29 January to 15 June.
- Debates of the Senate (Hansard). 1955. Third Session, 21 January to 23 June.
- Debates of the Senate (Hansard). 1956. First Session, 13 January to 14 June.
- Debates of the Senate (Hansard). 1956. Third Session, 13 January to 14 June. Tomlinson Commission Evidence, University of South Africa Library, Pretoria, South Africa.

Adam, Heribert. 1971. *Modernizing Racial Domination: The Dynamics of South African Politics*. Berkeley: University of California Press.

Agamben, Giorgio. 2005. *State of Exception*. Chicago: University of Chicago Press.

Akuupa, Michael U. 2011. "The Formation of 'National Culture' in Post-apartheid Namibia: A Focus on State Sponsored Cultural Festivals in Kavango Region." PhD diss., University of the Western Cape.

Alsop, Stewart. 1962. "Our New Strategy: The Alternatives to Total War." *Saturday Evening Post*, 1 December.

Alvesson, Mats, and André Spicer. 2016. *The Stupidity Paradox*. London: Profile.

Arendt, Hannah. 1981. *The Life of the Mind: The Groundbreaking Investigation on How We Think*. New York: Houghton Mifflin.

Asad, Talal, ed. 1973. *Anthropology and the Colonial Encounter*. London: Ithaca Press.

Backer, W. 1973. *Motivating Black Workers*. Johannesburg: McGraw-Hill.

Baehr, Peter. 2005. "The Sociology of Almost Everything: Four Questions to Randall Collins about *Interaction Ritual Chains*." *Canadian Journal of Sociology Online* (January–February): 1–11. https://core.ac.uk/download/pdf/49313436.pdf.

Baines, Gary. 2015. "SADF Soldiers' Silences: Institutional, Consensual and Strategic." *Acta Academica* 47, no. 1: 78–97.

Bakkes, Christiaan. 2014. *Krokodil aan my skouer*. Cape Town: Human and Rousseau.

Banghart, Peter D. 1969. "Migrant Labour in South West Africa and Its Effects on Ovambo Tribal Life." MA thesis, Stellenbosch University.

Barbash, Ilisa. 2017. *Where the Roads All End: Photographs and Anthropology in the Kalahari*. Cambridge: Peabody Museum Press.

Barth, Paul. 1926. *Südwestafrika*. Windhoek: John Meinert.

Baumann, Julius. 1965. *Mission und Ökumene in Südwestafrika*. Leiden: Brill.

Belmi, Peter, Margaret A. Neale, David Reiff, and Rosemary Ulfe. 2019. "The Social Advantage of Miscalibrated Individuals: The Relationship between Social Class and Overconfidence and Its Implications for Class-Based Inequality." *Journal of Personality and Social Psychology* 5 (November). https://doi.org/10.1037/pspi0000187.

Berger, Peter, and Anton Zijderveld. 2009. *In Praise of Doubt: How to Have Convictions without Becoming a Fanatic*. New York: Harper.

Bjerg, Ole, and Thomas Presskorn-Thygesen. 2017. "Conspiracy Theory: Truth Claim or Language Game?" *Theory, Culture and Society* 34, no. 1: 137–59. https://doi.org/10.1177/0263276416657880.

Bonn, Moritz J. 1909. "Siedlungsfragen und Eingeborenenpolitik: 1. Die Probleme Der Mischkolonie." *Archiv für Sozialwissenschaft und Sozialpolitik* 28: 654–92.

———. 1925. *The Crisis of European Democracy*. London: Oxford University Press.

———. 1938. *The Crumbling of Empire: The Disintegration of World Economy*. London: Allen and Unwin.

Bornemann, Fritz. 1970. "P. Martin Gusinde S.V.D. (1886–1969): Eine biographische Skizze." *Anthropos* 65, no. 5/6: 737–57.

Boswell, Christina. 2009. *The Political Uses of Expert Knowledge: Immigration Policy and Social Research*. London: Cambridge University Press.

Bradley, Jan E. 1970. "Die Mandlakazi: 'n ondersoek na enkele kultuuraspekte." MA thesis, Potchefstroomse Universiteit vir Christelike Hoër Onderwys.

Breytenbach, Jan. [1997] 2015. *Eden's Exiles*. Pretoria: Protea.

Bruwer, Johannes P. van S. 1957. *Die Bantoe van Suid-Afrika.* Johannesburg: Afrikaanse Pers.

———. 1961. *Ons Mandaat: Suidwes-Afrika.* Johannesburg: South African Broadcasting Corporation.

———. 1962. *The Kuanyama of South West Africa: A Preliminary Study.* Stellenbosch: Stellenbosch University.

———. 1965. "Die Khoisan- en Bantoebevolking van Suidwes-Afrika." In *Die Ethnischen Gruppen in Südwestafrika*, 45–84. Windhoek: SWA Wissenschaftlichen Gesellschaft.

———. 1966a. *South West Africa: The Disputed Land.* Cape Town: Nasionale Boekhandel.

———. 1966b. *Die matriliniêre orde van Okavangoland* [The matrilineal order of the Kavango]. Port Elizabeth: University of Port Elizabeth.

———. 1966c. "Volkere-aangeleenthede." Confidential mimeograph circulated to the Afrikaner Broederbond, 3 March.

Bruwer, Johannes P. van S., and M. J. Olivier. 1964. "Hedendaagse integrasie poginge: Is dit vernuwing of verraad?" *Tydskrif vir Rasse-Aangeleenthede* 15, no. 1: 64–78.

Budack, Kuno F. R. 1975. "Umgangsformen am Kavango." *Afrikanischer Heimatkalender*, 125–37.

Burger, Frederik Johannes. 1992. "Teeninsurgensie in Namibië: die rol van die polisie." MA thesis, University of South Africa.

Carr, E. Summerson. 2010. "Enactments of Expertise." *Annual Review of Anthropology* 39: 17–32. https://doi.org/10.1146/annurev.anthro.012809.104948.

Carroll, Faye. 1967. *South West Africa and the United Nations.* Lexington: University of Kentucky Press.

Cawthra, Gavin, 1986. *Brutal Force: The Apartheid War Machine.* London: International Defence and Aid.

Cloete, Fanie. 2018. "Oor Pik Botha se spin, filistyne en 'toordokters.'" *Die Vrye Weekblad*, 5 April. https://www.vryeweekblad.com/nuus-en-politiek/2019-04-05-oor-pik-botha-se-spin-filistyne-en-toordokters/.

Cockram, Gayle-Maryse. 1976. *South West African Mandate.* Cape Town: Juta.

Coertze, P. J., ed. 1964. *Inleiding tot die algemene volkekunde.* Johannesburg: Voortrekkerpers.

Coertze, Roelof D. 1991. "Aanvang van volkekunde aan afrikaanstalige universitieite in Suid-Afrika." *South African Journal of Ethnology* 14, no. 2: 25–34.

Coetzee, J. M. 1988. *White Writing: On the Culture of Letters in South Africa.* New Haven: Yale University Press.

———. 1996. *Giving Offense: Essays on Censorship.* Chicago: University of Chicago Press.

Cohen, Stanley. 2001. *States of Denial: Knowing about Atrocities and Suffering.* Cambridge: Polity.

Cohn, Bernard. 1996. *Colonialism and Its Forms of Knowledge: The British in India.* Princeton: Princeton University Press.

Collins, Joseph. 2016. "Jessica Mitford—Rebel with a Cause." Infinite Fire, 14 September. http://infinitefire.org/info/jessica-mitford-rebel-with-a-cause/

Collins, Randall. 1998. *The Sociology of Philosophies: A Global Theory of Intellectual Change.* Cambridge: Belknap Press.

———. 2004. *Interaction Ritual Chains.* Princeton: Princeton University Press.

Cooper, Allan D. 2001. *Ovambo Politics in the Twentieth Century*. Lanham: University Press of America.

Coser, Lewis A. 1974. *Greedy Institutions: Patterns of Undivided Commitment*. New York: Free Press.

Dale, Richard. 2014. *The Namibian War of Independence, 1966–1989*. Jefferson: McFarland.

Darnton, Robert. 2014. *Censors at Work: How States Shape Literature*. New York: Norton.

Davies, Robertson. 1974. *The Manticore*. New York: Penguin.

de Villiers, Dawid P. 1968. "The Moment of Truth." In *Ethiopia and Liberia vs. South Africa: The South West Africa Cases*. Occasional paper no. 5. Los Angeles: African Studies Center, UCLA.

de Visser, Lieneke. 2013. "Winning Hearts and Minds: Legitimacy in the Namibian War for Independence." *Small Wars and Insurgencies* 24, no. 4: 712–30. https://doi.org/10.1080/09592318.2013.857942.

de Vries, Roland. n.d. "Personal Impressions of the Commander: Operation Yahoo, 1982—We Will Never Forget." 61 Mech Battalion Group Veterans Association. Accessed 25 May 2015. http://www.61mech.org.za/operations/operation-yahoo.

de Waal, David. 1988. *Gemeenskapontwikkeling by Omega* [Community development at Omega]. MA thesis, University of Stellenbosch.

Dieckmann, Ute. 2007. *Hai‖om in the Etosha Region: A History of Colonial Settlement, Ethnicity and Nature Conservation*. Basel: Basler Afrika Bibliographien.

Douglas, Karen M., Robbie M. Sutton, and Aleksandra Cichocka. 2017. "The Psychology of Conspiracy Theories." *Current Directions in Psychological Research* 26, no. 6: 538–42. https://doi.org/10.1177/0963721417718261.

Du Toit, Brian M. 1965. *Beperkte lidmaatskap: 'n antropologies-wetenskaplike studie van geheime en semi-geheime organisasies*. Cape Town: John Malherbe.

Edelman, Murray. 1988. *Constructing the Political Spectacle*. Chicago: University of Chicago Press.

Eedes, Harold 1933. "Customs of the Okavango Natives." In *Report Presented by the Government of the Union of South Africa to the Council of the League of Nations Concerning the Administration of South West Africa for the Year 1932–*, 58–69. Pretoria: Government Printer.

Eirola, Martti, Jan Bradley, and Arto Laitinen. 1990. *The Way of Life of the Mupapama River Terrace Community: Kavango, the Sambiyu Tribe*. Rundu: Finn-Batt-Untag.

Ellis, John. 1975. *A Social History of the Machine Gun*. Baltimore: Johns Hopkins University Press.

Ellis, Stephen. 1998. "The Historical Significance of South Africa's Third Force." *Journal of Southern African Studies* 24, no. 2: 261–99. https://doi.org/10.1080/03057079808708577.

Els, D. 1977. "Etnoloë wen die Swartman se agting." *Paratus* (March): 19.

Els, Herman. 1992. *Akkulturasie: Teorie en Praktyk*. Pretoria: H. Els.

Els, Paul J. 2000. *We Fear Naught but God: The Pictorial Edition of the South African Special Forces "The Recces."* Johannesburg: Covos-Day

———. 2016. *Ons Was Daar: Sektor een Zero, Owambo, Kaokoland*. Pretoria: Pelsa.

Evans, Gavin. 1983. "The Role of the Military in Education in South Africa." BA (Hons) thesis, University of Cape Town.

Fallon, Sam. 2019. "The Rise of the Pedantic Professor: When Academic Self-Regard Becomes an Intellectual Style." *Chronicle of Higher Education*, 1 March. https://www.chronicle.com/article/The-Rise-of-the-Pedantic/245808.

Ferguson, James. 1994. *The Anti-Politics Machine: "Development," Depoliticization, and Bureaucratic Power in Lesotho*. Minneapolis: University of Minnesota Press.

Ferreira, O. J. O. 2018. *Broederskap: Eeufeesgeskiedenis van die Afrikaner-Broederbond en die Afrikanerbond, 1918–2018*, edited by Pierre F. Theron. Pretoria: Afrikanerbond.

Festinger, Leon. 1954. "A Theory of Social Comparison Processes." *Human Relations* 7, no. 2: 117–40.

Frey, Karl. n.d. "The Bushmen." *South African Trades Alphabet*, 14–15.

Fumanti, Mattia. 2016. *The Politics of Distinction: African Elites from Colonialism to Liberation in a Namibian Frontier Town*. Canon Pyon: Sean Kingston.

Geldenhuys, Jannie. 2009. *At the Front: A General's Account of South Africa's Border War*. Johannesburg: Jonathan Ball.

Gewald, Jan-Bart. 2002. "A Teutonic Ethnologist in the Windhoek District." In *Challenges for Anthropology in the African Renaissance: A Southern African Contribution*, edited by Debie LeBeau and Robert J. Gordon, 19–30. Windhoek: University of Namibia Press.

Giliomee, Hermann. 2004. *Die Afrikaners: 'n biografie*. Cape Town: Tafelberg.

Gill, E. L. 1926/27. "Biological Surveys." *Journal of the South West Africa Scientific Society* 2.

Gluckman, Max. 1949. "Social Beliefs and Individual Thinking in Tribal Society." *Memoirs of the Manchester Literary Society* 91, no. 5: 73–98.

Gockel, Klaus. 2010. *Mission und Apartheid: Heinrich Vedder und Hans Karl Diehl*. Cologne: Rüdiger Köppe Verlag.

Goffman, Erving. 1959. *The Presentation of Self in Everyday Life*. New York: Anchor.

———. 1961. *Asylums: Essays on the Social Situation of Mental Patients and other Inmates*. Chicago: Aldine.

———. 1967. *Interaction Ritual: Essays in Face-to-Face Behavior*. New York: Anchor.

Goldblatt, Israel. 1971. *History of South West Africa from the Beginning to the Nineteenth Century*. Cape Town: Juta.

González, Roberto J. 2018. "Beyond the Human Terrain System: A Brief Critical History (and a Look Ahead)." *Contemporary Social Science* (April). https://doi.org/10.1080/21582041.2018.1457171.

Gordon, Robert J. 1977. *Mines, Masters and Migrants: Life in a Namibian Mine Compound*. Johannesburg: Ravan.

———. 1991. "'Serving the Volk with *Volkekunde*': On the Rise of South African Anthropology." In *Knowledge and Power in South Africa*, edited by Jonathan D. Jansen, 79–97. Johannesburg: Skotaville.

———. 1992. *The Bushman Myth: The Making of a Namibian Underclass*. Boulder: Westview.

———. 1995. "Saving the Last South African Bushmen." *Critical Arts* 9, no. 2: 28–48. https://doi.org/10.1080/02560049585310111.

———. 2007. "'Tracks Which Cannot Be Covered': P. J. Schoeman and Public Intellectuals in Southern Africa." *Historia* 52, no. 1: 98–126.

———. 2009. "Hiding in Full View: The "Forgotten" Bushman Genocides in Namibia." *Genocide Studies and Prevention* 4, no. 1: 29–58.

————. 2014. "*Vogelfrei* and *Bestizlos*, with No Concept of Property: Divergent Settler Responses to Bushmen and Damara in German South West Africa." In *Genocide on Settler Frontiers: When Hunter-Gatherers and Commercial Stock Farmers Clash*, edited by Mohamed Adhikari, 108–34. New York: Berghahn.

————. 2017. "Protecting the Borders: Etiquette Manuals and Ethnology in the Erstwhile South African Defence Force." *Anthropology Southern Africa* 40, no. 3: 157–71.

————. 2018a. "Moritz Julius Bonn und die koloniale Bürokratie: Ein Schlüssel zu seinem Liberalismus?" In *Liberales Denken in der Krise der Weltkriegsepoche—Moritz Julius Bonn*, edited by Ewald Grothe and Jens Hacke, 149–70. Stuttgart: Steiner Verlag.

————. 2018b. "How Good People Become Absurd: J. P. van S. Bruwer, the Making of Namibian Grand Apartheid and the Decline of Volkekunde." *Journal of Southern African Studies* 44, no. 1: 97–113. https://doi.org/10.1080/0305707 0.2018.1403266.

Gordon, Robert J., Ciraj Rassool, and Leslie Witz. 1996. "Fashioning van Riebeeck's Bushmen." In *Miscast: Negotiating the Presence of the Bushmen*, edited by Pippa Skotnes, 257–70. Cape Town: University of Cape Town Press.

Gous, A. J. 1982. *Handleiding vir geestesweerbaarheid: Onderwysersgebruuik.* Windhoek: Gamsberg.

Graeber, David. 2012. "Dead Zones of the Imagination: On Violence, Bureaucracy, and Interpretive Labor; The 2006 Malinowski Memorial Lecture." *HAU: Journal of Ethnographic Theory* 2, no. 2 (Fall): 105–28. https://doi.org/10.14318/hau2.2.007.

Grundy, Kenneth W. 1986. *The Militarization of South African Politics.* London: I. B. Taurus.

"Haar liefde en lojaliteit jeens haar land ken geen grense." (Her love and loyalty towards her coutnry knows no borders). 1981. *Paratus* 50 (January).

Hahn, Carl H. L., Heinrich Vedder, and Louis Fourie. [1928] 1966. *The Native Tribes of South West Africa.* London: Cass.

Hailey, William M. 1957 [1938]. *An African Survey, Revised 1956: A Study of Problems Arising in Africa South of the Sahara.* London: Oxford University Press.

Hamilton, Carolyn, Bernard K. Mbenga, and Robert Ross, eds. 2011. *The Cambridge History of South Africa: 1885–1994.* 2 vols. Cambridge: Cambridge University Press.

Hammond-Tooke, David. 1997. *Imperfect Interpreters: South Africa's Anthropologists, 1920–1990.* Johannesburg: Witwatersrand University Press.

Harris, Marvin K. 1969. *The Rise of Anthropological Theory: A History of Theories of Culture.* New York: Crowell.

Hart, Paul't. 1991. "Irving L Janis' Victims of Groupthink." *Political Psychology* 12, no. 2: 247–78.

Harvey, John. 2019. "Rietbok Air Disaster Recalled." *Daily Dispatch*, 13 March.

Hašek, Jaroslav. [1923] 1974. *The Good Soldier Švejk: And His Fortunes in the World War.* New York: Penguin.

Hawley, Katherine. 2012. *Trust: A Very Short Introduction.* New York: Oxford University Press.

Hellberg, Carl-J. 1997. *Mission, Colonialism and Liberation: The Lutheran Church in Namibia 1840–1966.* Windhoek: New Namibia Books.

Henrichsen, Dag, Giorgio Miescher, Ciraj Rassool, and Lorena Rizzo, eds. 2015. "Rethinking Empire in Southern Africa." Special issue, *Journal of Southern African Studies* 41, no. 3.

Hoernlé, Winifred. 1987. *Trails in the Thirstland: The Anthropological Field Diaries of Winifred Hoernlé*, edited by Peter Carstens, Geoffrey Klinghardt, and Martin West. Cape Town: Centre for African Studies, University of Cape Town.

Hofstadter, Richard. 1964. "The Paranoid Style in American Politics." *Harper's Magazine* (November): 77–86.

Holleman, Hans. 1989. "The Great Purge." In *South African Perspectives: Essays in Honour of Nic Olivier*, edited by Pierre Hugo, 34–48. Cape Town: Die Suid-Afrikaan.

Hope, Christopher. 2018. *The Café de Move-on Blues: In Search of the New South Africa*. London: Atlantic Books.

Hugo, Pierre. 1998. "The Politics of 'Untruth': Afrikaner Academics for Apartheid." *Politikon* 25, no. 1: 31–55. https://doi.org/10.1080/02589349808705052.

Hunter, Monica. 1936. *Reaction to Conquest*. London: Oxford University Press.

ICJ (International Court of Justice). 1966. *South West Africa Cases (Ethiopia v. South Africa; Liberia v. South Africa) Volume X: Pleadings, Oral Arguments, Documents*. The Hague: International Court of Justice.

IOL. 2000. "Baboon Foetus Part of Kakiebos 'Witchcraft.'" 3 November. https://www.iol.co.za/news/south-africa/baboon-foetus-part-of-kakiebos-witchcraft-52187.

Irwin, Ryan M. 2012. *Gordian Knot: Apartheid and the Unmaking of the Liberal World Order*. Oxford: Oxford University Press.

Jaeger, Fritz. 1934. "Die geographischen Grundlagen der Kolonisation Afrikas." In *Afrika, Europa und Deutschland*, edited by Ernst E. Wunderlich, 105–7. Stuttgart: Fleischauer und Sohn.

Janis, Irving. 1982. *Groupthink*. Boston: Houghton Mifflin.

Jansen, Anemari. 2015. *Eugene de Kock: Assassin for the State*. Cape Town: Tafelberg.

Jansen van Rensburg, N. S. (Fanie). 2015. "Friedrich Rudolf Lehmann from Leipzig to Potchefstroom University: Scholarly Committed, Ethically Ambivalent." *Anthropology Southern Africa* 38, no. 3–4: 198–215. https://doi.org/10.1080/23323256.2015.1079140.

Jansen van Rensburg N. S., and C. S. van der Waal. 1999. "Continuity and Change in South African Cultural Anthropology (Volkekunde): Issues of Essentialism and Complexity." *South African Journal of Ethnology* 22, no. 2: 45–58.

Kahan, Dan M. 2018. "Why Smart People Are Vulnerable to Putting Tribe before Truth." *Scientific American*, 3 December. https://blogs.scientificamerican.com/observations/why-smart-people-are-vulnerable-to-putting-tribe-before-truth/.

Kahn, Ely J., Jr. 1968. *The Separated People: A Look at Contemporary Africa*. New York: Norton.

Kleynhans, Evert. n.d. "The 'Kavango Jeugbeweging' and the South African Counter-insurgency Campaign in Namibia—An Analysis." Mimeograph, Stellenbosch.

Koch, Eddie. 1992. "Dance Macabre of Colonels." *Weekly Mail*, 16–23 April.

Koestler, Arthur. 1964. *The Act of Creation*. London: Hutchinson.

Köhler, Oswin. 1956. "The Stage of Acculturation in South West Africa." *Sociologus*, n.s., 6, no. 2: 138–53.

Kolakowski, Leszek. 1968. *Marxism and Beyond: On Historical Understanding and Individual Responsibility*. London: Pall Mall.

Köpping, Klaus-Peter. 2002. *Shattering Frames: Transgressions and Transformations in Anthropological Discourse and Practice*. Berlin: Dietrich Reimer Verlag.

Kotzé, Johannes C. 1968. "Die Kuanyama van Ovamboland, Suidwes-Afrika: 'n studie van waarde opvattinge." MA thesis, Stellenbosch University.

Krige, Jack, and Eileen Jensen Krige. 1943. *Realm of the Rain Queen*. London: Oxford University Press.

Lantian, Anthony, Dominique Muller, Cécile Nurra, and Karen M. Douglas. 2017. "'I Know Things They Don't Know!': The Role of Need for Uniqueness in Belief in Conspiracy Theories." *Social Psychology* 48, no. 3: 160–73. https://doi .org/10.1027/1864-9335/a000306.

Larson, Thomas J. 2004. *The Great Adventure: The University of California Southern African Expedition of 1947–1948*. New York: iUniverse.

Lategan, Felix V. 1979. *P. J. Schoeman*. Johannesburg: Perskor.

Lau, Brigitte. 1995. "'Thank God the Germans Came': Vedder and Namibian Historiography." In *History and Historiography: 4 Essays in Reprint*, edited by Annemarie Heywood. Windhoek: Discourse/MSORP.

Lebzelter, Viktor. 1934. *Eingeborenenkulturen in Südwest- und Südafrika: Wissenschaftliche Ergebnisse einer Forschungsreise nach Süd- und Südwestafrika in den Jahren 1926–1928*. Leipzig: Hiersemann.

Lestrade, Gérard P. 1932. *Die naturellevraagstuk en die studie van die naturel*. Johannesburg: South African Institute for Race Relations.

Loeb, Edwin M. 1962. *In Feudal Africa*. Bloomington: Indiana University Research Center in Anthropology, Folklore and Linguistics.

Lösch, Niels C. 1997. *Rasse als Konstrukt: Leben und Werk Eugen Fischers*. Frankfurt am Main: Lang.

Loram, Charles T. 1917. *The Education of the South African Native*. London: Longmans.

Louw, Walter. 1967. "Die sosio-politieke stelsel van die Ngandjera van Ovamboland." MA thesis, University of Port Elizabeth.

MacLeod, Roy. 1987. "On Visiting the 'Moving Metropolis': Reflections on the Architecture of Imperial Science." In *Scientific Colonialism: A Cross-Cultural Comparison; Papers from a Conference at Melbourne, Australia, 25–30 May 1981*, edited by Nathan Reingold and Marc Rothenberg, 217–49. Washington, DC: Smithsonian Institute.

Mair, Lucy. [1936] 1980. *Native Policies in Africa*. New York: Negro Universities Press.

Malan, Johan S. 1980. *Peoples of South West Africa/Namibia*. Pretoria: HAUM. Translated by Kuno F. R. Budack as *Die Völker Namibias*. Windhoek: Hess, 1998.

———. 1982. "Political Attitudes and Opinions of the Wambo of SWA/Namibia." *Africa Insight* 12, no. 3: 189–98.

———. 1990. "Aspekte van identitieitsvorming en -verandering onder die Wambo." *South African Journal of Ethnology* 13, no. 1: 1–10.

———. 1995. *Peoples of Namibia*. Wingate Park: Rhino.

Malan, Magnus. 2006. *My Life with the SA Defence Force*. Pretoria: Protea.

Mallory, C. S. 1971. "Some Aspects of the Mission Policy and Practice of the Church of the Province of South Africa in Ovamboland." MA thesis, Rhodes University.

Mamdami, Mahmoud. 2012. *Define and Rule: Native as Political Identity*. Johannesburg: Wits University Press.

Maritz, Manie. 1938. *My lewe en strewe* [My life and striving]. Johannesburg: M. Maritz.

Marquez, Xavier. 2013. "Engines of Sacrality: A Footnote on Randall Collins' Interaction Ritual Chains." Abandoned Footnotes, 14 April. http://abandoned footnotes.blogspot.com/2013/04/engines-of-sacrality-footnote-on.html

Martin, Henno. 1956. *Wenn es Krieg gibt, gehen wir in die Wüste: Eine Robinsonade in der Namib*. Stuttgart: Union Deutsche Verlagsgesellschaft. Translated as *The Sheltering Desert* (London: Kimber, 1957) and as *Vlug in die Namib: 'n Robinsonade in die woestyn* (Cape Town: Tafelberg, 1959).

Mazower, Mark. 2012. *Governing the World: The Rise and Fall of an Idea*. New York: Penguin.

Memmi, Albert. 1964. *The Colonizer and the Colonized*. Boston: Beacon.

Metzger, Fritz. 1950. *Narro and His Clan*. Windhoek: South West Africa Scientific Society.

Mills, C. Wright. 1956. *The Power Elite*. Oxford: Oxford University Press.

Möller, P. W. Cmdt. 1975. "Die volkekunde is 'n magtige wapen." *Paratus* (November/December): 18–20, 24–25.

Möller, Pieter W. 1978. "Die aanwending van volkekundige kennis binne weermags-verband [The application of ethnological knowledge within a military context]." MA thesis, University of Port Elizabeth.

Mönnig, Hermann O. 1980. *Groepsidentiteit en groepswrywing: Enkele waarneminge oor ras en rassisme, volk en etnisiteit, nasie en nasionalisme*. Johannesburg: Perskor.

Moodie, Dunbar. 2017. "Separate Development as a Failed Project of Social Engineering: The Flawed Logic of Hendrik Verwoerd." *South African Historical Journal* 69, no. 2: 153–61. https://doi.org/10.1080/02582473.2017.1293720.

Morris, S. E. 1930. "At the Vacation Course of Bantu Studies, University of Cape Town." *Nada* 8: 30–45.

Mortimer, B., and SANDF Nodal Point. [1996]. *Submission in Respect of the Former SADF: SA Defence Force Involvement in the Internal Security Situation in the Republic of South Africa* (Submission to the Truth and Reconciliation Commission). [Pretoria]: [SANDF]. http://www.justice.gov.za/trc/hrvtrans/submit/sadf.htm.

Muirhead, Russell, and Nancy L. Rosenblum. 2019. *A Lot of People Are Saying: The New Conspiracism and the Assault on Democracy*. Princeton: Princeton University Press.

Munger, Edward S. 1956. "Suid-Afrikaanse Buro vir Rasse-angeleenthede (South African Bureau of Racial Affairs): An Intimate Account of SABRA's Origins, Leadership, Organization, and Views; and Its Interaction with Afrikanerdom's Church, Press, Party and Public." *American University Field Staff Reports* ESM 6.

———. 1959. "The 1959 Paradox in Afrikaner Nationalism." *American University Field Staff Reports* ESM 3.

Nader, Laura. 1969. "Up the Anthropologist: Perspectives Gained from 'Studying Up.'" In *Reinventing Anthropology*, edited by Dell Hymes, 285–311. New York: Pantheon.

Namuhuja, Hans D. 1996. *The Ondonga Royal Kings*. Windhoek: Out of Africa.

Naranch, Bradley, and Geoff Eley, eds. 2014. *German Colonialism in a Global Age.* Durham: Duke University Press.

Ndadi, Vinnia. 1974. *Breaking Contract: The Story of Helao Vinnia Ndadi.* Vancouver: LSM Press.

Nortje, Piet. 2012. *The Terrible Ones: A Complete History of 32 Battalion.* Cape Town: Zebra Press.

Olivier, Martinus J. 1961. "Inboorlingbeleid en -administrasie in die mandaatgebied van Suidwes-Afrika." PhD diss., Stellenbosch University.

O'Meara, Dan. 1983. *Volkskapitalisme: Class, Capital and Ideology in the Development of Afrikaner Nationalism, 1934–1948.* Johannesburg: Ravan.

Outis. 1931. "Von wilden und zahmen Buschleuten." *Meinerts Monats-Magazin* 2, no. 1: 41–43.

Palmié, Stephan. 2007. "Genomics, Divination, 'Racecraft.'" *American Ethnologist* 34, no. 2: 205–22. https://doi.org/10.1525/ae.2007.34.2.223.

Peacock, James. 2002. *The Anthropological Lens: Harsh Light, Soft Focus.* New York: Cambridge University Press.

Peberdy, Sally. 1996. "Not Quite White? Not Quite Black? Not Quite South African? Constructions of Race, Nation and Immigration in South Africa." Seminar paper presented to the Institute of Advanced Social Research, University of the Witwatersrand, 25 March.

Pedersen, Susan. 2015. *The Guardians: The League of Nations and the Crisis of Empire.* New York: Oxford University Press.

Pelzer, A. N. 1979. *Die Afrikaner-Broederbond: Eerste 50 jaar.* Johannesburg: Voortrekker

Penny, H. Glenn, and Matti Bunzl, eds. 2003. *Worldly Provincialism: German Anthropology in the Age of Empire.* Ann Arbor: University of Michigan Press.

PMC (Permanent Mandates Commission). 1923a. *Permanent Mandates Commission: Minutes of the Third Session, Held in Geneva, July 20th to August 10th, 1923.* Geneva: League of Nations.

———. 1923b. *Report of the Bondelzwarts Rebellion: Submitted to the Council of the League of Nations and Forwarded by the Council to the Assembly.* Geneva: League of Nations.

———. 1924. *Permanent Mandates Commission: Minutes of the Fourth Session, Held in Geneva, June 24th to July 8th, 1924.* Geneva: League of Nations.

———. 1928. *Minutes of the Fourteenth Session, Held at Geneva from October 26th to November 13th, 1928: Including the Report of the Commission to the Council and Comments by Various Accredited Representatives of the Mandatory Powers.* Geneva: League of Nations.

———. 1931. *Minutes of the Twentieth Session, Held at Geneva from June 9th to June 27th, 1931.* Geneva: League of Nations.

———. 1935. *Minutes of the Twenty-Seventh Session . . . Including Report of the Commission to the Council.* Geneva: League of Nations.

———. 1938. *Minutes of the Thirty-Fourth Session, Held at Geneva from June 8th to 23rd, 1938: Including the Report of the Commission to the Council.* Geneva: League of Nations.

Popper, Karl R. 1963. *Conjectures and Refutations: The Growth of Scientific Knowledge.* London: Routledge and Kegan Paul.

Porteus, S. D. 1960. "Ethnic Group Differences." *Mankind Quarterly* 1, no. 3: 187–200.

Potgieter, Evert F. 1955. *The Disappearing Bushmen of Lake Chrissie*. Pretoria: University of South Africa.

Pretorius, Louwrens. 1985. "Suid-Afrikaanse Kommissies van Ondersoek: 'n Sosiologiese Studie." DPhil diss., Stellenbosch University.

Proctor, Robert, and Londa L. Schiebinger. 2008. *Agnatology: The Making and Unmaking of Ignorance*. Stanford: Stanford University Press.

"Professor Dr. med. Dr. sc. h. c. Dr. med. h. c. Eugen Fischer: Das Lebenswerk des Forschers." 1964. *Mitteilungen der SWA Wissenschaftliche Gesellschaft* 5, no. 6–7: 1–4.

Pugach, Sarah. 2004. "Carl Meinhof and the German Influence on Nicholas van Warmelo's Ethnological and Linguistic Writing, 1927–1935." *Journal of Southern African Studies* 30, no. 4: 825–45. https://doi.org/10.1080/0305707042000313040.

———. 2012. *Africa in Translation: A History of Colonial Linguistics in Germany and Beyond, 1814–1945*. Ann Arbor: University of Michigan Press.

Ranger, Terence. 1979. "The Mobilization of Labour and the Production of Knowledge: The Antiquarian Tradition in Rhodesia." *Journal of African History* 20, no. 4: 507–24. https://doi.org/10.1017/S0021853700017515.

Raubenheimer, Ignatius van Wyk, and J. C. Kotzé. 1984. *Personeelbestuur en die swart werker*. Durban: Butterworths.

Rutherford, Danilyn. 2012. *Laughing at Leviathan: Sovereignty and Audience in West Papua*. Chicago: University of Chicago Press.

Sanders, James. 2006. *Apartheid's Friends: The Rise and Fall of South Africa's Secret Service*. London: John Murray.

Schapera, Isaac. 1939. "Anthropology and the Native Problem." *South African Journal of Science* 36: 89–103.

Schillinger, Liesl. 2019. "What Koestler Knew about Jokes." *New York Review*, 3 April. https://www.nybooks.com/daily/2019/04/03/what-koestler-knew-about-jokes/.

Schmidt, Bettina. 1996. *Creating Order: Culture as Politics in 19th and 20th Century South Africa*. Nijmegen: Third World Centre, University of Nijmegen.

Schoeman, Pieter J. 1941. "Territoriale segregasie: Enigste doeltreffende naturelle beleid vir Suid-Afrika." *Wapenskou*, June, 20–31, 34.

———. 1951. *Jagters van die Woestynland*. Pretoria: Protea. Translated as *Hunters of the Desert Land* (Cape Town: Howard Timmins, 1982).

———. 1971. "Weeskinders van Afrika." *Landbouweekblad*, 12 October, 10–15.

———. 1984. *Swerwersprokies*. Johannesburg: Perskor.

Schutte, Carl, Ian Liebenberg, and Anthony Minnaar, eds. 1998. *The Hidden Hand: Covert Operations in South Africa*. Rev. ed. Pretoria: Human Sciences Research Council.

Schwartz, Theodore. 1973. "Cult and Context: The Paranoid Ethos in Melanesia." *Ethos* 1, no. 2: 153–74. https://doi.org/10.1525/eth.1973.1.2.02a00020.

Scott, James C. 1998. *Seeing Like a State: How Certain Schemes to Improve the Human Condition Have Failed*. New Haven: Yale University Press.

Seegers, Annette. 1990. "If only . . . the Ongoing Search for Method in Counter-Insurgency." *Journal of Contemporary African Studies* 9, no. 2: 203–24. https://doi.org/10.1080/02589008908737489.

———. 1996. *The Military in the Making of the Modern South Africa*. London: IB Taurus.

Seiler, John. 1988. "South African Security Forces in Namibia: Unwitting Agents of Social Revolution." Mimeograph, Sterling Library, Yale University.

Sending, Ole Jacob. 2001. "The Effects of Knowledge: Making Space and Holding Things Together." Paper presented to the Norwegian Research Council's Multi-conference, 18–19 January.

Sennett, Richard. 2006. *The Culture of the New Capitalism*. New Haven: Yale University Press.

Shariatmadari, David. 2019. "Could Language be the Key to Detecting Fake News?" *The Guardian*, 2 September. https://www.theguardian.com/commentisfree/2019/sep/02/language-fake-news-linguistic-research

Shiweda, Napandulwe. 2011. "Omhedi: Displacement and Legitimacy in Oukwanyama Politics, Namibia, 1915–2010." PhD diss., University of the Western Cape.

Shutt, Alison K. 2015. *Manners Make a Nation: Racial Etiquette in Southern Rhodesia, 1910–1963*. Rochester: Rochester University Press.

Silberbauer, Raymond. 1968. *Understanding and Motivating the Bantu Worker*. Johannesburg: Publications Department.

Simmel, Georg. 1906. "The Sociology of Secrecy and of Secret Societies." *American Journal of Sociology* 11, no. 4: 441–98.

Simon, Herbert A. 1955. "A Behavioral Model of Rational Choice." *Quarterly Journal of Economics* 69, no. 1: 99–118.

Smith, Nico. 2009. *Die Afrikaner Broederbond: Belewinge van die binnekant*. Pretoria: LAPA.

Smuts, Jan C. 1936. Foreword to *Reaction to Conquest: Effects of Contact with Europeans on the Pondo of South Africa*, by Monica Hunter Wilson. London: Oxford University Press.

———. 1943. Foreword to *The Realm of the Rain Queen: A Study of the Pattern of Lovedu Society*, by Jack Krige and Eileen Jensen Krige. London: Oxford University Press.

———. 1966. *Selections from the Smuts Papers*. Vol. 4, edited by W. Keith Hancock and Jean van der Poel. Cambridge: Cambridge University Press.

South Africa. 1923. *Report of the Commission Appointed to Enquire into the Rebellion of the Bondelzwarts. (U.G. 16)*. Pretoria: Government Printer.

———. 1928. *Report of the Government of the Union of South Africa to the League of Nations Council concerning the Administration of South-West Africa*. Pretoria: Government Printer.

———. 1936. *Report of South West Africa Commission*. Pretoria: Government Printer.

———. 1964. *Commission of Enquiry into South West Africa Affairs*. Pretoria: Government Printer.

Stals, E. L. P. 1998. *Geskiedenis van die Afrikaner-Broederbond, 1918–1994*. Stellenbosch: Afrikaner-Broederbond.

———. 2008. *Wie is jy? 'n bundel historiese opstelle oor die Afrikaner in die voormalige Suidwes-Afrika*. Windhoek: Macmillan Namibia.

Stark, Peter. 2002. *Der weisse Buschmann Peter Stark: Vom Wilderer zum Wildhüter*. Windhoek: Kuiseb Verlag. Translated as *The White Bushman* (Pretoria: Protea, 2011) and *Die wit Boesman* (Pretoria: Protea, 2007).

Steinmetz, George. 2007. *The Devil's Handwriting: Precoloniality and the German Colonial State in Qingdao, Samoa, and Southwest Africa*. Chicago: University of Chicago Press.

———. 2008. "The Colonial State as a Social Field: Ethnographic Capital and Native Policy in the German Overseas Empire before 1914." *American Sociological Review* 73, no. 4: 589–612. https://doi.org/10.1177/000312240807300404.

Stoler, Ann L. 2016. *Duress: Imperial Durabilities in Our Times*. Durham: Duke University Press.

Sundermeier, Theo. 1973. *Wir aber suchten Gemeinschaft: Kirchwerdung und Kirchentrennung in Südwestafrika*. Erlangen: Luther-Verlag.

Swanepoel, Tienie. 1997. *My hart wil Afrika*. Cape Town: Queillerie.

Szakolczai, Arpad, and Bjørn Thomassen. 2019. *From Anthropology to Social Theory: Rethinking the Social Sciences*. Cambridge: Cambridge University Press.

Tiley, Alan S. 1974. *Bridging the Communication Gap between Black and White*. Cape Town: Tafelberg.

Tötemeyer, Andree-Jeanne. 1999. *The State of Museums in Namibia and the Need for Training for Museum Services*. Windhoek: University of Namibia.

Tötemeyer, Gerhard. 2015. *Das Werden und Wirken eines Rebellen: Autobiographische und historische Notizen eines Deutsch-Namibiers*. Windhoek: Kuiseb.

Travers, Mark, Leaf van Boven, and Charles Judd. 2014. "The Secrecy Heuristic: Inferring
Quality from Secrecy in Foreign Policy Contexts." *Political Psychology* 35, no. 1: 97–111.

TRC (Truth and Reconciliation Commission). 1992. *Truth and Reconciliation Commission of South Africa Report*. Department of Justice and Constitutional Development, South Africa. http://www.justice.gov.za/trc/report/index.htm.

Tuchman, Barbara W. 1984. *The March of Folly: From Troy to Vietnam*. New York: Ballantine.

Uys, Ian S. 1993. *Bushman Soldiers: Their Alpha and Omega*. Germiston: Fortress Publishers.

van der Merwe, Isak J. 1990. *The Role of War in Regional Development in Namibia*. Stellenbosch: Institute for Cartographic Analysis.

van der Merwe, J. H. 1983. *National Atlas of South West Africa (Namibia)*. Windhoek: Directorate Development Co-ordination, SWA.

van der Wath, J. G. H. 1983. *Johannes van der Wath van Suidwes-Afrika*. Windhoek: Auas.

van Deventer, Hennie. 2003. *In Kamera*. Pretoria: Protea.

Van Rooyen, Pieter H. 1977. *Die Inheemse Reg van die Kavango* [Indigenous law of the Kavango]. MA thesis, University of Stellenbosch.

van Warmelo, Nicolaas J. [1951] 1962. *Notes on the Kaokoveld (South West Africa) and Its People*. Pretoria: Government Printer.

———. 1960. "The Inhabitants of South West Africa from an Ethnological Point of View." First draft, February 1960, NTS 9715 01 807/400, SANA.

———. 1961. "Memo: On Inhabitants of South West Africa from an Ethnological Point of View." A591 van Warmelo Collection, National Archives of Namibia.

———. 1969. *Guide and Questions on History, Law and Custom*. Pretoria: Department of Bantu Administration and Development.

———. 1977. *Anthropology of Southern Africa in Periodicals to 1950: An Analysis and Index*. Johannesburg: Witwatersrand University Press.

van Wyk, J. J. 2000. "Huldeblyk A. O. Jackson, 1930–1998." *South African Journal of Ethnology* 23, no. 1: 39–41.

Veblen, Thorstein. 1900. *The Theory of the Leisure Class*. Chandi Chowk: Global Media.

Vedder, Heinrich. 1934. *Das alte Südwestafrika*. Berlin: Warneck. Translated as *Die voorgeskiedenis van Suidwes-Afrika* (Windhoek: Meinert, 1937) and *The Early History of South West Africa* (London: Oxford University Press, 1938).

———. [1953] 1957. *Kort verhale uit 'n lang lewe*. Cape Town: Balkema.

Verdery, Katherine. 2012. "Observers Observed: An Anthropologist under Surveillance." *Anthropology Now* 4, no. 2: 14–23. https://doi.org/10.1080/19492901.2012.117 28357.

Verwoerd, Wilhelm J., ed. 2018. *Verwoerd aan die Woord II: Die laaste vier jaar*. Pretoria: Protea.

Visser, Gideon E. 2000. "Die geskiedenis van die Suid-Afrikaanse Militêre Akademie, 1950–1990." DPhil diss., Stellenbosch University.

Visser, J. A. 1984. *The South African Defence Force's Contribution to the Development of South West Africa*. Pretoria: SADF Military Information Bureau.

Visser, Salomé M. G. 1982. *Die mense van SWA: 'n geo-etnologiese oorsig*. Windhoek: South West Africa Territorial Force.

Voipio, Rauha. 1972. *Kontrak soos die Owambo dit sien*. Karibib: Evangelical Lutheran Owambo-Kavango Church and Evangelical Lutheran Church of South West Africa.

von Schumann, Gunther. 2011. "Dr Kuno Franz Robert Budack: Ein Leben für die Wissenschaft in Namibia." *Journal of the Namibian Scientific Society* 59: 5–13.

Wagner, Günter. 1949. *The Bantu of North Kavirondo*. Vol. 1. London: Oxford University Press.

———. 1956. *The Bantu of North Kavirondo*. Vol. 2. London: Oxford University Press.

Walton, Edgar. 1923. *Comments of the Accredited Representative of the Union of South Africa on the Commission's Report on the Bondelzwarts Rebellion*. Geneva: League of Nations.

Wanless, Ann. 2007. "The Silence of Colonial Melancholy: The Fourie Collection of Khoisan Ethnologica." PhD diss., University of the Witwatersrand.

Watt, J. S. 1951. "President Watt's Report to the Annual General Meeting." Edited by SWA Scientific Society. Mimeograph, Windhoek.

Weidenreich, Franz. 1946. "Letter to the Editor." *Science* 104: 399.

Wilkins, Ivor, and Hans Strydom. 1978. *The Super-Afrikaners*. Johannesburg: Jonathan Ball.

Wilson, Woodrow. 1919. *Addresses of President Wilson*. Washington DC: Government Printing Office.

Woods, Dennis. 1977. "'Nakale' Harold Eedes: A Legend of His Time: The Last of the Lords of the Frontier." *SWA Annual*.

Index

WHAM (Winning the Hearts and
  Minds initiative), 6, 105–7, 110,
  137, 139
"white man's burden," 10, 15n4, 23, 27
Wilson, Woodrow, 17
Winning the Hearts and Minds initiative
  (WHAM), 6, 105–7, 110, 137, 139
women (native)
  ambivalence about role of, 29, 116,
    141

etiquette towards, 52, 124
plight of Bushmen, 69–70, 123
views on, 30, 154n1
World Court (International Court of
  Justice), 2, 6, 13, 88–89, 93–97,
  98, 101

youth, countermobilization and,
  105–114, 116, 126, 128, 130n9,
  130n11, 130n13